J.K. LASSER

TAXES MADE EASY FOR YOUR HOME-BASED BUSINESS

Look for these and other titles from J.K. Lasser™—Practical Guides for All Your Financial Needs.

J.K. Lasser's Pick Winning Stocks by Edward F. Mrkvicka Jr.

J.K. Lasser's Invest Online by LauraMaery Gold and Dan Post

J.K. Lasser's Year-Round Tax Strategies by David S. De Jong and Ann Gray Jakabcin

J.K. Lasser's Taxes Made Easy for Your Home-Based Business by Gary W. Carter

J.K. Lasser's Finance and Tax for Your Family Business by Barbara Weltman

J.K. Lasser's Pick Winning Mutual Funds by Jerry Tweddell with Jack Pierce

J.K. Lasser's Your Winning Retirement Plan by Henry K. Hebeler

J.K. Lasser's Winning With Your 401(K) by Grace Weinstein

J.K. Lasser's Winning With Your 403(b) by Pam Horowitz

J.K. Lasser's Strategic Investing After 50 by Julie Jason

J.K. Lasser's Winning Financial Strategies for Women by Rhonda Ecker and Denise Gustin-Piazza

J.K. Lasser's Online Taxes by Barbara Weltman

J.K. Lasser's Pick Stocks Like Warren Buffett by Warren Boroson

J.K. Lasser's The New Tax Law Simplified

J.K. Lasser's New Rules for Retirement and Tax by Paul Westbrook

J.K. Lasser's New Rules for Small Business Taxes by Barbara Weltman

J.K. Lasser's Investor's Tax Guide by Elaine Floyd

J.K. Lasser's Choosing the Right Long-Term Care Insurance by Ben Lipson

J.K. Lasser's Winning Ways to Save for College by Barbara Wagner

J.K. Lasser's Financial Basics for Business Managers by John Tracy

J.K. LASSER'S™

TAXES MADE EASY FOR YOUR HOME-BASED BUSINESS

Fifth Edition

The Ultimate Tax Handbook for the Self-Employed

Gary W. Carter, PhD, MT, CPA

John Wiley & Sons, Inc.

Published by John Wiley & Sons, Inc., Hoboken, New Jersey.
Published simultaneously in Canada.

For general information on our other products and services, or technical support, please contact our Customer Care Department within the U.S. at 800-762-2974, outside the United States at 317-572-3993 or fax 317-572-4002.

Wiley also publishes its books in a variety of electronic formats. Some content that appears in print may not be available in electronic books.

Library of Congress Cataloging-in-Publication Data:

Carter, Gary W.
    J.K. Lasser's taxes made easy for your home based business : the ultimate tax handbook for the self-employed / Gary W. Carter.—5th ed.
      p. cm.
    Includes index.
    ISBN 0-471-23504-0 (pbk. : alk. paper)
    1. Income tax—Law and legislation—United States—Popular works.   2. Home-based businesses—Taxation—Law and legislation—United States—Popular works.   3. Self-employed—Taxation—Law and legislation—United States—Popular works.   4. Tax returns—United States—Popular works.   I. Title: JK Lasser's taxes made easy for your home based business.   II. Title: Taxes made easy for your home-based business.   III. Title.

KF6369.6 .C37 2002
343.7305′2—dc21

2002032386

Printed in the United States of America.

10 9 8 7 6 5 4 3 2 1

To Ben and Deanna

Acknowledgments

My thanks to Steve Warren, CPA, and Paul Gutterman, Esq., CPA, for their helpful comments on various sections of this book, and to my wife, Deanna, for improving the readability of the book.

G.W.C.

Contents

Introduction: Before We Get Started

> I can go to work in my underwear when it's 40 below, without fear of frostbite or being arrested.
>
> —A Minnesota home-office user

What a great time for running a home-based business! Advances in telecommunication and Internet technology have made working from home easier than ever before. On top of that, legislation that became effective in 1999 has made the home-office deduction rules less restrictive than at any time since 1976. You will learn from this Fifth Edition of *Taxes Made Easy for Your Home-Based Business* how virtually any home-based business owner can qualify for important tax benefits.

The fact that you have chosen to make your livelihood from home is enlightening. First of all, it's clear that you are no dummy. (If you were, you would have bought that other tax book for dummies.) It is also obvious that you are self-sufficient and self-motivated. You like to be in charge and in control. With the help of this book, you can be in charge when dealing with the Internal Revenue Service (IRS). These pages will guide you through the federal income tax issues typically faced by home-based business owners.

It is simply prudent business management to minimize your tax liability when possible. Money you save through legitimate tax-reduction techniques is worth more than the same amount of additional income. Additional income must be taxed at your top rate. Furthermore, if your income is high enough, each additional dollar reduces deductions subject to phaseouts (such as your personal exemptions). That increases your tax burden even more. Saving a dollar of tax, on the other hand, means keeping every penny of it.

Learn all you can about your tax situation. As the one item that affects your bottom line more than any other, your tax obligation deserves more than just grudging indulgence during the filing season. You might view it as a very profitable hobby. Even if you engage a professional to actually prepare your return, your tax knowledge will save you money. The next few paragraphs describe what you will learn from each of the following chapters.

Chapter 1 provides an overview of the structure of our federal income tax system, and generally describes the role of Congress, the IRS, and the courts. Your options in responding to an audit are discussed, from the administrative appeals process to litigation in court.

Chapter 2 describes in detail what the IRS and the courts consider to be a trade or business. This is important because you can deduct home-business expenses only if you have a trade or business. The difference between an investment activity and a business is explained, as is the difference between a business and a hobby. The general rules for identifying deductible business expenses are also explained.

Chapter 3 talks about your choices for a business entity if you are self-employed. Your business could be organized as a sole proprietorship, a partnership, a limited liability company, a limited liability partnership, a regular C corporation, or an S corporation. The general features of each business form are explained, along with their advantages and disadvantages for tax purposes.

Chapter 4 describes your choices of accounting methods and taxable years. Determining the proper year to report an item of income or a deduction is sometimes a little tricky. Therefore, the general requirements for when to report income and deductions under the cash and accrual methods are discussed.

Chapters 5 and 6 offer the most detailed explanation you will find of how home-office deductions are treated. Chapter 5 tells you what expenses are subject to the limitations, and how the limitations work. The new relaxed standards for 1999 and later years are explained in detail. Then in Chapter 6 you are guided line-by-line through Form 8829, "Expenses for Business Use of Your Home." Chapter 6 is designed as a reference tool for actually filling out the form.

Chapter 7 gives you the rules for deducting travel and local transportation expenses. Car expenses can be pretty confusing, so most of the chapter is devoted to them.

Chapter 8 tells you about other common business deductions that are not limited by the home-office deduction rules. Depreciation of your business property is another area that is confusing, so this chapter takes you through the rules in detail. Other costs discussed include software, books, subscriptions, telephone services, insurance, wages for office workers, and retirement plans.

Chapter 9 tells you about self-employment tax, your obligation to make estimated tax payments if you are self-employed, and employment taxes if you have employees. It also describes how to keep your annual estimated tax payments to a minimum while avoiding the underpayment penalty.

Chapter 10 describes in detail how claiming home-office deductions affects the reporting of the sale of your home. You are taken step-by-step through the reporting requirements.

Chapter 11 tells you about the records you should keep and how long you should keep them. Read this chapter before you throw any of that stuff away.

Chapter 12 contains a comprehensive example of how to fill out Schedule C (Profit or Loss From Business), Form 8829 (Expenses for Business Use of Your Home), Form 4562 (Depreciation and Amortization), and Schedule SE (Self-Employment Tax). You are then shown how to determine your estimated tax payments for the following year.

You will notice that each chapter contains endnote references to the text. They are filled with cites to Internal Revenue Code sections, court decisions, Treasury regulations, and IRS rulings. These are the primary sources of authority for the rules of federal taxation (discussed in Chapter 1). If you wish to read any of the references for yourself, visit any library that maintains legal publications. Some of the references are also available on the Internet. Specific guidance on how and where to find this material is provided in Chapter 1. It is not necessary to read the endnotes as you study this book, but they are important to fully document the advice and suggestions offered. If the IRS ever challenges your deductions, you will be able to back them up with the appropriate legal authority.

Both pitfalls and opportunities await the millions of home-based business owners who must confront their income tax return each year. Many blindly trust a tax preparer, never knowing if their return is accurate or if they are truly paying the least tax possible. With the aid of this book, you will know how to properly minimize your income tax obligation relating to your home-based business. You will also learn how to plan your future home-office activities for the desired tax advantages. Above all, you will gain the confidence of being knowledgeable about home-office deductions and your rights as a taxpayer, and need never fear a tax audit again.

J.K. LASSER'S™

TAXES MADE EASY FOR YOUR HOME-BASED BUSINESS

CHAPTER 1

The Lay of the Land

The Tax Code, once
you get to know it,
embodies all the
essence of life:
greed, politics,
power, goodness,
charity.

—Sheldon Cohen
(Former IRS
Commissioner)

Some folks view our tax rules as an edict from the IRS. That's not quite the case. It is true that the IRS is an ominous bureaucracy with broad powers. Nevertheless, the IRS is not the law maker but the administrator of a tax system enacted by Congress. The purpose of this chapter is to give you fundamental knowledge of the legal system relating to federal taxation and to explain the interrelationship between the IRS, the courts, and Congress. It is not necessary to read this chapter to fill out your tax return. However, it is a must read if you ever receive an audit notice from the IRS.

Legislative, Administrative, and Judicial Authority

Our government was established under the Constitution with a system of checks and balances. The Legislative Branch (Congress) enacts the laws, the Administrative Branch (the President and cabinet) enforces the laws, and the Judicial Branch (the courts) makes sure the other two branches are operating legally and within their constitutional authority. The President delegates the administration of tax laws to the U.S. Treasury Department, which includes the IRS. You have recourse in the courts if the IRS tries to deny you rights (like deductions, exemptions, and credits) that Congress has authorized.

Now for the tricky part: How do you know if the IRS is denying you a legitimate right? The answer to that question requires a closer look at the Legislative, Administrative, and Judicial Branches as they pertain to taxation.

When tax legislation is enacted by Congress and signed into law by the President, it adds to or amends the Internal Revenue Code of 1986 (which is Title 26 of the U.S. Code). The Internal Revenue Code (Code) contains all of our country's tax laws, which the IRS is required to administer and enforce.

Often the laws written by Congress are either unclear or are not specific enough to apply to particular circumstances. To enforce these laws, it is necessary for the Treasury Department and the IRS to provide interpretations. These interpretations generally come in the form of *regulations* from Treasury and *revenue rulings* and *letter rulings* from the IRS. The IRS also publishes *revenue procedures,* which tell taxpayers about IRS administrative practices.

Regulations

The Treasury Department issues tax regulations under authority granted by Congress.[1] The purpose of regulations is to explain, in relatively normal language, the meaning of all or part of a Code section. They generally expand on the language and provide examples to help taxpayers comply with the Code section. Some regulations merely interpret what the Code section itself says. These are called *interpretive* regulations. In some Code sections, Congress provides authority for the Treasury to come up with certain rules on its own, as long as they comply with the overall intent of the Code section. These are called *legislative* regulations. Regulations are the highest form of administrative authority and carry considerable weight with the courts. Legislative regulations carry the force and effect of the law itself, as long as they comply with the intent of the Code section under which they are issued. Regulations are not law, however. The validity of a regulation can be questioned. Courts are not bound by regulations and can overrule them if they are unreasonable and plainly inconsistent with the Code.

You can tell when a regulation is being referred to, as opposed to a Code section, because it will begin with the number one (if issued under an income tax Code section) followed by a decimal, then the number of the Code section. For example, Regulation Section 1.61-1 is the citation for the first regulation issued under Section 61. You will also see it cited as Reg. § 1.61-1.

Revenue Rulings

The National Office of the IRS issues revenue rulings. These are generally official replies by the IRS to specific questions raised by taxpayers. They also interpret tax law, but are not as authoritative as regulations (meaning the courts are more likely to disagree with them). They tend to deal with much more limited issues than regulations, often addressing a specific legal question. They are published to provide guidance in cases having similar facts to those presented in the rulings and are generally only one or two pages long.

Here's an example of the citation for a revenue ruling: Rev. Rul. 80-52, 1980-1 C.B. 100. The "80-52" means it was the 52nd revenue ruling issued in the year 1980. The "1980-1 C.B." means this ruling can be found in the first volume of the 1980 *Cumulative Bulletin.* The "100" at the end means it can be found on page 100 of that Cumulative Bulletin. After 1999, revenue rulings have four digits representing the year rather than two. An example is Rev. Rul. 2000-10. For the most recent rulings, you see "I.R.B." instead of "C.B." for the citation reference. That means it can be found in the *Internal Revenue Bulletin* rather than the Cumulative Bulletin. What the Cumulative Bulletin and the Internal Revenue Bulletin are, and where they can be found, is discussed later under "Where to Find This Stuff" on page 8.

Letter Rulings

Letter rulings are issued to a particular taxpayer at the taxpayer's request, and describe how the IRS will treat a proposed transaction. If the taxpayer carries through with the transaction exactly as described in the ruling request, the IRS is bound to abide by the ruling. If the taxpayer changes any of the facts of the transaction, the IRS is no longer obligated to follow the ruling. This is a way for you to get the IRS to tell you in advance what the tax effects of a particular transaction will be. The IRS limits its letter rulings to only certain types of transactions, though.[2] Also, the answer better be pretty important to you. Most ruling requests cost $5,000. However, ruling requests are only $500 if your gross income is less than $150,000. And if your ruling request involves a business-related tax issue, such as home-office expenses or residential rental property issues, you can get one for $500 if your gross income is less than $1 million.[3]

Letter rulings used to be called private letter rulings, because they were not available to the public. Since 1976, however, they have been available to read, after all the information that could identify the taxpayer has been deleted. They are still private in another sense though: A letter ruling is a two-party contract between the IRS and the taxpayer who requested the ruling. The IRS is not obligated to treat a similar transaction by another taxpayer in the same way.[4] That means you cannot rely on someone else's letter ruling with certainty; you've got to get your own. With this in mind, letter rulings still provide evidence to the public of how the IRS will handle a transaction. Tax practitioners tend to use them to support their treatment of similar transactions. If enough taxpayers request rulings on the same question, the IRS will issue a *revenue ruling* stating its position, which can be relied on by all taxpayers.

Here's an example of the citation for a letter ruling: LTR 9624010. It is always a seven-digit number if it was issued prior to 1999, and a nine-digit number if it was issued since. The first two numbers (first four after 1998) indicate the year the ruling was issued, the next two indicate the week of the year the ruling was issued, and the last three numbers indicate the number among the rulings issued that week. So the letter ruling cited was issued in 1996 during the 24th week, and it was the 10th ruling issued that week.

Revenue Procedures

Revenue procedures are issued in the same manner as revenue rulings, but they deal with different issues. They tell you about IRS practices and procedures instead of answering specific legal questions. The IRS has its own peculiar way of doing things, and revenue procedures tell you how to do things the IRS's way. A revenue procedure is also used to provide the annual inflation adjustments for everything in the Code that is supposed to be adjusted for inflation. These include individual tax rates, exemptions, the standard deduction, and several other things. This is useful information for doing tax planning for the current year. Rev. Proc. 2001-59[5] shows what these amounts are for 2002.

Revenue procedures are cited just like revenue rulings, except they begin with "Rev. Proc." rather than "Rev. Rul." They are found in the Internal Revenue Bulletin (I.R.B.) and the Cumulative Bulletin (C.B.), which are discussed under "Where to Find This Stuff" on page 8.

An Example of Interpreting a Code Section

Here's an example of a Code section that has fairly simple wording. IRC Section 61 provides a definition of *gross income* (the term Congress uses to define income subject to tax, before being reduced by allowable deductions). This is part of what it says:

Sec. 61. Gross Income Defined

(a) General Definition—Except as otherwise provided in this subtitle, gross income means all income from whatever source derived, including (but not limited to) the following items:

1. Compensation for services, including fees, commissions, fringe benefits, and similar items
2. Gross income derived from business
3. Gains derived from dealings in property . . .

This Code definition of gross income might seem understandable enough, but now let's try to apply it to an actual situation. Let's say you are in the business of selling newspapers. You have sold $500 worth of newspapers for cash during the year and your cost of the papers was $250. In addition, some guy came by one day on his way to work, carrying his lunch in a paper bag. He had forgotten his wallet, but really wanted to buy a paper. You, being an astute businessperson, traded the guy a newspaper for his lunch. We'll assume the lunch had a value of two dollars.

What is your gross income? Does it include the value of the guy's lunch? Does it include gross cash sales or cash sales minus the cost of the papers? Here are the options. It could be: (a) $500, or (b) $502, or (c) $250, or (d) $252. The wording of Section 61 does not make it entirely clear which answer is correct, does it? This is where Treasury regulations come in handy.

There are several interpretive regulations issued under Section 61. Regulation Section 1.61-1 provides a general definition, and Regulation Section 1.61-3 tells what "gross income derived from business" means. Regulation Section 1.61-1 says in part:

> Gross income includes income realized in any form, whether in money, property, or services. Income may be realized, therefore, in the form of services, meals, accommodations, stock, or other property, as well as in cash.

Since the guy's lunch is property, the regulation says its value is included in your gross income. That narrows down the answer to either (b) $502, or (d) $252. Regulation Section 1.61-3 says in part:

> In a manufacturing, merchandising, or mining business, "gross income" means the total sales, less the cost of goods sold . . .

This regulation excludes the cost of sales from the term gross income, thus giving us the correct answer to our question—$252 ($500 sales less $250 for cost of goods sold plus a $2 lunch). Note that the cost of sales is not a *deduction* like other normal costs of operating your business; it is an *exclusion*, which is an amount that is never included in gross income in the first place.

We found some issues here that were not addressed in the Code section, but were explained in the regulations. Other issues might not be discussed in the regulations, but are found in revenue rulings or letter rulings. The answers provided by these documents are opinions of the IRS—they are not the law. Once in a while taxpayers disagree with the IRS and choose to have the courts decide who is right. The courts sometimes interpret the law differently than the regulations and rulings. That means it is important to consider judicial interpretation contained in the many volumes of opinions that have been handed down over the years.

Judicial Authority

If you disagree with the amount of tax the IRS thinks is due, does that mean you must automatically fork over whatever the IRS says to pay? Heck no! That's what the judicial system is for—to settle disputes between the IRS and taxpayers.

Sometimes the dispute relates to a *factual* issue, such as the amount a taxpayer has incurred for a business expense, or the value of an art object donated to charity. Other times the argument relates to a *legal* issue, such as the proper interpretation of a particular Code section.

THE TRIAL COURTS

If a taxpayer and the IRS can't come to some agreement during the administrative appeals process (discussed next), a taxpayer has a choice of three judicial forums to begin litigation. They are the United States Tax Court, the United States Court of Federal Claims, and the United States District Court for the district in which the taxpayer lives.

The United States Tax Court (Tax Court) is the court of choice for most taxpayers. It is a court of national jurisdiction, and it hears only tax cases. The judges are very knowledgeable in tax matters, so its opinions tend to be more highly regarded as precedent than decisions of the other two trial courts. Its decisions are appealable to the regional court of appeals having jurisdiction where the taxpayer lives, as discussed next.

District courts are regional courts, and their judges hear an array of federal issues. There is at least one district court in each state, and the more populous states have more than one. Decisions from these courts are appealable to the regional court of appeals in the same manner as Tax Court decisions.

The United States Court of Federal Claims (commonly called the Court of Claims) is a national court like the Tax Court. The difference is, the Court of Claims sits in Washington, DC, while the Tax Court hears cases all over the country. This court hears most types of federal tax cases, in addition to other cases in which there is a claim against the federal government. The Court of Claims has its own appeals court; its decisions are appealable to the United States Court of Appeals for the Federal Circuit.

THE APPELLATE COURTS

The loser in the trial court, be it the taxpayer or the IRS, has the right to appeal the decision to an appellate court. A trial court decision can only be appealed to the appellate court that has jurisdiction over the case. If the trial court is the Tax Court or a district court, the case must be appealed to the regional appellate court having jurisdiction where the taxpayer lives. Cases from the Court of Claims can only be appealed to the Court of Appeals for the Federal Circuit.

With the exception of the Court of Appeals for the Federal Circuit, our federal appellate system is a territorial arrangement. It is made up of twelve courts of appeal, each having jurisdiction over a particular area of the country. For instance, if you happen to live in Texas, Louisiana, or Mississippi, you are under the jurisdiction of the Fifth Circuit Court of Appeals. If you live in Minnesota, North

Dakota, South Dakota, Nebraska, Iowa, Missouri, or Arkansas, you are subject to the Eighth Circuit Court of Appeals. Each of these appellate courts is an independent jurisdiction, and they do not have to agree with one another. Consequently, a question considered by the Ninth Circuit Court of Appeals might be decided differently than the same question considered by the Second Circuit Court of Appeals. If an appellate court has issued an opinion on a particular issue, the trial courts whose decisions are appealable to that appellate court are obligated to follow the opinion. If an issue is handled differently by different circuit courts, the IRS will treat taxpayers in those jurisdictions accordingly. Taxpayers will not be treated uniformly in such cases unless the Supreme Court settles the dispute or Congress clarifies the law.

As an example, several years ago the singer Ethel Merman performed on Broadway for a little over two years in the musical *Gypsy*. During the run of the play on Broadway, Ethel lived in New York, but her permanent residence at the time was in Colorado. So she deducted her meals and lodging expenses while in New York as traveling expenses while *away from home* under the authority of Code Section 162(a). The IRS interpretation was that her tax home had become New York, so she was not away from home and her expenses were not deductible. Ethel took the issue to court in New York, and after being denied the deductions by the trial court, appealed the case to the Second Circuit Court of Appeals. The Second Circuit held that *home* means a taxpayer's permanent abode, and allowed Ethel the deductions because she was away from her home in Colorado.[6] In doing so, it created a rule that conflicted with the opinions of six other appellate courts.[7] The IRS did not request a hearing before the Supreme Court on this issue, but later Congress amended Code Section 162(a) to deny a deduction for away-from-home expenses for "any period of employment if such period exceeds 1 year."

THE SUPREME COURT

This is the only Court that lays down precedent that must be followed by all of the lower courts. The IRS must also follow rulings of the Supreme Court as precedent. This would clear up much confusion in our tax laws except for a couple of problems.

First, the Supreme Court has complete discretion over whether it will hear a case. A party requests a hearing by Writ of Certiorari. If at least four members of the Court believe the issue is of sufficient importance to be heard by the Court it will grant the Writ (*cert. Granted*). Most often, however, it will deny jurisdiction (*cert. Denied*). It is generally persuaded to hear a tax case only when there is a conflict on the issue among the appellate courts (that is, two or more appellate courts have decided the issue differently). Even then, sometimes the Supreme Court will not hear the case.

Furthermore, even when the Supreme Court steps in and handles a tax case, its decision often has the effect of muddling the issues rather than clarifying them, leaving us even more confused and bewildered.

With all this in mind, you can see that the answers to tax questions often are not clear-cut. Sometimes when the IRS says no, the courts say yes; or some courts say yes and other courts say maybe. Having an appreciation for this puts you at an advantage when dealing with the IRS. You should never submit to an IRS agent's adjustment on your return unless it is backed up by appropriate authoritative support. The next section tells you how to find the various sources of authority.

Where to Find This Stuff

People who are not tax professionals generally have no interest in reading tax cases or IRS rulings. However, you might get the urge to look up one of the sources cited in this book just to see for yourself what it says. If you have a particular burning question, you might even become inspired to go further and explore the tax services discussed next. This might even lead to an intriguing new hobby for you. So if you're in the mood for sleuthing, slip on your trench coat and keep reading.

You could start by looking up the government documents department of any public library. Call and ask if they have current IRS rulings and Treasury regulations. If you are near a university that has a business school, its library probably has a *Business Reference* section that contains these documents. Or if you are close to a law school, call its library and ask if it has a tax reference section, and whether you can gain access to it. The completeness and currency of the documents will vary among these locations, so try to find the best one.

THE CUMULATIVE BULLETIN AND INTERNAL REVENUE BULLETIN

Now that you have found a place that has tax documents, ask if it has the Cumulative Bulletin and the Internal Revenue Bulletin. The Internal Revenue Bulletin is published on a weekly basis. Each weekly volume is a small pamphlet that contains everything issued by the IRS during that week. Included are revenue rulings, revenue procedures, and other pronouncements. Every six months these bulletins are gathered together, reorganized by Code section, and published in a bound volume. The bound volume is the Cumulative Bulletin. That means there are at least two Cumulative Bulletins per year. The first volume contains IRS pronouncements from the first half of the year, and the second volume has the stuff from the second half.

Besides rulings issued by the IRS, the Cumulative Bulletin also contains the entire text of any tax legislation enacted during the year and the *committee reports* that accompany it. Committee reports are written by the tax legislative committees of Congress, and provide explanation and insight into the congressional intent of the legislation. If there is major legislation during the year, there might be additional volumes of the Cumulative Bulletin to handle the legislation.

TAX SERVICES

Tax services are multivolume references to Code sections that provide commentary and explanation. They are also updated regularly, and refer you to the most recent cases and rulings affecting a particular subject. A library might have these tax services in the same area as the Cumulative Bulletin, or they might be shelved separately in the business section.

A popular tax service is the *Standard Federal Tax Reporter* published by Commerce Clearing House (CCH). Another is the *United States Tax Reporter* by Research Institute of America (RIA). These volumes are organized by Code section and have a topical index. For each Code section, you will find the law itself, regulations, selected Committee Reports, a plain language explanation by the publishers, and references to all the cases and rulings pertaining to that Code section.

COURT CASES

Both CCH and RIA also reproduce federal court decisions dealing with tax issues. All federal tax cases, other than those from the Tax Court, are found in *United States Tax Cases* (CCH) and the *American Federal Tax Reporter* (RIA). The "Citator" for each of these services provides an alphabetical index to the cases.

Tax Court decisions are divided into two categories: "Regular" decisions are published by the U.S. Government Printing Office in volumes called the *U.S. Tax Court*. "Memorandum" decisions are not published by the government, but are published by private tax services like CCH and RIA. Memorandum decisions are just like regular decisions, but they are designated by the Chief Judge of the Tax Court as less precedential. This is because they either deal with factual issues, or address questions that have been answered before by the Tax Court.

ONLINE RESOURCES

There are many sites on the World Wide Web that offer tax information. The contents and addresses of these sources change all the time, so if the addresses given here don't work, just do a web search. For forms, publications, current news, and tax regulations in plain English, visit the IRS Web site at *www.irs.gov.* A site that links you to just about every other tax site that's useful is *www.taxsites.com.* This site, maintained by University of Northern Iowa Professor Dennis Schmidt, will lead you to federal, state, and city tax resources. My web site at *www.thetaxguy.com* gives you links to resources for home-based business owners and updates on the contents of this book.

If you are a member of an online service, such as America Online or CompuServe, you will find a wealth of tax information by using a key-word search for "tax" or "taxes," though finding an answer to a particular burning question might prove frustrating. Two virtual law libraries operated by private companies are *Lexis* and *Westlaw.* These provide online access to every tax resource available in a law school library. These services are primarily used by attorneys and tax professionals, and are expensive. However, you might find a law school or business library in your area that makes these services available to the public free of charge.

Now that you know where the rules come from and how to look them up, you might like to know how the IRS administers them on an individual basis. The next section describes what you have to look forward to if you are audited, and what your rights are if you disagree with the results.

The Audit Process and Your Appeal Rights

We all have our own particular phobias. What might frighten one person, someone else can take in stride. But the one thing that seems to traumatize just about all of us is the prospect of an audit from the IRS. Perhaps the greatest fear of this process is not knowing what to expect. If that's the case, this section should ease your mind somewhat.

Only a small percentage of U.S. taxpayers are audited each year. Those who run a small, unincorporated business are better candidates than other individuals, but even they have about a 95 percent chance of *not* getting audited. The IRS has limited resources, so it tries to make its audit program as efficient as possible. It does this by selecting returns for audit that appear to be the best prospects for additional tax.

This is done through a computer program called the "Discriminant Function System" (DIF). This program scores each return for potential error based upon prior experience. For example, let's say you decide to cheat, and you claim exemptions for a few of the neighborhood kids in addition to your own. Your return will receive a large DIF score. That will make it pop out of the computer like a piece of burnt toast, right into the waiting hands of your friendly neighborhood IRS agent.

The Examination

Many examinations are done strictly by mail. This is called a correspondence examination. You get a letter asking for documentation or additional information on a particular line item of your return. If you provide the requested information, the IRS might agree with you. If it does not, it should explain the reasons for any changes. Do not hesitate to ask questions if you do not understand the changes. If you have questions you cannot resolve through the mail, you can request a personal interview with an agent.[8] Additionally, if you feel that handling the examination through correspondence is impractical or places you at a disadvantage, you can request an office examination conference immediately.

If an examination is conducted through a personal interview with an agent, you have the right to ask that it take place at a convenient time and place. It might take place at the IRS office, your home or place of work, or the office of your accountant or attorney. If you are claiming home-office deductions, the agent will likely want to visit your home office. If you had someone prepare your return for you, make sure they show up, too. If you would like to let your representative handle it, you could even grant your attorney or accountant a "power of attorney" (IRS Form 2848, *Power of Attorney and Declaration of Representative*) and let him or her meet with the agent alone.

At the end of the examination, the agent will give you a report if there are any proposed changes to your return. Remember that the IRS must follow the Internal Revenue Code and Supreme Court decisions. But the IRS does not have to follow the precedent of lower court decisions, and may still apply its own interpretation to your situation.[9] If you do not agree with the report after the agent has explained the adjustments and your available appeal rights, you can request a meeting with the agent's supervisor. As a tactical strategy, sometimes an agent will discover one point but fail to develop another point that could result in even more tax. Here it may be advisable to accept the proposed adjustment because carrying the case forward might lead to the opening of other items on the return.

APPEAL WITHIN THE IRS

If you cannot resolve the dispute with the supervisor, the agent will send you a notice of proposed deficiency, commonly called a *30-day letter.* This letter tells you about your right to appeal the proposed changes within 30 days to the IRS Appeals Office. Accompanying the letter you will receive:

- A copy of the examination report explaining the agent's proposed changes.
- An agreement or waiver form (Form 870).
- A copy of IRS Publication 5, Appeal Rights and Preparation for Unagreed Cases.

You have the option of accepting the proposed adjustments by signing the waiver form and paying the tax, or you can appeal the proposed changes. The letter will explain what steps you should take, depending on which action you choose.

The regional IRS Appeals Office, which is independent of the District Director or the Service Center, is the only level of appeal within the IRS. You may or may not be required to file a written protest, and the conference is conducted in an informal manner. Most disputes are settled at this level. The appeals officer has the authority to compromise, and the IRS is generally not interested in going to court if it doesn't have to. Many legal issues are not amenable to compromise, however, and the IRS is not likely to back down. That means if you want to press the issue, you will have to go to court.

THE 90-DAY LETTER

If you cannot come to terms with the appeals officer, the IRS will send you a statutory notice of deficiency, commonly called a *90-day letter.* If you do not respond within 90 days of the date this letter is mailed, the IRS can issue an assessment and begin collection proceedings. Don't put yourself in this position—collection people are not fun to deal with. If you do not want to go to court, and you do not have the money to pay, ask the IRS for Publication 594, *Understanding the Collection Process.* This tells you about arranging installment payments, delaying collection action, and submitting an offer in compromise.

A proper response to the 90-day letter is your only way of preserving your right to litigate the issues. Your options within the 90-day period are to: (1) pay the tax and be done with it, (2) not pay the tax and file a petition with the Tax Court, or (3) pay the tax to stop the accrual of interest;[10] then file a petition with the Tax Court. If you do not file a petition with the Tax Court within this 90-day period, you lose your right to litigate the case in the Tax Court. If you pay the tax and later decide to litigate one or more of the issues, you can still take your case to the Court of Claims or your district court. To do this you must file a claim for refund with the IRS; then you can sue for the refund if it is denied.

Taking Your Case to the Tax Court

Over 95 percent of tax litigation begins in the Tax Court. This is probably because when you file a petition with the Tax Court, you do not have to pay the disputed tax until after *final determination.* Final determination means you have exhausted all your appeal rights, and the courts still say you owe the tax. You can stop the accrual of interest by prepaying the tax if you wish, but only after you have received the 90-day letter. If you pay the tax prior to receiving the 90-day letter, you might ruin your chances of taking your case to the Tax Court. This is because if you send in the entire amount due, the IRS will not send you a 90-day letter, and you can only file a petition in the Tax Court after receiving a 90-day letter.[11]

If your petition is properly filed within the 90-day period, the court will schedule your case for trial at a location convenient to you. You can represent yourself in court or you can hire an attorney to argue your case.

The Tax Court is a national court, with judges who travel the country to hear cases. There are 19 regular judges who are appointed by the president, and a number of special trial judges who are also authorized to hear cases. One judge presides over each case, and the trial judge's opinion is reviewed by the Chief Judge before it is final. If the Chief Judge believes the case deals with issues that are controversial or particularly important, the case will be reviewed by all 19 regular judges.

Tax Court judges are very knowledgeable of tax issues. Many are former IRS or Justice Department litigators. Because of this, some say the Tax Court is biased in favor of the IRS. It is true that the IRS tends to win more cases in the Tax Court than taxpayers. On the other hand, you would be surprised at some of the cases in which the court seems to bend over backwards to give the taxpayer a fair shake.

THE SMALL CASE PROCEDURE

A unique feature of the Tax Court is its *Small Case Procedure.* If the amount of tax in dispute is $50,000 or less for any tax year, the Tax Court will hear your case in an informal setting. That means you do not have to comply with a lot of formal legal procedures making it easy to present your case in court without having to hire an attorney or an accountant. The downside of using the Small Case Procedure is that the judge's opinion is final, and *there is no right to appeal.* You can get more information on the Tax Court procedures by writing the United States Tax Court, 400 Second Street, N.W., Washington, DC 20217.

Litigating in Your District Court or the Court of Claims

Perhaps you have paid the tax and failed to file a petition in the Tax Court, but you still believe the IRS is wrong and you want your money back. You start by filing a claim for refund with the IRS. This will not get you your money unless someone at the IRS sends it back by mistake. However, this enables you to sue the IRS for a refund when it rejects your claim, or does not act within six months from the date you file the claim. To enforce your claim, you must file suit in your United States district court or in the Court of Claims within two years after your claim is rejected by the IRS. The Tax Court is not an option at this point.

Litigating in the district court might be an advantage if you think you could benefit from a jury trial. This is only an option in a district court (not the Tax

Court or Court of Claims), and the jury can only decide issues of *fact*, not *law*. On the other hand, taking your case to the Court of Claims might be best if the argument you wish to make has been heard in a previous case and rejected by the Tax Court, your district court, or the court of appeals in your area. If your argument has not been rejected by the Court of Claims, that court does not have to follow the precedent of the other courts.

You can get more information about procedures for filing suit in either court by contacting the clerk of your district court or the clerk of the Court of Claims. The address for the Court of Claims is: United States Court of Federal Claims, 717 Madison Place, N.W., Washington, DC 20005. Addresses for all district courts are listed in IRS Publication 556, *Examination of Returns, Appeal Rights, and Claims for Refund*.

Recovering Litigation or Administrative Costs

Although it is possible to represent yourself in court, it is not advisable unless you happen to be an attorney and are familiar with courtroom procedures. (Being a regular viewer of *Law and Order* doesn't make it.) The only situation in which you are not at a disadvantage in representing yourself in a tax case is if you are litigating in the Tax Court under the Small Case Procedure. Litigation is therefore costly, even if you win, because you will have attorney fees and other costs to pay. To prevent the IRS from using this fact to coerce taxpayers into submitting to trumped up charges, Congress passed a law that requires the IRS to refund you for reasonable litigation or administrative costs under certain circumstances.[12]

You may be able to recover these litigation or administrative costs if you are the *prevailing party* and if:

- You have exhausted your administrative remedies within the IRS.
- Your net worth is not more than $2 million ($7 million if the taxpayer is a business) when the litigation or administrative proceedings began.
- You do not unreasonably delay the proceedings.

You are considered the *prevailing party* if:

1. You have substantially prevailed with respect to the amount in controversy or with respect to the most significant issues.
2. You establish that the position of the IRS in the proceedings was not substantially justified.

If the controversy has gone to court, the court will decide whether or not you are the prevailing party. If it is an administrative action, the IRS will decide, subject to appeal by you to the Tax Court.

What Costs Are Recoverable?

As long as they are reasonable, you can generally recover the following:

- Attorney fees that generally may not exceed $150 per hour (for 2002).
- The costs of studies, analyses, engineering reports, and other projects that are necessary to prepare your case.
- Court costs.
- Expenses for expert witnesses.
- Administrative fees charged by the IRS for administrative proceedings.

To find out more, see IRS Publication 556.

Additional Resources

Although the IRS presents only its point of view on legal issues, its tax publications provide useful general guidance in a variety of areas. Additional information on the examination and appeal process and access to the courts can be found in IRS Publication 556, *Examination of Returns, Appeal Rights and Claims for Refund*. Publication 1, *Your Rights as a Taxpayer*, explains your rights at each step in the tax process. Publication 594, *Understanding the Collection Process*, explains IRS procedures after you have been issued an assessment notice. Publication 910, *Guide to Free Tax Services*, provides a list of free tax publications and an index of tax topics and related publications. It also describes other free tax information available from the IRS, including tax education and assistance programs.

You can get these publications free by calling the IRS at (800) TAX-FORM [(800) 829-3676]. If you have access to TTY/TDD equipment, you can call (800) 829-4059. To download them from the Internet, go to *www.irs.gov* (World Wide Web), or *ftp.irs.gov* (FTP). If you would like to get forms and instructions (not publications) by FAX, dial (703) 368-9694 to reach IRS Tax Fax.

Notes

[1] IRC § 7805.

[2] See Rev. Proc. 2000-3, 2000-1 I.R.B. 103 for the latest list of areas in which the IRS will not issue advance rulings.

[3] Rev. Proc. 2000-1, 2000-1 I.R.B. 4.

[4] IRC § 6110(j)(3).

[5] 2001-52 I.R.B. 1.

[6] *Robert F. Six and Ethel Merman Six v. United States,* 450 F 2d 66 (2d Cir. 1971).

[7] *Coerver v. Commissioner,* 297 F.2d 837 (3d Cir. 1962); *Bercaw v. Commissioner,* 165 F.2d 521 (4th Cir. 1948); *Commissioner v. Mooneyman,* 404 F.2d 522 (6th Cir. 1968); *England v. United States,* 345 F.2d 414 (7th Cir. 1965); *Jenkins v. Commissioner,* 418 F.2d 1292 (8th Cir. 1969) *Wills v. Commissioner,* 411 F.2d 357 (9th Cir. 1969); and *York v. Commissioner,* 160 F.2d 385 (D.C. Cir. 1947).

[8] See IRS Publication 1, *Your Rights as a Taxpayer.*

[9] See IRS Publication 556, *Examination of Returns, Appeal Rights, and Claims for Refund.*

[10] Ibid.

[11] Ibid.

[12] IRC § 7430.

CHAPTER 2

What Is a Business for Tax Purposes?

> The chief business of the American people is business.
>
> —Calvin Coolidge

The Internal Revenue Code requires that you be engaged in a trade or business in order to claim trade or business deductions on Schedules C, C-EZ, F, or E of Form 1040, or employee business deductions on Schedule A of Form 1040. Deductions for the use of a home office are a special kind of trade or business deduction. In this chapter, you will learn how to structure an activity so that it qualifies as a trade or business, and how to identify legitimate trade or business deductions.

Although the term *trade or business* is used hundreds of times in the Code and IRS regulations, neither Congress nor the IRS has provided us with a general definition. Over the years, the IRS and taxpayers have had differences of opinion about what this term means, and occasionally the dispute has wound up in the Supreme Court.

In considering the meaning of trade or business, the Supreme Court has given us some guidance, but no precise or unequivocal rules. In 1911, for example, when the Court dealt with the issue for the first time, it simply looked up the definition in the dictionary, which said a business is "[t]hat which occupies the time, attention, and labor of men for the purpose of a livelihood or profit."[1] In a more recent decision, the Court narrowed the concept a little when it said:

> We accept the fact that to be engaged in a trade or business, the taxpayer must be involved in the activity with continuity and regularity, and that the taxpayer's primary purpose for engaging in the activity must be for income or profit. A sporadic activity, a hobby, or an amusement diversion does not qualify.[2]

17

So generally, if you are engaged in an activity on a regular and continuous basis, and your main purpose is to earn an income, you have a trade or business. (Exceptions to this rule are discussed next.) Your business need not be full-time, and you could be engaged in several businesses at once. Being engaged in a trade or business does not presume that you are actually earning an income, or generating any revenue at all—only that you are trying. However, your main purpose for engaging in the activity must be to earn a profit, and the best way to indicate this is to actually show a profit at some point. If you run a sole proprietorship (discussed in Chapter 3) income and deductions of your business are reported on Schedule C, "Profit or Loss from Business." Even if you work for someone else as an employee you are deemed to be engaged in a trade or business for tax purposes, but unreimbursed employee business expenses must be reported as "miscellaneous itemized deductions" on Schedule A, and are reduced by 2 percent of your Adjusted Gross Income.

Investing Cannot Be a Business

An exception to the previous definition of trade or business is the activity of investing in securities or collectibles to generate long-term profits. In 1941, the Supreme Court held that the activity of investing is not a trade or business.[3] Consequently, as an investor, you may not deduct the costs of an office at home regardless of what you are investing in, whether it is stocks and bonds or rare beer cans.

An investor might spend a substantial amount of time investing, but no matter how much time is spent, an investor is never considered to be engaged in a trade or business with respect to his or her investment activities.[4]

This is not to say that investment related expenses are not deductible; only that home-office deductions cannot be claimed as investment expenses. Section 212 of the Code allows investment-related expenses to be deducted by individuals. These are generally included on Schedule A (line 22) as miscellaneous itemized deductions. Gains and losses from the investments are generally capital gains and losses and are reported on Schedule D ("Capital Gains and Losses").

If you are a *trader* or a *dealer* in securities or commodities, your activities probably qualify as a business, and you can report your income and deductions on Schedule C. Now the question is: How do you tell whether you are an investor, a trader, or a dealer?

Dealing or Trading Could Be a Business

If you buy and sell regularly on an exchange (for securities) or any other active market (commodities, for example), you might be either a dealer or a trader. If you buy with the expectation of reselling at a profit not because of a rise in value between the purchase and resale, but merely because you have a market of buyers who will purchase from you at a price in excess of your cost, you are a dealer. The markup between your purchase price and your selling price represents compensation for your service in bringing buyers and sellers together.[5]

Traders, on the other hand, do not perform a merchandising function, because their source of supply is not significantly different from that of those to whom they sell. That is, they trade in an open market and perform no services that need to be compensated for by a markup in price. If you are a trader, you depend on such circumstances as a rise in value or an advantageous purchase to be able to sell at a price in excess of your cost.[6] As a trader, you seek profit from short-term market swings and receive income principally from the activity of buying and selling rather than from dividends, interest, or long-term appreciation.[7]

The primary distinction, for tax purposes, between a trader and a dealer is that a dealer reports gains and losses as ordinary business gains and losses on Schedule C, while a trader generally reports gains and losses as capital gains and losses on Schedule D.[8] Nevertheless, if you are either a dealer or a trader, you will be deemed to be engaged in a trade or business if your trading is frequent and substantial.[9] This also means that if you deal or trade out of your home, your home-office expenses are deductible.

The difference between an investor and a trader relates to your motive for buying and selling. While a trader seeks profit from short-term market swings rather than from dividends, interest, or long-term appreciation, an investor makes purchases for capital appreciation and income, usually without regard to short-term developments. If you are actively buying and selling securities or other property as a dealer or trader, it doesn't mean that you cannot also be an investor with respect to some of your transactions, but those transactions should not be considered part of your business.

Being a trader implies more frequent and substantial purchases and sales than being an investor.[10] Activities that are sporadic, in the sense that they are not regular and continuous, do not qualify as a trade or business.[11] For example, in *Paoli v. Commissioner*,[12] the taxpayer maintained a private telephone line with a stock brokerage house and had frequent conversations with brokers. A machine in the taxpayer's home produced current stock prices (this was before the Internet), and he also obtained information regarding his investments from periodicals and company reports. The taxpayer consummated 326 securities sales during the year at issue involving approximately $9 million worth of securities. Between January 12 and February 11, the taxpayer consummated 125 of the 326 sales of stocks made during the year. During January, February, March, and May, the taxpayer reported 233 sales, about 72 percent of the total sales for the year. From the volume of the transactions, it would seem that Paoli would qualify as a trader. But the Tax Court concluded that he failed to prove that his pattern of buying and selling stocks was sufficiently regular and continuous during the entire year to constitute a trade or business, so Paoli was classified as an investor.

As you can see, the distinction between being a trader (having a business) and being an investor (not having a business) is a pretty fuzzy one. It is a factual question that depends on your own situation and personal motivation. You bear the burden of proving that your activities constitute a trade or business.[13] Therefore, if you decide that you're a trader, you should be prepared to back up your conclusion if questioned by an IRS agent.

Rents from Real Estate

If you are a dealer or trader in real estate, and you receive rents from property you are holding for resale, the rental income and deductions are reported on Schedule C (Form 1040) along with your other business income and deductions.[14] If you run a hotel, a boarding house, or an apartment house where you provide hotel services to the occupants, or if you provide space in parking lots, warehouses, or storage garages, the income and deductions are also reported on Schedule C.[15] To provide hotel services to occupants of an apartment house means to provide maid services and other services for the convenience of the occupants. But the normal services rendered to occupants of apartments, like furnishing heat and light and cleaning the public areas, are not considered hotel services.

In contrast, if you do not provide services to tenants and you are neither a dealer nor a trader, your income and deductions from rental real estate are reported on Schedule E, Part I ("Income or Loss from Rental Real Estate and Royalties"). Even if your real estate rental activities take a lot of time, and even if you rent appliances and furniture with your buildings, you still use Schedule E as long as you do not provide services to the renters.[16]

Because income reported on Schedule E is generally considered investment income, you don't pay self-employment tax (social security tax) on Schedule E net income. However, depending on your degree of involvement, rental activities reported on Schedule E can be considered a business rather than an investment activity. The courts have held that renting even a single property can constitute a business for various purposes.[17] In the 1980 case of *Curphey v. Commissioner*,[18] the Tax Court held that the rental activities of a dermatologist who was employed full time by a hospital, but who also owned and managed six rental properties, constituted a business for the purpose of claiming home-office deductions. The Tax Court made it clear that ownership and management of such properties will not always qualify as a business, and that the scope of a taxpayer's management activities will be the deciding factor.

In spite of the *Curphey* decision, the unofficial position of the IRS is that home-office deductions are not available in connection with rental real estate. Therefore, even if you satisfy the Tax Court's trade or business requirement, and all the other requirements under Section 280A, you still might have to butt heads with an IRS agent over home-office deductions on Schedule E. Perhaps the IRS will soften its position now that the new relaxed standards for home-office deductions are in effect (see Chapter 5).

Is It a Hobby or a Business?

A rule laid down by the Supreme Court is that a business cannot be merely a hobby.[19] Having a hobby means that your primary objective in engaging in the activity is to have a little fun rather than to be profitable. So the deciding factor in distinguishing a business from a hobby is whether the activity is engaged in for profit.

This is not to say that your business must generate a profit in order to be considered a business, or even that there be a reasonable expectation of a profit.[20] But if you do incur losses, you must be able to demonstrate that your primary motive in running the business is to produce income. The IRS loves to disallow losses to small business owners on the assertion that they are hobby losses rather than business losses.

Relevant Factors in Determining a Profit Motive

The IRS has specified nine factors in the regulations that it will use to determine a profit motive.[21] It stipulates, however, that whether a profit motive exists depends on the circumstances of each case, and all relevant information beyond the factors specified will be taken into account. The IRS has cautioned that it places greater weight on objective facts than the taxpayer's mere statement of subjective intent. Nine factors listed in the regulations include:

1. *The manner in which the taxpayer carries on the activity.* If you take your business seriously by operating in a businesslike manner and maintaining a complete and accurate set of books, you would appear to have a profit motive. Additionally, carrying on your business in substantially the same way as others in the same business who are profitable would indicate a profit motive. You would also demonstrate a profit motive if you change your operating procedures, adopt new techniques, or abandon old methods in an effort to improve your profitability.

   Here are a few things you can do to help satisfy this requirement. Get an Employer Identification Number (see Chapter 9) and apply to the Secretary of State (for your state of business) for an assumed business name.

Become aware of all the state and local requirements for home-based businesses and comply with them. Have a separate checking account for your business and use it only for business transactions. Most importantly, set up a formal bookkeeping system, even if it is a simple single-entry system (see Chapter 11).

2. *The expertise of the taxpayer or his advisors.* Preparation before commencing the business activity through extensive study of its accepted business, economic, and scientific practices, or consultation with experts, may indicate a profit motive if you carry on the activity in accordance with such practices. On the other hand, if you consult with experts and don't do what they say, it might indicate a lack of profit motive, unless it appears you are attempting to develop superior techniques.

For example, if you think it would be a good idea to raise Giant African Bullfrogs so you can sell their big juicy legs to restaurants, don't just run out and start buying frogs. Come up with a business plan detailing how you will become profitable in the frog business. Do some reading about the frogs first. Learn how to care and feed the frogs. Learn what kind of environment the frogs are comfortable in and come up with an adequate facility. Talk to Giant African Bullfrog experts, if you can find any. Most importantly, see if their legs are tasty and find out if anyone else likes them. To claim business deductions you must be able to demonstrate to the IRS that you thoroughly researched the business that you are in and have adequate knowledge of the business to make it profitable.

3. *The time and effort expended by the taxpayer in the activy.* The fact that you devote much of your personal time and effort to the activity, particularly if the activity is not a lot of fun, may indicate a profit motive. Quitting your day job to devote more time to your business is another indication of a profit motive. However, the fact that your business is part-time and you only have limited time to devote to it does not necessarily indicate lack of profit motive.

4. *Expectation that the assets used in the activity will appreciate in value.* The term *profit* includes appreciation of your business assets. So even if you have losses from current operations, your expectation that your business property will appreciate over time to produce an overall profit, will demonstrate a profit motive.

5. *The success of the taxpayer in carrying on other activities.* Entrepreneurial success in the past with other business ventures might indicate a profit motive in your current activity, even if the activity is currently unprofitable.

6. *The taxpayer's history of income or losses with respect to the activity.* If losses are sustained after the time that is usually necessary to make the operation profitable, such losses might be an indication of lack of profit motive. However, if such losses result from circumstances that are beyond your control, such as natural disasters, fire, theft, disease, or depressed market conditions, such losses would not be indicative of lack of profit motive.

   Remember that a reasonable expectation of profit is not required. For example, suppose you think you're going to make a killing in a wildcat oil well operation that produces large losses year after year, even if everyone thinks you're crazy and should get out of the investment while you still have your shirt. Regardless of how speculative the investment, the oil well activity would be considered engaged in for profit.

7. *The amount of occasional profits, if any.* Generating an occasional small profit is not necessarily indicative of a profit motive, especially if your investment is large or you have sustained large losses in other years. However, a large profit, though only occasional, would indicate a profit motive when the investment or losses in other years are comparatively small. Also, the opportunity to eventually earn substantial profit in a highly speculative venture is usually sufficient to indicate a profit motive.

8. *The financial status of the taxpayer.* The fact that you do not have substantial income or capital from sources other than the activity might indicate that the activity is engaged in for profit. In other words, if you are going to have to generate income from your activity in order to eat, that's a pretty good indication that you expect to make a profit. On the other hand, if you or your spouse has a well-paying job, or if you have a lot of money stashed away, it might be an indication you do not have a profit motive. This is especially true if you are claiming large losses and the business you are engaged in is fun.

9. *Elements of personal pleasure or recreation.* If your business activity involves doing what you love to do for recreation, that might indicate a lack of profit motive. In contrast, if your business activity is not any fun at all, that might indicate a profit motive. Nevertheless, personal enjoyment is not sufficient to tip the scales either way; you are not expected to be motivated strictly by profit and to do work that is not enjoyable.

   For example, suppose you have enjoyed fishing as a hobby for years. If you become a professional fishing guide and incur start-up losses, the fact that you love to fish might be one indication that you are not engaged in the activity for profit. However, if you carry on in a businesslike manner, are knowledgeable in what you do, and have quit your other job to pursue your new business, you will demonstrate a profit motive.

What to Do if All You Have Is a Hobby

There is actually a section in the Internal Revenue Code that allows the deductibility of expenses incurred in connection with a hobby. This is a Code section that you want to utilize only if you lose the argument that your activity is a business. It only applies if the hobby is conducted by an individual, an S corporation, or a partnership. It is Section 183 and it allows you to deduct your hobby expenses to the extent that your hobby generates income. These expenses are only deductible as Miscellaneous Itemized Deductions on Schedule A, subject to the reduction by 2 percent of your Adjusted Gross Income. Any expenses in excess of income that are not otherwise deductible are lost forever.

Under Section 183, there is a presumption that your activity is engaged in for profit if gross income from the activity exceeds expenses attributable to the activity for three out of five consecutive years (two out of seven years for breeding, training, showing, or racing horses).[22] The presumption generally applies to the third profit year (second year for horses) and all years subsequent to the third profit year within any five-year period. Still, this does not mean that losses will automatically be allowed. The IRS may try to rebut the presumption by showing a lack of profit motive.

If you have losses in the first few years of an activity that is less than five years old, and the IRS tries to disallow them as hobby losses, you can elect to postpone the determination of whether the activity is engaged in for profit until after the fifth year (seventh year for horses). The election applies to all the years in this initial five- (or seven-) year period. The election is made on Form 5213, "Election to Postpone Determination (as to Whether the Presumption Applies That an Activity Is Engaged in for Profit)." It must be made by the earlier of three years after the due date of the return for your first business year, or 60 days after receiving a 30-day letter from the IRS proposing to classify your activity as a hobby. If you make the election, the IRS has an additional two years after the five- (or seven-) year period in which to audit your initial return.

If you file your first year's return on time and you believe your activity is a business, you should never make this election unless and until you have received the 30-day letter from the IRS. *Read that again.* You should always treat your activity as a business until the IRS asserts that it is a hobby. Filing Form 5213 before being contacted for audit simply tells the IRS that you think you have a hobby rather than a business, and that maybe they should send someone over right away to look into it. Filing Form 5213 before being contacted for audit also gives the IRS an additional two years to issue deficiencies related to the activity.

Identifying Deductible Business Expenses

"Can I write this off?" That's a question that has been asked of tax accountants countless times since the enactment of our income tax in 1913. It often relates to whether an amount qualifies as a deductible business expense. Sometimes the answer is not easy.

The first issue to consider is whether a taxpayer is conducting a business as opposed to an investment activity or a hobby. Some investment and hobby expenses are deductible, but they are subject to separate limitations and reporting requirements, as discussed earlier.

Some business expenses, like entertainment and travel expenses, are subject to special record-keeping requirements. Still others, like home-business deductions, are limited by special rules. These topics are addressed in later chapters. Before the limitations apply, however, a cornerstone section of the Code provides the basic foundation of deductibility. It is IRC Section 162. Here is the pertinent part:

> Sec. 162. Trade or Business Expenses.
>
> (a) In General—There shall be allowed as a deduction all the ordinary and necessary expenses paid or incurred during the taxable year in carrying on any trade or business, ...

There is a lot more to Section 162 than shown here, but within this phrase are all the general criteria. Each item must meet the four conditions specified in this phrase to be deductible as a business expense. It must be (1) an *expense* as opposed to a capital expenditure, (2) *ordinary* and *necessary*, (3) *paid or incurred*, and (4) for *carrying on* a *trade or business*.

Is It an Expense?

An expense is a cost that primarily benefits the immediate taxable year, in contrast with a cost that will benefit your business for several years to come. For example, a car repair is an expense, while a new car is not—it is a capital expenditure. The monthly phone bill is an expense, while the cost of purchasing your phone is not. The cost of a business car or a business phone might be deductible as depreciation over the years they are used for business. These assets might even be deductible in full in the year of purchase under a special Code provision (Section 179). But they do not qualify as Section 162 deductions. See Chapters 6 and 8 for more detailed information.

Is It Ordinary and Necessary?

The meaning of ordinary and necessary has been left to the courts to interpret. These are terms that have never been defined by the Code or regulations.

"Ordinary," according to the Supreme Court, means "normal, usual, or customary."[23] The Court also said an expense may be ordinary even though it happens only once in a taxpayer's lifetime. An example would be the cost of defending your business against a lawsuit.

"Necessary," according to the Supreme Court, means no more than "appropriate and helpful"[24] in running your business. For example, if you embark on a massive TV advertising campaign because you believe it will increase your net income, the IRS does not have the right to disallow the expense because the agent believes it to be a bad business decision. The courts have tended to accept the judgment of taxpayers regarding the business value of expenditures; they don't want IRS agents acting as business efficiency experts.

Deductions have also been disallowed under the ordinary and necessary standard if they are incurred primarily for personal reasons rather than for a business purpose.[25] There is a pretty fuzzy line between what the IRS and the courts consider primarily personal and what they consider to be an ordinary and necessary business expense. Although there are no clear standards for separating the two, the history of court decisions on this issue suggests that you ask yourself the following questions:

1. Would the expense have been incurred were it not for the business purpose?
2. Do you receive any significant personal satisfaction from the expenditure beyond its business purpose?
3. Does the Code specifically provide for the expense as an itemized deduction (like medical expenses and home mortgage interest, implying that it is not available as a business expense)?

If your answer is "no" to all of these questions, you have a good argument for claiming a business deduction, provided the expense meets the other conditions of Section 162. The IRS and the courts will not necessarily agree, but at least you have a legitimate defense. Here is an example:

Example 2.1

Bubba was the manager of a fashion boutique and was required to purchase and wear boutique clothes at work. But Bubba was not a boutique kind of guy, and would not be caught dead wearing boutique clothes outside the shop. Bubba went to work in blue jeans and cowboy boots and changed into his boutique clothes after he got to work. Bubba deducted his boutique clothes as an ordinary and necessary business expense under Section 162. The IRS said the cost of the clothes was a personal, nondeductible expense.

A case similar to Bubba's was heard in the Tax Court, which allowed the deduction.[26] The Tax Court said the deduction should be allowed as an ordinary and necessary business expense if: (1) the clothing was required or essential in the taxpayer's employment, (2) the clothing was not suitable for general or personal wear, and (3) the clothing was not so worn. The Tax Court used a subjective approach to determine suitability for personal wear, basing its decision on the lifestyle of the taxpayer.

The case was appealed by the IRS, however, to the Fifth Circuit Court of Appeals, which held for the IRS.[27] The appellate court used an objective approach, and said the cost of such clothes was not deductible because the clothes were commonly adaptable to general usage. Still, the Tax Court's reasoning remains valid outside the jurisdiction of the Fifth Circuit Court of Appeals.

Ordinary and necessary also implies that an expense be reasonable in amount.[28] This is a test primarily used to determine if the full amount paid for goods and services from related taxpayers is legitimate. Sometimes overpayments are used to disguise gifts from family members or dividends from closely held corporations.

Is It Paid or Incurred During the Taxable Year?

This requirement relates to the method of accounting you use for your business. If you are on the cash method, it is not good enough to have *incurred* an expense; you must pay it to deduct it. Likewise, if you are on an accrual method, you must have incurred an expense according to the rules for accrual method taxpayers to deduct it. See Chapter 4.

Are You Carrying on a Trade or Business?

An expense is not a deductible business expense unless you are *carrying on* your business at the time it is paid or incurred. To be carrying on means to be actually conducting business rather than preparing to conduct business. For example, let's say you are opening a travel agency in your home. The first month you decorate your office, install a phone line, set up your computer system, and send out promotional literature. It is not until the second month that you begin to accept clients. Any ordinary and necessary business expenses incurred during the first month are not incurred in *carrying on* a trade or business. That means you can't deduct them as business expenses. A separate provision in the Code (Section 195) allows you to amortize them over a 60-month period beginning with the month you begin business.

Does It Pay to Be Creative?

Does it pay to be creative? The answer is—it depends. If you lack sufficient knowledge of the income tax laws and your purpose is to evade paying taxes, your creativity could land you in jail. On the other hand, tax law is constantly evolving in the courts and in Congress because of the legitimate creativity of taxpayers and their advisors. If you have a deduction that you believe meets the requirements of Section 162, and no one can tell you why it doesn't—go for it! Here is an example of a taxpayer who believed she was right and prevailed.

Mrs. Green Really Poured Herself into Her Work

Mrs. Green sold her blood plasma to a local laboratory. She possessed a rare blood type (AB negative), so her blood plasma was a scarce commodity. She marketed her plasma for a number of years as her primary source of income. She would drive to the lab, which was about 20 miles away from her house, about once a week. At the lab, they would take out some blood, put it through a process called plasmapheresis to remove the plasma, then put back into her what was left.

Before this process began, the lab always tested her blood for the desired concentration of iron, protein, and antibodies. If her blood had a low concentration of these items, she was not allowed to give plasma. Therefore, to maintain a marketable product, she took vitamins and minerals, and ate a special high-protein diet.

On her tax return, Mrs. Green reported her income from plasma donations as business income. She deducted the following expenses as business expenses: (1) the excess cost of a high-protein diet over her normal diet, (2) vitamin and mineral supplements, and (3) car expenses to and from the lab.

THE IRS PUT A TOURNIQUET ON THE DEDUCTIONS

The IRS said the food eaten at home was a personal expense and not deductible. For some reason, it allowed part of the vitamins, but disallowed the rest. The travel to and from the lab, it said, was commuting and nondeductible. Mrs. Green, not being one of faint heart, was convinced that the expenses were sufficiently related to her blood business to be deductible. She therefore took her claim to the Tax Court and argued her case before the court herself.

THE TAX COURT LOOSENED THE KNOT

To convince the court that her deductions were legitimate business expenses, Mrs. Green was first required to show that the sale of her blood was a business. This she did by showing that she engaged in the blood-giving activity on a regular and continual basis for the purpose of deriving an income. The Court decided that her blood donations were comparable to the selling of a product, which required removal and processing in the laboratory. After proving that her blood was a marketable product, Mrs. Green had to show that she incurred the costs of a high-protein diet and vitamins, not for her personal benefit, but because her product would not be marketable without these supplements. On this issue the Tax Court ruled:

> [T]he additional expense of a high-protein diet is a deductible business expense . . . when the diet is intimately related to [Mrs. Green's] production of acceptable blood plasma and [Mrs. Green] has incurred the additional expense of this special diet solely in furtherance of her business of selling blood plasma. . . . In the unique situation presented by the instant set of facts, the special foods expense incurred in addition to that necessary for [Mrs. Green's] personal needs crosses "the line" and becomes a business expense deduction.[29]

Having persuaded the Tax Court that her high-protein food and vitamins were deductible as business expenses, Mrs. Green then turned to the task of showing that her trips to and from the lab were also business expenses, and not merely commuting expenses as contended by the IRS. Commuting expenses are clearly personal expenses and are not deductible.[30]

The trips, said Mrs. Green, were not the same as driving to and from work. Because she was selling a tangible product to the lab, the trips were equivalent to transporting a product to market. The nature of her product was such that she could not transport it to market without her accompanying it. She was, in effect, the container in which the product had to be transported. The Court bought this argument, and reasoned that "[h]ad she been able to extract the plasma at home and transport it to the lab without her being present, such shipping expenses would have been deductible as selling expenses."[31] The Court therefore allowed her to deduct her transportation expenses.

This is a case with a unique factual pattern involving expenses that are normally considered nondeductible. Because the taxpayer focused on what she believed legitimately satisfied the requirements of a deductible business expense, and used creative arguments to make her case, she was able to win over the Tax Court.

Additional Resources

Additional information on business and investment expenses is found in Publication 535, *Business Expenses;* and Publication 550, *Investment Income and Expenses.* Publication 910, *Guide to Free Tax Services,* provides a list of free tax publications and an index of tax topics and related publications. It also describes other free tax information available from the IRS, including tax education and assistance programs.

You can get these publications free by calling the IRS at (800) TAX-FORM [(800) 829-3676]. If you have access to TTY/TDD equipment, you can call (800) 829-4059. To download them from the Internet, go to *www.irs.gov* (World Wide

Web), or *ftp.irs.gov* (FTP). If you would like to get forms and instructions (not publications) by FAX, dial (703) 368-9694 to reach IRS Tax Fax.

Notes

[1] *Flint v. Stone Tracy Co.*, 220 U.S. 107, 171 (1911).

[2] *Commissioner v. Groetzinger*, 480 U.S. 23, 35 (1987).

[3] *Higgins v. Commissioner*, 312 U.S. 212 (1941).

[4] Ibid.

[5] *King v. Commissioner*, 89 T.C. 445, 457 (1987).

[6] Ibid.

[7] *Groetzinger v. Commissioner*, 771 F.2d 269, 274-275 (7th Cir. 1985), affd. 480 U.S. (1987).

[8] *King v. Commissioner*, note 5.

[9] *Groetzinger v. Commissioner*, note 7.

[10] *King v. Commissioner*, note 5 at 458.

[11] *Polakis v. Commissioner*, 91 T.C. 660, 670-672 (1988); *Steffler, et ux. v. Commissioner* (T.C. Memo. 1995-271).

[12] *Paoli v. Commissioner*, T.C. Memo. 1991-351.

[13] *Estate of Yaeger, v. Commissioner*, T.C. Memo. 1988-264; *Mayer v. Commissioner*, T.C. Memo. 1994-209.

[14] Treas. Reg. § 1.1402(a)-4(a).

[15] Treas. Reg. § 1.1402(a)-4(c)(2).

[16] Treas. Reg. § 1.1402(a)-4(c)(1).

[17] See, e.g., *Hazard v. Commissioner*, 7 T.C. 372 (1946), acq. 1946-2 C.B. 3; *Post v. Commissioner*, 26 T.C. 1055 (1956), acq. 1958-2 C.B. 7; *Fegan v. Commissioner*, 71 T.C. 791 (1979), aff'd 81-1 U.S.T.C. ¶ 9436 (10th Cir. 1981); *Lagreide v. Commissioner*, 23 T.C. 508 (1954); *Pinchot v. Commissioner*, 113 F.2d 718 (2d Cir. 1940).

[18] *Curphey v. Commissioner*, 73 T.C. 766 (1980), appeal dismissed (9th Cir. 1983).

[19] *Commissioner v. Groetzinger*, note 2.

[20] Treas. Reg. § 1.183-2.

[21] Treas. Reg. § 1.183-2.

[22] IRC § 183(d).

[23] *Deputy v. DuPont*, 308 U.S. 488, 495-96 (1940).

[24] *Welch v. Helvering*, 290 U.S. 111, 113 (1933).

[25] IRC § 262 expressly denies a deduction for all "personal, living, or family expenses."

[26] *Pevsner v. Commissioner,* T.C. Memo 1979-311.

[27] *Pevsner v. Commissioner,* 628 F.2d 467 (5th Cir. 1980), rev'g T.C. Memo 1979-311.

[28] *Commissioner v. Lincoln Electric Co.,* 176 F.2d 8815 (6th Cir. 1949).

[29] *Green v. Commissioner,* 74 T.C. 1229, 1237 (1980).

[30] *Commissioner v. Flowers,* 326 U.S. 465 (1946).

[31] *Green v. Commissioner,* 74 T.C. at 1238.

CHAPTER 3

Choices for Business Organization

<blockquote>
It's a game. We [tax lawyers] teach the rich how to play it so they can stay rich—and the IRS keeps changing the rules so we can keep getting rich teaching them.

—John Grisham
</blockquote>

Whether you currently own and operate a home-based business, or anticipate starting one, you should carefully think about what form of business organization is best for you. If you are by yourself, you could operate as a sole proprietor or a limited liability company (LLC), or you could incorporate and operate as a C corporation or an S corporation. If you have partners or associates, you could operate as a corporation, a partnership, or as an LLC or limited liability partnership (LLP). Both LLCs and LLPs are treated as partnerships for tax purposes when there is more than one owner. This chapter discusses the characteristics of the various forms of business and compares their benefits and drawbacks.

Sole Proprietorships

A sole proprietorship is any unincorporated business owned entirely by one individual. It is the simplest form of business and has the advantage of low cost in its formation, operation, and termination. If you are just going into business, you might want to choose a name for your business that is different from your own. Contact your state's Secretary of State and ask how to do this. You should contact the state and city or county department of revenue to find out about sales tax and other filing requirements.

General Tax Treatment

Sole proprietors file Schedule C ("Profit or Loss from Business") with their Form 1040. Proprietors who are farmers file Schedule F ("Profit and Loss from Farming") with their Form 1040. Owners of rental real estate, who are not otherwise in the real estate business, report rental income and expenses on Schedule E ("Supplemental Income and Loss") to be filed with Form 1040. Royalties from nonworking interests in oil, gas, or mineral properties, copyrights and patents are also reported on Schedule E. The income or loss from the business is combined with the taxpayer's other income and deductions and taxed at the individual rates.

Self-Employment Tax

Sole proprietors must also pay self-employment tax on the entire net income from Schedule C or Schedule F (but not Schedule E), one-half of which they can deduct on page one of Form 1040. For 2002, up to $84,900 of net income is subject to SE tax, which consists of Social Security and Medicare tax, at the combined rate of 15.3 percent. Net income in excess of $84,900 is subject only to Medicare tax at the rate of 2.9 percent. You could be an employee for your regular job in addition to having a part-time business, the net income from which is subject to self-employment tax. Any wages you earn reduce the self-employment tax base for retirement and disability benefits. For example, if you earned over $84,900 in wages in 2002, and had Schedule C income in addition, the Schedule C income is only subject to SE tax at the rate of 2.9 percent. See the expanded discussion of SE tax in Chapter 9.

Who Can Be a Sole Proprietor?

The word *proprietor* might bring to mind a shop owner, but you can operate any business under this form as long as you are the only owner. You could operate a large company with hundreds of employees as a sole proprietorship, or you could be a one-person consulting firm. You could operate a sole proprietorship on a full-time or part-time basis, and you can have more than one proprietorship if you want. A sole proprietorship must be a business—not an investment activity or a hobby. (See Chapter 2.)

If you work primarily or exclusively for one company, but are not classified as an employee for income tax purposes, you are a type of sole proprietor referred to as an *independent contractor.* Sometimes there is a very fuzzy line between being an independent contractor and being an employee, but the distinction has important tax implications. As an independent contractor, your business expenses are deductible "above-the-line" on Schedule C (Form 1040). This means they are deductible even if you claim the standard deduction. As an employee, on the other hand, all of your unreimbursed employment-related expenses must be deducted on Schedule A (Form 1040) as "Miscellaneous Itemized Deductions," which means that you don't get the full benefit of these deductions because they are subject to the 2 percent floor.

An advantage of being an employee is that you pay only one-half of your social security tax—the other half is paid by your employer. You also qualify for employee benefits offered by your employer that you don't get as an independent contractor. The determination of whether you are an employee or an independent contractor generally follows the same tests for both income tax and social security tax purposes, but there are differences. If you are unsure of whether you should be classified as an independent contractor or an employee, see Chapter 9 under "Who Must Pay Self-Employment Taxes?"

Tax Accounting Methods and Periods

ACCOUNTING METHODS

A sole proprietorship is not an entity separate from the individual proprietor, so any income or loss from the proprietorship is combined with income and deductions from other sources on Form 1040. However, you can choose a method of accounting for your business that is different than the method used for your other income and deductions.[1] In fact, you can run several businesses as sole proprietorships and use a different accounting method for each one. For example, you are a cash method taxpayer when you report wage income and nonbusiness deductions; but you can adopt an accrual method for your sole proprietorship. If you have two separate businesses, you can use the cash method for one and an accrual method for the other. You should report each business on a separate Schedule C. The general rules for the cash and accrual methods are discussed in Chapter 4.

TAXABLE YEAR

Wouldn't it be neat if you could adopt January 31 as the year-end for your Schedule C, so eleven months of your income from this year would not be reported until you file next year's return? Forget it—you can't do that. Unlike the rule for accounting methods, as an individual you can use only one accounting period for all your income and deductions.[2] Individuals are required to use a calendar year unless, when they file their first return, they have a bookkeeping system in place and adopt a fiscal year. As a practical matter, individuals rarely meet this requirement. As a result, they are required to use the calendar year. Once adopted, a taxable year cannot be changed without the approval of the IRS.

Retirement Plans

As a sole proprietor, you can set up a Simplified Employee Pension (SEP) plan, a Keogh plan, or both, and make deductible retirement contributions for yourself and your employees. Alternatively, you may be able to set up a Savings Incentive Match Plan, known as the SIMPLE retirement plan, for yourself and your employees (if you have any). Enacted as part of the Small Business Job Protection Act of 1996, this type of plan does not have to meet many of the requirements of qualified plans. Deductible contributions to these plans and the earnings on them remain tax free until you or your employees receive distributions from the plans in later years. These plans are available for your own retirement even if you do not have employees. See Chapter 8 under "Retirement Plans for the Self-Employed" for details on these plans. Contributions for employees are claimed on Schedule C (Form 1040) or Schedule F (Form 1040), but your own contributions are deductible on page one of Form 1040. That means contributions for your account do not reduce self-employment income in computing self-employment tax.

Health Insurance

You can also deduct from your gross income a percentage of the amount you pay during the year for health insurance for yourself, your spouse, and your dependents. This above-the-line deduction cannot exceed your earned income from the business for which the plan was established. Also, you cannot deduct health insurance premiums above-the-line if you are eligible to participate in a health insurance program sponsored by your own or your spouse's employer. The portion of health insurance costs that are not deductible above-the-line are deductible on Schedule A as medical expenses, subject to the 7.5 percent of Adjusted Gross Income (AGI) reduction. The above-the-line portion is deductible on page one of Form 1040 rather than on Schedule C, so it does not reduce your self-employment income in computing self-employment tax.

Under Section 162(l) of the Code, as amended by the Trade and Tax Relief Extension Act of 1998, the above-the-line percentage for 1999 through 2001 was 60 percent. It increased to 70 percent for 2002, and becomes 100 percent for 2003 and thereafter.

Liability for Sole Proprietorship Debts and Claims

Because a sole proprietorship is not a separate legal entity, the owner has unlimited liability for debts and other claims against the business, so it would be wise to review your insurance policies. If you are doing business from your home, you might want a business liability policy separate from your homeowner's policy. If you are dealing with customers, at least be sure to have the *office, school, or studio* option in effect with your homeowner's policy.

The quest for limited liability is the most common reason some small business owners believe it is prudent to incorporate, or to form a limited liability company (LLC). C corporations, S corporations, and LLCs are entities independent from their owners and are legally responsible for their own debts and liability claims. However, creditors of home-based businesses typically require the owners to cosign for any significant debt. Also, if a civil action is brought against a home-based business, the claimant will typically seek action against the individual owner or owners as well. That means the promise of limited liability by these more complex forms of business is often illusory.

Partnerships

A partnership is an association of two or more persons to carry on a business, with each contributing money, property, labor, or skill and expecting to share in the profits and losses. There are four types of entities that are treated as partnerships for tax purposes: general partnerships, limited partnerships, limited liability partnerships (LLPs), and limited liability companies (LLCs).

A general partnership consists of one or more general partners, each of whom is personally liable for the debts of the partnership. A general partner can be held personally liable for a malpractice judgment brought against the partnership, even though the partner is not the one who committed the malpractice. Limited partners and members of LLPs and LLCs are protected against personal liability.

Like a sole proprietorship, a partnership is not considered a separate entity for computing income tax, but acts as a conduit through which income and deductions are passed to the partners. For certain other purposes, however, a partnership is considered an entity separate from its partners. Although the theory of partnerships seems simple enough, it can be an extremely complex way to conduct business from a tax standpoint. This section highlights only the general rules and concepts for partnerships. You will find additional resources at the end of this chapter. If you are doing business as a partnership, or are contemplating forming one, you should get a tax accountant involved early.

Family Partnerships

Most home-based business owners are not candidates for forming a partnership because they are going it alone. However, if you and your spouse, or another member of your immediate family, carry on a business together and share in the profits and losses, you might be partners whether or not you have a formal partnership agreement. This could reduce your family's tax burden. For example, if you could make your three kids partners in your business, and shift income to them so that business profits are being split four ways, your family's combined tax liability might be lower than if all the income was taxed to you. This will work as long as it is a legitimate partnership and not a facade to reduce taxes. If the kids are still being visited by the Tooth Fairy, and have no equity in the partnership, don't count on the IRS allowing you a tax break. The government makes it difficult to establish family partnerships for tax purposes precisely because of this tax avoidance potential. Family members are considered to be legitimate partners only in the following cases:

- Capital is a material income-producing factor in the partnership, and the family member has bona fide ownership and control of a capital interest (even if the interest was acquired by gift from another family member).
- Capital is not a material income-producing factor, but the family member contributes services that are substantial and vital to the partnership.[3]

Capital is a material income-producing factor when the business depends on machinery and equipment or inventories to generate a substantial portion of gross income, rather than services of the partners.

General Tax Treatment

A partnership does not pay any income tax at the partnership level. Its income or loss is reported on Form 1065 (U.S. Partnership Return of Income) that informs the IRS of partnership profit or loss and each partner's share on Schedule K-1 (Partner's Share of Income, Credits, Deductions, etc.). Each partner reports his or her share of partnership net profit or loss as shown on Schedule K-1, regardless of whether or not distributions are made by the partnership. Income that is not distributed or withdrawn increases the basis of a partner's partnership interest. The character of any item included in each partner's share is the same as if the partner recognized it directly. So things like tax exempt income, interest, dividends, royalties, long-term and short-term capital gains and losses, and charitable contributions are stated separately on Schedule K-1.

THE PARTNERSHIP AGREEMENT

This can be as simple or as convoluted as the partners wish to make it. A partnership affords great flexibility in how gains, losses, assets, and liabilities are shared by the partners. Each partner has a capital-sharing ratio, which is the partner's percentage of ownership in the assets and liabilities of the partnership, and a profit-and-loss sharing ratio. The partnership agreement can provide for special allocations of certain items to specific partners, or it can allocate items in a different proportion than the general profit-and-loss sharing ratios. For a special allocation to be recognized for tax purposes, it must have *substantial economic effect,*[4] meaning it must not simply be a tax reduction scheme. If you form a partnership, it's a good idea to have professional tax help in writing the partnership agreement, especially if you want special allocations.

REPORTING INCOME AND DEDUCTIONS

Partners report their share of partnership income and deductions on their Form 1040, even if a distribution has not been made. The partners' share can include several types of income that may have to be reported in separate places on their tax return. For example, ordinary business income or loss from the partnership is reported on Schedule E (Supplemental Income and Loss), whereas capital gains and losses are reported on Schedule D and charitable contributions are reported on Schedule A.

SELF-EMPLOYMENT TAX

General partners must pay self-employment tax on their net earnings from self-employment allocated to them from the partnership, even if their participation is passive.[5] Net earnings from self-employment include an individual's share, whether or not distributed, of income or loss from any trade or business carried on by a partnership.[6] An exception excludes a limited partner's distributive share of partnership income or loss,[7] but guaranteed payments as compensation for services are classified as earnings from self-employment, whether made to a general or limited partner.[8]

Partnership Contributions and Basis in the Partnership

CONTRIBUTIONS

When partners contribute property or money to a partnership in exchange for an interest in the partnership, they generally do not recognize gain or loss.[9] The partnership simply takes the property with the same basis as it had when owned by the contributing partner. There are exceptions to this rule, however. For example, if the partner contributes property and receives property or money in addition to an interest in the partnership, the transaction is treated as a sale in which gain or loss is recognized. Also, if a partner contributes property that is subject to a liability greater than the basis of the contributed property, the partner might recognize gain. Further, any partner who contributes services (rather than money or property) to the partnership in exchange for a partnership interest must generally recognize income equal to the value of the partnership interest received.

BASIS IN THE PARTNERSHIP INTEREST

Partners must each keep track of their basis in their partnership interest because they cannot deduct losses from the partnership in excess of their basis. A partner's basis in the partnership is increased by the sum of money contributed, the adjusted basis of property contributed, and the amount of any income recognized from the contribution of services to the partnership.

Liabilities also affect the partners' basis—and this gets a little tricky. Because a partnership is an aggregation of the partners' assets and liabilities, any increase in a partner's share of partnership liabilities is considered a contribution of money to the partnership,[10] and increases the partner's basis in the partnership. Conversely, any decrease in partnership liabilities, or an assumption by the partnership of a partner's liabilities, decreases the partner's basis.[11] Here's an example:

Example 3.1

Raoul and Ramona contribute property to become equal general partners in the RR Partnership. Raoul contributes cash of $30,000. Ramona contributes land with a fair-market value of $45,000 and an adjusted basis of $12,000. The land is subject to a liability of $15,000 that the partnership assumes. The partnership borrows $100,000 to finance the construction of a building on the contributed land. Raoul and Ramona's bases in their partnership interests are determined as follows:

RAOUL'S BASIS		RAMONA'S BASIS	
Contributed cash	$30,000	Basis in contributed land	$12,000
Share of construction loan	50,000	Share of construction loan	50,000
Share of debt on land	7,500	Share of debt on land	7,500
		Less: debt assumed	
		by partnership	(15,000)
Total	$87,500	Total	$54,500

Once a partner's initial basis in the partnership is determined, it is subject to continual change. It is increased by the partner's share of partnership income and additional contributions by the partner, and it is decreased by the partner's share of partnership losses and distributions of money and property to the partner. If money is distributed to a partner in excess of the partner's partnership basis, the partner must recognize gain on the distribution.

(Remember that a decrease in partnership liabilities is considered a distribution of money to the partners.) Here's another example:

Example 3.2

Assume the same facts as in Example 3.1, except the partnership incurred an ordinary loss of $100,000 in the first year of operation. Raoul and Ramona each deduct a $50,000 loss, and their respective bases are $37,500 and $4,500. In the second year, the partnership generated no income or loss, but repaid $40,000 of the construction loan. The $20,000 reduction of each partner's share of liabilities is treated as a money distribution to the partners. As a result, Raoul's basis is reduced to $17,500 and Ramona's basis is reduced to zero. (It can never be less than zero.) In addition, Ramona must report $15,500 of gain, because she is deemed to have received a money distribution of $15,500 in excess of her partnership basis.

ALLOCATION OF DEBT

There are actually two types of debt that a partnership could owe. *Recourse debt* is debt for which the partnership or at least one of the partners is personally liable. *Nonrecourse debt* is secured only by a particular partnership asset, so creditors can have no claim on other assets of the partnership or of the partners. The two types of debt are allocated differently for purposes of determining each partner's partnership basis. This used to be fairly straightforward; recourse debt was shared among the partners according to their loss-sharing ratios and nonrecourse debt was shared according to the way the partners shared profits. The rules are much more difficult than that now, since a complex set of regulations were issued a few years ago regarding nonrecourse debt.[12] IRS Publication 541, *Tax Information on Partnerships,* gives limited information on this, and then refers you to the regulations. If your partnership owes nonrecourse debt, hire a tax accountant. Be sure to find one who is familiar with the Section 752 regulations.

Tax Accounting Methods and Periods

ACCOUNTING METHODS

A partnership is treated as an entity for purposes of adopting accounting methods in computing its taxable income. As with a sole proprietor, the partnership can adopt a separate accounting method for each separate business of the partnership.

Most small-business partnerships can use the cash method of accounting if they wish, except when accounting for the purchase and sale of inventory. But Section 448 of the Code bars use of the cash method for certain partnerships with losses. These partnerships must use an accrual method, which makes the tax accounting process a little more complicated. See Chapter 4 for more information.

TAXABLE YEAR

A partnership is considered a separate entity for the purpose of adopting a taxable year, but its taxable year generally must be the same as its partners. So if you are a partner on a calendar year, and all of your partners are on a calendar year, the partnership is generally required to be on a calendar year.[13] If you and your partners are on different taxable years, the Code provides specific rules for what taxable year the partnership generally must adopt.[14] See IRS Publication 541.

There are two exceptions to the requirement that the partnership be on the same taxable year as its partners. One allows the partnership to establish a *business purpose* for being on a different taxable year. It is not easy to establish what the IRS considers a business purpose for being on a different taxable year. Usually the only way you can qualify for this is if you have a seasonal business, such as a golf course or a ski resort, where there is a natural business year corresponding to the season.

The second exception allows a newly organized partnership to make a "Section 444 election." A Section 444 election is complicated and costly and usually isn't worth the effort. It allows the partnership year to differ from the taxable year of the partners by as much as three months, but requires the partnership to make tax deposits for income that is deferred to the partners. You will find more on the Section 444 election in Chapter 4 under "Accounting Periods" on page 75.

Retirement Plans and Health Insurance

Partnerships can set up a Keogh plan, a Simplified Employee Pension (SEP) plan, or a SIMPLE plan in the same manner as a sole proprietor. Contribution limits for the partners are based on their net earnings from self-employment from the partnership. These plans are discussed more fully in Chapter 8 under "Retirement Plans for the Self-Employed" on page 194.

If the partnership pays health insurance premiums and other fringe benefits for its partners, the partners must include the amount of such payments in their gross income. The deduction for a percentage of health insurance premiums above-the-line is available to partners in the same manner as sole proprietors.[15] The above-the-line deduction cannot exceed a partner's net earnings from self-employment derived from the partnership.

Liability for Partnership Debts and Claims

GENERAL PARTNERSHIPS

There is a diversity among the entities that are taxed as partnerships with respect to who is ultimately responsible to pay the bills. All *general partners* are subject to the same personal liability for partnership debts and malfeasance claims as sole proprietors, even if the claims are due to the actions of one of the other partners. That's why it is wise to check out anyone with whom you plan to enter into a *general partnership*.

LIMITED PARTNERSHIPS

In contrast, *limited partners* are liable only to the extent of their investment in the business and their obligation to make further investments. Limited partners cannot take an active part in the management of the partnership. A limited partnership must have at least one general partner (which could be a corporation) but can have as many limited partners as it wants. Limited partnerships are popular for financing things like movies and real estate developments.

LIMITED LIABILITY PARTNERSHIPS (LLPS)

A type of entity that has only recently been authorized by state statutes is the LLP. It is just like a general partnership except for one important difference: In most states, partners in a registered LLP are jointly and severally liable for commercial partnership debt, but are not personally liable for the malpractice and torts of their partners. In some states, LLP partners are granted complete limited liability. In 1994, all of the then Big Six accounting firms (now Big Four) changed from general partnerships to LLPs.

LIMITED LIABILITY COMPANIES (LLCS)

This is another new kid on the block. It combines partnership tax treatment with limited personal liability for all the owners of the entity. All states have passed legislation permitting the establishment of LLCs in some form. More details are provided later in the chapter.

C Corporations

When you form a corporation, you create a separate tax-paying entity. Unlike sole proprietorships and partnerships, income earned by a regular corporation is taxed at corporate rates, unless the corporate shareholders elect to be an S corporation. Regular corporations are called C corporations because Subchapter C of Chapter One of the Internal Revenue Code is where you find all the general tax rules affecting corporations and their shareholders. The rules for S corporations are found in—you guessed it!—Subchapter S.

Forming a Corporation

This is a fairly straightforward process. It involves submitting articles of incorporation to the Secretary of State of the state in which you want to incorporate. The articles contain the name and purpose of the corporation, the name of a registered agent in the state where mail can be sent, the name of the incorporator, the number of shares authorized, and the classes of stock authorized. The state of incorporation does not have to be the state in which you will be conducting business. For example, a lot of businesses incorporate in the state of Delaware because of that state's flexible, well-developed, and corporate friendly laws. Before you jump into this, however, read the rest of this chapter. Also, be sure to check the franchise tax and filing requirements for the state in which you choose to incorporate. You might find that your small business will pay a lot of extra money to the state just for being a corporation.

If you hire a lawyer to file the articles of incorporation, the lawyer will probably do what lawyers do best—charge you a lot of money. Since incorporating is a straightforward process, you might want to save on the lawyer fees and just do the incorporation yourself. The Secretary of State's office in most states will send you a form Articles of Incorporation that allows you to simply fill in a few blanks, pay a fee, and voilá!—you're a corporation.

On the other hand, you might still want to hire an attorney if you have questions about which state of incorporation is best, the liability protection granted, and how to make an "S election" (discussed later). Also, if other shareholders are involved, considerations like buy-sell agreements come into play where legal advice might be crucial.

NOTE

Taxable income of certain corporations, substantially all the activities of which involve the performance of services in the fields of health, law, engineering, architecture, accounting, actuarial science, performing arts, or consulting ("qualified personal service corporations") is taxed at a flat rate of 35 percent.

Reporting Taxable Income

A C corporation reports taxable income on Form 1120 (U.S. Corporation Income Tax Return) or Form 1120-A (the corporate short form), and pays tax on its taxable income using the rate schedule for corporations. The top corporate tax rate imposed on C Corporations with income under $100,000 is 34 percent (qualified personal service corporations are subject to a flat tax rate of 35 percent) which is over 4 percent less than the top individual rate in 2002 of 38.6 percent. It may not be advantageous to be taxed as a corporation, however, because corporations have a two-tier tax structure. This means that if earnings are paid to an owner (shareholder) as a dividend, the money is taxed once at the corporate level and again at the shareholder level. Therefore, you should carefully consider how the corporate tax regime will affect you before deciding to incorporate. Here are the rates for corporations:

CORPORATION INCOME TAX RATES FOR 2002

TAXABLE INCOME OVER	NOT OVER	TAX RATE
$0	$50,000	15%
50,000	75,000	25
75,000	100,000	34
100,000	335,000	39
335,000	10,000,000	34
10,000,000	15,000,000	35
15,000,000	18,333,333	38
18,333,333	. . .	35

Example 3.3

Ed's Corporation files Form 1120, and reports taxable income of $50,000 after paying its shareholder-employee, Ed, his wages. The corporation pays corporate income tax of $7,500. The balance of its taxable income, $42,500 is distributed as a dividend to Ed. Ed is in the 38.6 percent tax bracket, and pays tax of $16,405 on the dividend. The total income tax paid on the $50,000 of corporate earnings is $23,905 ($7,500 + $ 16,405). If Ed operated instead as a sole proprietorship, income tax on the $50,000 of income would be only $19,300 ($50,000 × 38.6%).

If Ed, in Example 3.3, had the corporation pay him an additional $50,000 of wages, the corporation would have zero taxable income after wages, which would eliminate the double taxation. Wages are deductible by the corporation under Section 162 of the Code only if they are "reasonable." If the IRS thinks Ed has received more in pay than his services are worth, the IRS will reclassify the money as a dividend and the reclassified amount will still be subject to the two-tier tax system.

EMPLOYMENT TAXES

Employment taxes are another consideration in deciding how corporate earnings should be distributed.

A corporate shareholder pays social security and Medicare taxes only on compensation for services, not on dividends. If the shareholder is an employee, the corporation and the employee each pay one half of these taxes, and the corporation can deduct its half. Another look at Ed's situation is shown in Example 3.4.

Example 3.4

If Ed's Corporation in Example .3 used its $50,000 of taxable income as wage expense, the corporation would have no taxable income, so it would not pay corporate income tax. However, the combined corporate/employee liability for Social Security taxes on the additional wages to Ed would be as much as 15.3 percent or as little as 2.9 percent. The rate depends on whether Ed had already been paid the base amount of wages ($84,900 in 2002) for retirement and disability benefits. If the entire $50,000 was subject to tax at 15.3 percent, the additional tax would be $7,106 ($3,553 FICA paid by the corporation and $3,553 FICA paid by Ed on $46,447 of wages). Note that Ed would not get the full $50,000, because the corporation would need $3,553 for its share of the Social Security tax, which it could also deduct ($46,447 + $3,553 = $50,000). In addition, Ed would pay income tax on the additional $46,447, unreduced by the Social Security tax. So total Social Security and income tax on the additional $46,447 of wages would be $25,035 ($46,447 × 15.3% + $46,447 × 38.6%). This is more in total tax than if the corporation had simply paid Ed the $50,000 as a dividend. If Ed operated, instead, as a sole proprietorship, his combined tax on the additional $50,000 would be about the same, considering self-employment tax of 15.3 percent and Ed's allowable deduction of one-half of it.

Accumulating Earnings for Future Expansion

Another option available for excess corporate earnings is to retain them in the corporation for future expansion. The corporate tax rate on taxable income up to $50,000 is only 15 percent, which is generally lower than what a shareholder would pay if the money was paid out in wages. If your goal is to build equity in the company and eventually to use the money for expansion, this is the cheapest way to do so. Also, any investment earnings on the excess capital will be taxed at the lower corporate rates. There is a special "dividends received deduction" available to C corporations that receive dividends from other domestic corporations.[16] The deduction is generally 70 percent of the dividends received. That puts the tax rate on dividends, for a corporation with taxable income of $50,000 or less, at 4.5 percent (15% × 30%). If you were to build up the value of the corporation in this way, you could eventually sell the stock at a price reflecting the increased value and be taxed at the favorable capital gains rates. Alternatively, you could just keep the stock and pass it on to your heirs when you pass away. That way, no one would pay tax at the individual level on the built up income in the corporation because the heirs would get fair market value bases in their stock. You would have to figure a potential estate tax liability into this plan, however.

NOW HERE IS THE CATCH

Congress realized that it is more attractive from a tax perspective for shareholders of a corporation to accumulate earnings in the corporation rather than to distribute them as dividends. That's why there is an "accumulated earnings tax" on every corporation "formed or availed of for the purpose of avoiding the income tax with respect to its shareholders . . . by permitting earnings and profits to accumulate instead of being . . . distributed."[17] This penalty tax is imposed at the top rate for individuals on undistributed current year earnings that are not necessary for the reasonable needs of the business. A corporation is not subject to this tax until it accumulates over $250,000 of earnings in the business.[18] Even if a corporation has more than $250,000 of earnings, it will not be subject to the tax if it can prove that the accumulation is for reasonable business needs.[19]

There is another penalty tax imposed at the top rate for individuals on undistributed income of a "closely held corporation" that is a "personal holding company."[20] A corporation is closely held if over 50 percent of its stock is owned, directly or indirectly by five or fewer individuals. It is a personal holding company only if at least 60 percent of its income (with a few adjustments) is from dividends, interest, royalties and other types of investment income.[21]

This tax is to prevent high-income individuals from building up their investment portfolio in a corporation and avoiding the tax at the individual level, then selling the stock and recognizing long term capital gain. In any one year, however, the IRS cannot impose both the accumulated earnings tax and the personal holding company tax. Also, both of these taxes can easily be avoided by making appropriate distributions to the shareholders.

Contributions to the Corporation

A newly formed corporation is no more endowed than a new born baby—with financial assets that is. To start the new entity out in life, operating assets and money are contributed by its organizers in exchange for stock in the corporation. If a business is already being run as a sole proprietorship or partnership when it is incorporated, assets of the business must be transferred to the corporation in order for the corporation to claim any related deductions.

The general rule, when two parties exchange assets, is that gain or loss is recognized by both of them, just as in a sale.[22] Each transferor reports as gain or loss the difference between the basis of the asset given up and the value of the asset received. However, there are several special situations in which the recognition of gain or loss is not justified. The contribution of property to a corporation is one of them.

When a corporation receives money or property in exchange for its own stock, the corporation never recognizes any gain or loss.[23] Also, Section 351 of the Code says the shareholders do not recognize gain or loss on property transferred in exchange for stock if they are "in control" (explained a little later) of the corporation after the exchange.[24] Property received by the corporation takes the same basis as it had in the hands of the shareholder who transferred it, increased by any gain recognized to the shareholder. A separate rule says that losses are never recognized by an individual on property contributed to a corporation if the individual owns, directly or indirectly, over 50 percent of the outstanding stock of the corporation.[25]

For purposes of Section 351, the term *property* is pretty comprehensive, including both tangible and intangible assets. Yet, one item that the Code specifically excludes from the definition of property is services rendered to the corporation. So any shareholder who contributes services (rather than money or property) to the corporation in exchange for stock must recognize income equal to the value of the stock received.

THE 80 PERCENT TEST

Section 351 of the Code says that no gain or loss is recognized to the contributing shareholders if they are "in control" of the corporation "immediately after the exchange."[26] That means that the person or persons transferring the property must own eighty percent of the stock of the corporation immediately after the transfer. This test applies either to a single transferor, or to several people transferring property for stock at about the same time. Transfers by several people in an integrated transaction do not have to be simultaneous to satisfy the "immediately after the exchange" requirement, but they have to be fairly close together. If the control test is not met, the transferors must recognize any gain on the property transferred, just as if cash was received instead of stock. See Examples 3.5 and 3.6.

Example 3.5

Betty exchanges property with a basis of $50,000 and fair market value of $80,000 for 70 percent of the stock of B&D Corporation. The other 30 percent of the stock is owned by Don, who acquired it several years ago. Betty receives stock with a fair market value of $80,000, and recognizes taxable gain of $30,000 on the transfer. The 80 percent control test is not satisfied.

Example 3.6

Larry, Moe, and Curly incorporate their respective businesses and form the Stooge Corporation. Larry exchanges his property for 333 shares of Stooge stock on July 1. Moe contributes his property for 333 shares of Stooge stock on July 10, and Curly transfers his property for 333 shares of Stooge stock on August 15, all of the same year. The three exchanges are part of a prearranged plan, so none of the shareholders recognize gain or loss on the exchange; the control requirement is met.

WHEN "BOOT" IS RECEIVED IN ADDITION TO STOCK

When a shareholder receives anything other than corporate stock from the corporation as compensation for the property transferred, it is referred to as *boot*. Whenever boot is received, the shareholder must recognize any gain on the transfer up to the amount of boot received.[27] A loss is never recognized.[28] See Example 3.7.

BASIS IN CORPORATE STOCK

Shareholders receive basis in their stock equal to the basis of the property they contribute to the corporation, reduced by any boot received from the corporation, and increased by any gain recognized on the exchange. If the corporation makes a distribution of money or property that is not out of corporate earnings, it is nontaxable to the shareholders only to the extent of the basis of their stock. Any distribution in excess of basis is taxable as capital gain. Also, the shareholders must keep track of their stock basis in order to determine gain or loss on the sale of their stock.

Example 3.7

Julie owns all the stock of Julie's Corporation. She transfers a computer to the corporation that has a basis of $1,000 and is valued at $3,000. In exchange, the corporation gives Julie $500 in cash, a note for $1,000, and issues her stock worth $1,500. Because the cash and note are boot, Julie must recognize gain of $1,500, which is the smaller of her realized gain ($2,000) and the amount of boot received ($1,500).

TREATMENT OF GAIN OR LOSS ON DISPOSITION OF STOCK

The general rule when corporate stock is sold or exchanged is that the gain or loss is capital gain or loss. The maximum rate on *long-term* capital gains (the asset is owned for over a year for sales after 1997) is 20 percent.[29] The top rate on ordinary income, on the other hand, is 38.6 percent in 2002 and 2003, with a scheduled drop to 35 percent after 2005. Capital losses are fully deductible against capital gains, but if losses exceed gains you can only deduct up to $3,000 of the excess loss against ordinary income. Capital losses that cannot be deducted in the current year are carried over to future years. The $3,000 limit is reduced to $1,500 for married persons filing separately.

A special rule in Section 1244 of the Code allows shareholders of certain small business corporations to deduct a loss from the sale or worthlessness of their stock as an ordinary loss rather than a capital loss. That means the loss can be deducted in full rather than being subject to the limitations on capital losses. There is another special break in Section 1202 of the Code that says you can exclude from income 50 percent of the gain on "qualified small business stock" held for more than five years at the time of sale. In general, qualified small business stock must be issued after August 10, 1993, in a C corporation that is conducting an active business and does not have gross assets in excess of $50 million. There are a lot of picky little rules on this in Section 1202, so consult a tax adviser if you have stock that you think qualifies.

Tax Accounting Methods and Periods

ACCOUNTING METHODS

As a separate taxable entity, a corporation can adopt any acceptable accounting method. There is one limitation on accounting methods for C corporations that does not apply to other entities. The cash method is generally not allowed for corporations with gross receipts greater than $5 million.[30] As with sole proprietorships and partnerships, a corporation can adopt a separate accounting method for each separate business of the corporation.

TAXABLE YEAR

Most new C corporations can adopt either a calendar year or any fiscal year, regardless of the taxable years of their shareholders. They are even permitted to change their fiscal or calendar year after 10 years without permission from the IRS, if they meet some conditions contained in the regulations.[31]

A "personal service corporation" is the one type of C corporation that is required to adopt a calendar year.[32] The definition of a personal service corporation for this purpose is a little complex. Generally it is a C corporation that has employee owners who perform services in the fields of health, law, engineering, architecture, accounting, actuarial science, performing arts or consulting. If it looks like your corporation might be a personal service corporation, you can find a more comprehensive definition in IRS Publication 538, *Accounting Periods and Methods.*

The two exceptions to the requirement that a personal service corporation be on a calendar year are the same requirements that apply to partnerships and S corporations. The first allows the corporation to establish a "business purpose" for being on a different taxable year. The second allows the corporation to make a "Section 444 election." As discussed under *Partnerships,* it is usually not easy to establish what the IRS considers a business purpose for being on a different taxable year, and making a Section 444 election is not generally worth the trouble. You will find more on the business purpose exception and the Section 444 election in Chapter 4 under "Accounting Periods" on page 75.

Retirement Plans and Health Insurance

There is a variety of qualified retirement plans available for corporate employees. Qualified plans must meet stringent requirements under the Code with respect to participation, contributions, and distributions. They have the advantage of providing tax deferred retirement benefits to employees while allowing the corporation a current deduction for contributions. It used to be that corporate plans allowed greater contributions than retirement plans for unincorporated businesses, but that isn't the case any longer. Keogh plans for self-employed people are now subject to the same general rules as qualified corporate plans. One difference is that owners in corporate plans can borrow from the plan, with certain restrictions, but loans from Keogh accounts are prohibited. A corporation that does not want to be bothered with the complexities of a qualified plan can set up a simplified employee pension (SEP) plan or a SIMPLE plan, which are discussed more fully in Chapter 8 under "Retirement Plans for the Self-Employed" on page 194.

An advantage of being a corporate employee is that you can have the corporation pay and deduct all of your family's health insurance premiums. Self-employed individuals can deduct 70 percent of their health insurance premiums as a business expense in 2002, and 100 percent in 2003 and beyond.[33]

Liability for Corporate Debts and Claims

A corporation is a legal entity, chartered under state law, that is separate and distinct from its shareholders and officers. It is a vehicle designed to foster investment by protecting the investors from liabilities of the business. Limited liability is probably the chief reason most businesses incorporate (although I am convinced that a lot of people incorporate just to be the president of something).

Shareholders and officers of a corporation are usually not personally responsible for creditor claims unless they provide a personal guarantee. Unfortunately, for home-based businesses with few assets, a personal guarantee is exactly what many creditors demand. Bankers will tend to treat your fledgling corporation more like a minor child than a separate business entity. As the corporation acquires more assets and a good credit rating, there will be fewer creditor demands for personal guarantees.

Even if there are no personal guarantees from shareholders, creditors are sometimes allowed under common law to "pierce the corporate veil." That means they can pursue corporate owners directly for corporate claims. In some states, shareholders can be sued directly for unpaid wages and employee benefits. Shareholders can also be held liable for corporate debts when the corporation has not been operated in a manner that indicates it is truly separate from the personal finances of its stockholders.

Additionally, if you perform services for the corporation that result in some kind of civil action, you will be sued along with your corporation. State laws used to prohibit professional individuals (like accountants, attorneys, architects, and doctors) from incorporating. Now they are allowed to incorporate, but they are not provided limited liability for the performance of professional services.

In summary, if your primary purpose for incorporating your home-based business is to gain limited liability, you might be better advised to save all the accounting and attorney's fees and purchase additional business liability insurance instead. If you are a service professional, you will probably be unable to create liabilities for which the corporation alone will be responsible. Of course, if your *real* purpose for incorporating is to be called Mr. or Ms. President, none of this advice really matters.

S Corporations

Operating as an S corporation combines the advantages of a single level of taxation at the shareholder level with limited liability for corporate shareholders. An S corporation has the same corporate characteristics as a C corporation. It is a legal entity, chartered under state law, that is separate and distinct from its shareholders and officers. The only difference is that, after incorporating, it has filed an election with the IRS to be treated differently for federal tax purposes. The election generally permits the income of the S corporation to be taxed to the shareholders of the corporation rather than to the corporation itself. The election can be made for a new entity, or it can be made for an existing corporation that has been taxed as a C corporation. When S status is no longer an advantage to the corporate shareholders, the election can be revoked.

S status has been available ever since the late 1950s, and its use enjoyed a steady increase over the years. It was in the late 1980s, though, that it became really popular. That's because for a few years after the Tax Reform Act of 1986, the top individual tax rate was less than the top corporate rate. Now the top rate for individuals is several points above the top rate paid by most small corporations (34 percent), and LLCs, which are authorized in all states, offer more advantages than S corporations for many taxpayers. Nevertheless, the popularity of S corporations has not diminished. The IRS projects S corporations will be the fastest growing type of business tax entity through 2005.

Doing business as an S corporation is complex from a tax standpoint. Tax accountants drool over clients with S corporations. You should hire one who has had plenty of experience—not with drooling, but with dealing with S corporations. This section highlights only the general rules and concepts. Additional resources are suggested at the end of this chapter.

Making the Election

A corporation will not be treated as an S corporation unless a proper election is made in a timely manner. The election is made on Form 2553 (Election by a Small Business Corporation), which must be filed with the IRS before the sixteenth day of the third month of the corporation's tax year for which the election will be effective. An election made after the fifteenth day of the third month but before the end of the taxable year is generally effective for the next year. However, as part of the changes made by the Small Business Job Protection Act of 1996, the IRS is granted authority to cut taxpayers some slack if they make a late election, or inadvertently fail to make an election. The IRS may treat a late election or a nonexistent election as timely made if the IRS determines that there was reasonable cause for the failure to file the election on time.[34] See the instructions to Form 2553. Each shareholder must consent to and sign the election.

An S election made with the IRS might not be effective for state tax purposes. While most states simply follow the federal law on this, some don't. A state that allows S status might require a separate election to be filed with the state. Be sure to check the laws of your state before making an S election.

Who Can Make the Election?

A corporation can be an S corporation only if it meets the following tests:

1. It is a domestic corporation.
2. It has no more than 75 shareholders (increased from 35 in 1996). A husband and wife are treated as one shareholder for this purpose, but everyone else is a separate shareholder.

CHOICES FOR BUSINESS ORGANIZATION

3. It has only individuals, estates, or certain trusts, financial institutions and tax-exempt entities as shareholders. The types of eligible S corporation shareholders were significantly expanded for 1997 and later years by the Small Business Job Protection Act of 1996.

4. It has no nonresident alien shareholders.

5. It has only one class of stock.

6. It has a "permitted tax year." That means its tax year is the calendar year, unless the corporation establishes a business purpose for a fiscal year that satisfies the IRS, or makes a Section 444 election. The rules for taxable years are the same as discussed for partnerships.

If the corporation violates any of these rules while it is an S corporation, the S election will automatically terminate and the corporation will be taxed as a C corporation, unless steps are taken by the shareholders to correct the problem. If there is no violation of the rule the election stays in effect until the shareholders choose to terminate it.

General Tax Treatment

An S corporation is treated much the same as a partnership, in that it generally does not pay tax at the corporate level. Its income or loss is reported on Form 1120S (U.S. Income Tax Return for an S Corporation), and flows through to be reported on the shareholders' individual returns. Schedule K-1 (Shareholder's Share of Income, Credits, Deductions, etc.) is completed with Form 1120S for each shareholder. These schedules tell the shareholders their allocable share of corporate income and deductions. Shareholders, therefore, must pay tax on their share of corporate income, regardless of whether it is actually distributed.

A potential disadvantage, for an S corporation with more than one shareholder, is that income and deductions from an S corporation must be allocated according to the shareholder's ownership interest. They cannot be specially allocated to shareholders like they can from a partnership.

There is one exception to this rule that prevents tax avoidance by family members, similar to the family partnership rules. Any individual who is a member of a family of S corporation shareholders must receive adequate compensation for services or capital provided to the corporation. For example, if you are allocating corporate profits among your six minor children, the IRS is authorized to allocate more profits to you to adequately reflect the services and capital you provide to the corporation.[35]

BASIS IN STOCK AND DEBT

A shareholder's basis in an S corporation's stock is adjusted in much the same way a partner's partnership interest is adjusted. Losses from the S corporation attributable to a shareholder are limited to the shareholder's stock basis. There is a major difference, though, in the way corporate debt is treated. Remember that a partner's basis in the partnership interest includes the partner's direct investment plus a ratable share of any partnership liabilities. For S corporation shareholders, however, corporate borrowing has no effect on their stock basis. S corporation shareholders get a separate tax basis in any debt the corporation owes *directly to them,* but not in any other corporate debt. Here's a tip: If you form an S corporation that you expect to incur losses, and the corporation needs to borrow money, *don't have it borrow money directly from someone else* if you are going to have to guarantee the loan anyway. A loan from a third party does not increase your basis for deducting losses. Borrow the money yourself and lend it to the corporation.

Losses allocated to shareholders in excess of their stock basis are suspended until their basis is increased. Shareholders who have outstanding loans to the corporation can deduct additional losses to the extent of the loans. This feature of S corporations gives individual shareholders a lot of flexibility in choosing when to recognize losses from the corporation.

CORPORATE LEVEL TAXES

Unlike partnerships, there are some special situations in which tax is paid directly by an S corporation. One involves built-in gains of a C corporation that converts to an S corporation.[36] Built-in gains are gains related to appreciation on assets held by a C corporation that converts to S corporation status. Another applies when passive investment income of an S corporation having C corporation earnings and profits exceeds 25 percent of gross receipts.[37] The last corporate level tax applies when a C corporation using LIFO (last-in-first-out) inventory converts to an S corporation.[38] All of these special taxes affect S corporations that were formally C corporations. If you form a corporation and immediately elect S status, the S corporation will never be taxed at the corporate level.

Reporting Income and Deductions

The income and deductions from an S corporation are reported by the shareholders in much the same way as partnership income and deductions are reported. The character of any item included in each shareholder's pro rata share is the same as if the shareholder recognized it directly. So things like tax exempt income, interest, dividends, royalties, long-term and short-term capital gains and losses, and charitable contributions are stated separately on each shareholder's Schedule K-1. Individual shareholders report their share of ordinary business income or loss from the corporation on Schedule E (Supplemental Income and Loss). The separately stated items are reported on the appropriate schedules of Form 1040.

EMPLOYMENT TAXES

S corporation employee/shareholders are treated the same as if they were employees of a C corporation. Income or loss of the corporation is allocated to the shareholders after the deduction for wages. The shareholders are not subject to self-employment tax on any income they receive from the corporation.

This is a potentially lucrative advantage of doing business as an S corporation. For a sole proprietor, the entire net income on Schedule C is subject to self-employment tax. General partners and active limited liability shareholders must also pay self-employment tax on their share of partnership income. But S corporation employee/shareholders who are paid a reasonable wage will escape employment taxes on the remaining income of the corporation. This benefit might be as high as 15.3 percent or as low as 2.9 percent, depending on the amount of wages the shareholder has received from the corporation and other sources. Caution is in order here, though. If you are the sole shareholder of an S corporation earning income from your services, the IRS could argue that all of the corporate service income should reasonably be recognized by you as wages.

Although Laura, in Example 3.8, saves over $4,700 in taxes by treating only $50,000 of her corporate income as wages, she is vulnerable to the IRS treating all of the corporate income attributable to her services as wages.

Tax Accounting Methods and Periods

ACCOUNTING METHODS

An S corporation adopts its own accounting methods in computing its taxable income. Similar to partnerships, most S corporations are permitted to use the cash method of accounting if they wish, with the exception of accounting for the purchase and sale of inventory for which an accrual method must be used. However, Section 448 of the Code denies the use of the cash method to certain S corporations that have incurred losses. These corporations are required to use an overall accrual method. See Chapter 4.

TAXABLE YEAR

S corporations have a required taxable year, like partnerships and personal service corporations. They are required to adopt a calendar year unless they can establish a business purpose for being on a different taxable year, or make a Section 444 election.

Retirement Plans and Health Insurance

The variety of qualified retirement plans available to employees of C corporations is also available to employees of S corporations. A simplified employee pension (SEP) plan is also an option for S corporations.

Example 3.8

Laura owns all the stock of Laura's S Corporation. The corporation earned net income of $100,000 from Laura's services as a consultant in 2002, and paid Laura $50,000 in wages for her services. The remaining corporate income is taxed to Laura as a dividend. Assuming Laura is in the 35 percent tax bracket, and ignoring personal deductions, Laura's after tax corporate income is about $3,700 greater than if all of the service income was treated as wages to Laura.

Total earned	**$100,000**
Less:	
$50,000 × 15.3% (corporate and employee FICA)	($7,650)
$50,000 × 35% (income tax on wages)	($17,500)
$46,175 × 35% (income tax on corporate income after wages and employer FICA)	($16,161)
After tax corporate income	**$58,689**
If Laura's S corporation paid Laura all of its income in wages, Laura's after tax corporate income would be:	
Total earned	**$100,000**
Less:	
$84,900 × 15.3% (corporate and employee FICA)	($12,990)
$15,100 × 2.9% (corporate and employee Medicare tax after corporate FICA)	($438)
$93,286 × 35% (income tax on wages after employer FICA)	($32,650)
After tax corporate income	**$53,922**

Remember that an advantage of being an employee of a C corporation is that you can have the corporation pay and deduct all of your family's health insurance premiums, and some other benefits, without the amounts being included in your gross income. That doesn't apply for S corporation shareholders who own more than two percent of the corporation's outstanding stock. They are treated like partners for this purpose.[39] If the corporation pays health insurance premiums for these shareholders, the amount is deducted by the corporation as wages and included in the shareholders' gross income. The deduction for a percentage of health insurance premiums above-the-line is available to the shareholders in the same manner as partners and sole proprietors.[40]

Liability for Corporate Debts and Claims

An S corporation offers shareholders the same limited liability protection that a C corporation does. See the discussion under *C Corporations*.

Limited Liability Companies (LLCs)

Background

The LLC is a fairly recent phenomenon in the United States, though European countries have been using the concept for quite a while. Wyoming passed the first LLC legislation in the United States in 1977. Now all the states and the District of Columbia have LLC statutes.

Limited liability companies are organizations that are formed under state law to provide limited liability for their owners, who are called *members,* in the same way corporate shareholders are protected. They are not corporations under state law, however, and the IRS has ruled that they may be treated as partnerships rather than corporations for federal income tax purposes.[41] This ruling was necessary under regulations in effect prior to 1997 when the IRS could tax any unincorporated entity as a corporation if had more corporate characteristics than noncorporate characteristics. The four characteristics that were used to distinguish an association taxable as a corporation from an association taxable as a partnership were: (1) centralized management, (2) continuity of life, (3) free transferability of interests, and (4) limited liability.[42] These factors were given equal weight so that an organization was classified as a partnership if it lacked at least two of them.[43]

Beginning in 1997, the IRS has decided to use a much simpler approach. The regulations have been changed to allow most unincorporated businesses the choice of whether they will be taxed as a corporation or not, even if all the owners have limited liability.[44] Except for a business entity that is automatically classified as a corporation under the revised regulations, an entity with at least two members can choose to be classified as either an association taxable as a corporation or a partnership. A business entity with a single individual owner can choose to be taxed as a corporation or treated as a sole proprietorship. These business entities are automatically taxed as either a partnership (if the entity has more than one member) or a sole proprietorship (if the entity only has one member) unless Form 8832 is filed by the entity's owner(s) electing to have the entity taxed as a corporation.

The Advantages

An ideal financial structure for a business entity would provide limited liability for its owners, a single level of taxation, maximum flexibility in dividing profits and losses and uncomplicated rules for tax compliance. The LLC provides most of these attributes.

An LLC has characteristics of both a partnership for tax purposes and a corporation for liability purposes. An LLC functions like a partnership in that it provides single level taxation for an entity with more than one owner; it provides flexibility in dividing profits and losses, and it allows partners to increase the basis of their partnership interest with third-party debt of the partnership. An LLC functions like a corporation in that it provides limited liability to its members. The same benefits apply to a single member LLC. The owner can achieve limited liability, maintain a single level of taxation and avoid the complexities of S corporation status.

The Drawbacks

STATE TAX ISSUES

State statutes differ in their treatment of LLCs, and state law is still evolving to determine treatment of LLCs formed in one state but doing business in another state. Some states, like Texas, tax LLCs as corporations. Other states, such as Michigan, Illinois, New Hampshire, and the District of Columbia, impose entity level taxes on LLCs.

Under the revised federal regulations discussed above, an LLC owned by a single individual is treated as a sole proprietorship for federal tax purposes by default. That means you file Schedule C and treat your LLC just like an unincorporated sole proprietorship for federal tax purposes. For a time, several states refused to allow single member LLCs. However, most states have now indicated through regulations or public rulings that they will conform to the simplified federal classification for single member LLCs. As noted earlier, though, some impose a tax at the entity level. Currently, in Idaho, Massachusetts, and Pennsylvania, state statutes either specifically do not allow or are ambiguous with respect to domestic single-member LLCs, possibly requiring a single member firm to file a partnership return for state tax purposes.

If you wish to be an LLC and are performing professional services that require licensing under state law, you are typically required to form a professional limited liability company (PLLC or PLC) under separate statutes. A PLLC is granted the same limited liability as a corporation for creditor claims, but there is no limited liability with respect to claims arising out of your professional services. In other words, being an LLC will not prevent your clients from suing you personally for malpractice. Professional services generally include accountancy, architecture, engineering, law, medicine and surgery, chiropractic, registered nursing, psychology, dentistry and dental hygiene, pharmacy, veterinary medicine, surveying, landscape architecture, and certified interior design.

If you are considering LLC status, be sure to check the LLC provisions of your state and any state in which you plan to do business.

SELF-EMPLOYMENT TAX

Self-employment income, on which self-employment (SE) tax must be paid, includes the gross income derived by an individual or partner from any trade or business.[45] However, a *limited* partner's share of partnership income, except for guaranteed payments, is not subject to SE tax.[46] There is no definition of the term limited partner in the Code or regulations. That brings up the question of whether, as an LLC member, you are considered a general or limited partner for this purpose.

A regulation proposed by the IRS in January of 1997 addressed this question.[47] The proposed regulation said that generally, an individual will be treated as a limited partner for self-employment tax purposes unless the individual (1) has personal liability for the debts of or claims against the partnership by reason of being a partner, (2) has authority to contract on behalf of the partnership under the statute or law pursuant to which the partnership is organized, or (3) participates in the partnership's trade or business for more than 500 hours during the taxable year. The regulation added that if substantially all of the activities of a partnership involve the performance of services in the fields of health, law, engineering, architecture, accounting, actuarial science, or consulting, any individual who provides services as part of that trade or business will not be considered a limited partner.

This proposed regulation caused quite an uproar. It was thought by some that the regulation exceeded the regulatory authority of the IRS, and that it would effectively change the law administratively without congressional action. Therefore, as part of the Taxpayer Relief Act of 1997, Congress provided that no regulation can be issued or made effective by the IRS on the definition of limited partner for self-employment tax purposes before July 1, 1998. That means the IRS must now go back to the drawing board and come up with some rules that are not so expansive in imposing self-employment tax on LLC members and limited partners in general. New regulations have yet to be proposed.

LOSS LIMITATIONS

The rules restricting passive activity losses have not been discussed previously because they usually affect taxpayers who are not active participants in their business, which generally include limited partners. In general, a passive activity is a business in which the taxpayer is a passive investor and does not "materially participate" in management activities.[48] A taxpayer's passive activity loss (PAL) is not allowed to offset income which is not from a passive activity in computing taxable income.[49] A PAL that is disallowed can be carried forward to reduce passive income in the following year.[50]

The passive loss rules are particularly restrictive for LLC members, because LLC members are classified as limited partners for this purpose, even when they are active in the business.[51] A stricter test is required for limited partners to determine if they materially participate in the business. Basically, a business is considered a passive activity for any member of an LLC who devotes less than 500 hours per year to the business.[52] Consequently, any LLC member who participates on a part-time basis (under 500 hours per year) and incurs losses might not be allowed to deduct them under the passive loss rules.

Which Form Is Best?

The answer to that question is completely dependent upon your particular circumstances and objectives. If you are the sole owner of a business and your primary goal is to keep things as simple as possible, there are surprisingly few tax advantages to organizing as anything other than a sole proprietorship. You can achieve limited liability and still file as a sole proprietor by forming a single member LLC, but beware of the state tax pitfalls mentioned above. If you form an S corporation to achieve limited liability you can say so long to simplicity. Yet, a potential advantage of an S corporation is the ability of S shareholders to avoid employment taxes on their share of corporate income above a reasonable wage.

If you have partners or associates, a general partnership provides the maximum flexibility in dividing profits and losses while allowing a single level of taxation. If you are going to have a general partnership, there are very few reasons not to organize as an LLC or LLP if your state permits it. Organizing as an LLC or LLP provides limited liability and partnership tax treatment.

If you are producing or manufacturing a product and you wish to build capital in the business for eventual worldwide domination of the market (why not be optimistic?), the corporate form is probably best. It might be prudent, however, to delay incorporating for a year or two, or to initially elect S status, or form an LLC and then convert it to a corporation, so you can take advantage of start-up losses on your personal return.

Additional Resources

For additional information on doing business as a sole proprietor, a good IRS publication for general guidance is Publication 334, *Tax Guide for Small Business*. IRS Publication 541, *Partnerships*, provides guidance in filing Form 1065 and the related Schedules K and K-1. For information on the tax requirements of S corporations, the best IRS source is the *Instructions for Form 1120S.* Also see the instructions for Form 2553 (S election). Tax information on doing business as a C corporation is in Publication 542, *Corporations.*

You can get these publications free by calling the IRS at (800) TAX-FORM [800 829-3676]. If you have access to TTY/TDD equipment, you can call (800) 829-4059. To download them from the Internet, go to *www.irs.gov* (World Wide Web), or *ftp.irs.gov* (FTP). If you would like to get forms and instructions (not publications) by FAX, dial (703) 368-9694 to reach IRS Tax Fax.

As an alternative to downloading files from the Internet, you can order *IRS Federal Tax Products* on CD-ROM. This CD includes over 2,000 tax products, including all of the above publications and forms. It can be ordered by calling (800) 233-6767. Also, Publication 3207, *Small Business Resource Guide,* is an interactive CD-ROM that contains information important to small businesses. It is available in mid-February. You can get one free copy by calling (800) 829-3676.

Notes

[1] Reg. § 1.446-1(c)(1)(iv)(b).

[2] See Rev. Rul. 57-389, 1957-2 C.B. 298.

[3] IRC § 704(e).

[4] IRC § 704(b).

[5] *Matthew Norwood and Linda Kramer v. Comm.,* T.C. Memo 2000-84.

[6] IRC § 1402(a).

[7] IRC § 1402(a)(13).

[8] Ibid.

[9] IRC § 721.

[10] IRC § 752(a).

[11] IRC § 752(b).

[12] See Reg. § 1.752-1 through § 1.752-5, generally effective for liabilities incurred or assumed by a partnership on or after December 28, 1991.

[13] IRC § 706(b).

[14] IRC § 706(b)(1)(B).

[15] Rev. Rul. 91-26, 1991-1 C.B. 184. Self-employed individuals can deduct 60 percent of their health insurance premiums as a business expense in 1999 through 2001, 70 percent in 2002 and 100 percent in 2003 and later years.

[16] IRC § 243.

[17] IRC § 532.

[18] IRC § 535(c)(2).

[19] IRC § 535(c)(1).

[20] IRC § 541.

[21] IRC § 543.

[22] IRC § 1001.

[23] IRC § 1032.

[24] IRC § 351(a).

[25] IRC § 267(a).

[26] IRC § 351(a).

[27] IRC § 351(b)(1).

[28] IRC § 351(b)(2).

[29] IRC § 1(h) as amended by the Internal Revenue Service Restructuring & Reform Act of 1998.

[30] IRC § 448.

[31] See Treas. Reg. § 1.442-1(c).

[32] IRC § 441(i).

[33] IRC § 162(I). The balance of the premium may be claimed as a medical expense on Schedule A, subject to the 7.5 percent of adjusted gross income floor.

[34] IRC § 1362(b)(5), as amended by the Small Business Job Protection Act of 1996.

[35] IRC § 1366(e).

[36] IRC § 1374.

[37] IRC § 1375.

[38] IRC § 1363(d).

[39] IRC § 1372.

[40] Rev. Rul. 91-26, 1991-1 C.B. 184. Self-employed individuals can deduct 60 percent of their health insurance premiums as a business expense in 1999 through 2001, 70 percent in 2002 and 100 percent in 2003 and later years.

[41] Rev. Rul. 88-76, 1988-2 C.B. 360.

[42] Treas. Reg. § 301.7701-2 effective prior to 1997.

[43] *Larson v. Commissioner,* 66 T.C. 159 (1976).

[44] Treas. Reg. § 301.7701-1 through 3.

[45] IRC § 1402(a).

[46] IRC § 1402(a)(13); Reg. § 1.1402(a)-1(b).

[47] Prop. Treas. Reg. § 1.1402(a)-2

[48] IRC § 469(c).

[49] IRC § 469(a).

[50] IRC § 469(b).

[51] Temp. Reg. § 1.469-5T(e)(3)(i)(B).

[52] Temp. Reg. § 1.469-5T(a)(1).

CHAPTER 4

Tax Accounting Methods and Periods

Anyone may so arrange his [or her] affairs that his [or her] taxes shall be as low as possible.

—Judge Learned Hand

Regardless of what kind of business you have, or whether you run it as a sole proprietorship, partnership, or corporation, you are required to declare the method of accounting used for your business on your tax return. If you look at Schedule C ("Profit or Loss from Business") for example, on Line F you are asked if your method of accounting is cash, accrual, or other. This is a question you should take a little time with. Using the SWAG (scientific wild-ass guess) method to figure out what box to check is not recommended. This is one of the most important questions you are asked on your tax return and you had better get it right the first time. Why? Because you are generally not allowed to change an accounting method without permission from the IRS, which it often will not grant.

In this chapter you will learn what a method of accounting is, the general requirements for each overall method you are allowed to use, and which method is best for you. You will also learn what taxable years are permitted.

What Is a Method of Accounting?

A method of accounting is any consistent treatment from year to year of when you report an item of income or expense. A method of accounting could refer to your overall method of reporting income and deductions, or it could refer to any particular item.

For example, when you buy a EE U.S. savings bond, you pay less than face value for the bond. The face value is payable at maturity. The difference between your purchase price and the redemption value of the bond is taxable interest. You could choose to report the annual interest earned as income each year, or you could wait and report it all in the year you cash in the bond.[1] Whichever method you choose is your method of accounting for interest on EE savings bonds. Either method is proper, but you have to choose one method for all of your EE bonds. If you want to change from one method to the other, you have to follow the rules that the IRS prescribes.

The Code provides a general rule that says you cannot change a method of accounting without permission from the IRS.[2] You request a change in method of accounting by filing Form 3115, "Application for Change in Accounting Method," and generally paying a filing fee. If the folks at the IRS like the current method you are using, it might be difficult or even impossible to get them to agree to a change. If they do agree to the change, another Code section[3] provides for an adjustment to your income so that it is not over or under reported during the years affected by the change. In certain situations, in order to save taxpayers and the government time and expense, automatic change procedures are provided. In these cases, if you follow the rules the IRS lays out, you are automatically granted a change in accounting method.

Getting back to the EE bond, let's say you originally decided to report all the interest when you cash in the bond, and not report it during the years it accrues. Then, after a few years of not reporting any interest income from the bond, you decide you would rather report the interest in the years it accrues.

There happens to be a special rule in the Code for this situation.[4] It says you can make this change in any year without permission from the IRS. But the change must apply to all similar bonds that you own or will buy in the future. Also, for the year of the change, you are required to include in income the interest that had accrued and had not been reported in the previous years, even if those years are closed by the statute of limitations. This is equitable, because otherwise you would never have to report that interest as income at all.

If you wish to change from reporting interest each year as it accrues to reporting it all when you cash in the bond, the procedure is not quite so simple. In this case you have to file Form 3115 with your return, and agree to some conditions specified by the IRS.[5]

If you want to learn more about changing an accounting method, you will find additional resources at the end of this chapter. Next is a discussion of the overall methods of accounting you are permitted to use for tax purposes, and the general requirements of those methods.

The Cash Receipts and Disbursements Method

This is the simplest of the accounting methods. Under this method of accounting, income is recorded when cash is received and a deduction is recorded
when an expense is paid. This is the method individuals use to report nonbusiness income and deductions. It can also be used for most businesses for tax
purposes. But in certain circumstances you are not allowed to use the cash
method, and must use an accrual method (discussed later).

Who Cannot Use the Cash Method?

TAXPAYERS SELLING INVENTORY WITH RECEIPTS OVER $1 MILLION

A taxpayer that purchases or manufactures products to sell is generally required
to maintain inventories of the products. Maintaining an inventory means that
costs of goods purchased or produced can be deducted only when the merchandise is sold, rather than when it is purchased or manufactured. Any taxpayer required to maintain inventories is also generally required to use an accrual
method of accounting with regard to purchases and sales of the merchandise.[6]
Accrual accounting means that all sales during the year are included in income,
even though the money has not yet been received, and expenses, other than inventory, are deductible, even though not yet paid.

In 2000 the IRS announced that merchants and manufacturers with average
annual gross receipts of $1 million or less are not required to use an accrual
method of accounting or to maintain inventories.[7] To qualify, you must have average annual gross receipts of $1 million or less for each prior tax year ending
on or after December 17, 1998. Average annual gross receipts for a particular
year are based on the three-year period ending with that year. For example, to
see if you qualify to use the cash method and not maintain an inventory for
2003, you must test the average annual gross receipts for all prior years from
1998 on. You qualify if your average annual gross receipts for 1996, 1997, and
1998 are $1 million or less (1998 test), your average annual gross receipts for
1997, 1998, and 1999 are $1 million or less (1999 test), your average annual
gross receipts for 1998, 1999, and 2000 are $1 million or less (2000 test), your
average annual gross receipts for 1999, 2000, and 2001 are $1 million or less
(2001 test), and your average annual gross receipts for 2000, 2001, and 2002 are
$1 million or less (2002 test).

If you qualify and choose not to maintain an inventory, you will deduct the
cost of the items you would otherwise include in inventory in the year they are
sold or the year you pay for them, whichever is later. If you are a producer, you
can use any reasonable method to estimate the raw material in your work in
process and finished goods at the end of the year to determine the raw material used to produce finished goods that were sold during the year. For more

information on the requirements and changing to the cash method, see IRS Publication 538, *Accounting Periods and Methods,* and Revenue Procedure 2001-10 in Internal Revenue Bulletin 2001-2.

Contractors, such as plumbers, painters, remodelers, electricians, and roofers, among others, have traditionally used the cash method of accounting for tax purposes. At one time the IRS allowed contractors to use the cash method, even though they purchase products to sell to their customers. In recent years, however, the IRS has been busy denying these taxpayers the use of the cash method, and the courts have been supportive of the IRS.[8] This can be costly for a contractor who has large receivables. While receivables are not income in the current year under the cash method, they are income under an accrual method, meaning that the contractor must pay tax on income not yet received. The recent relaxation of the rules by the IRS is great news for those contractors with receipts of $1 million or less.

TAX SHELTERS

Any entity that is classified as a "tax shelter" cannot use the cash method.[9] When you think of the term *tax shelter* you probably envision some phony scheme cooked up by an unscrupulous promoter. Unfortunately, the definition is much broader than that for determining who is denied use of the cash method. If you operate your business as a partnership or S corporation, and more than 35 percent of the losses for any tax year are allocated to partners or shareholders who are inactive investors, your business is a tax shelter—at least according to the Internal Revenue Code.[10] This is a real trap for the unwary.

CERTAIN C CORPORATIONS

If you operate your business as a C corporation, or as a partnership with a C corporation as a partner, and it has had average annual gross receipts of $5 million or more for at least three years, it generally cannot use the cash method.[11] This rule does not apply to a *qualified personal service corporation.* A qualified personal service corporation is any corporation substantially all the activities of which are in the fields of health, law, engineering, architecture, accounting, actuarial science, performing arts, or consulting and substantially all of the stock is held by employees or former employees.

If you think you might be subject to the $5 million rule, put this book down and spend some of those bucks on a good accountant who can figure this stuff out for you.

Income under the Cash Method

Income is generally reported in the taxable year in which "actually or constructively received" under the cash receipts and disbursements method.[12] The name

Example 4.1

Jane provides management consulting services for Ralph's Appliances and Television. Ralph pays Jane with a brand new television set with a value of $600 rather than with cash. Jane has income in the amount of $600 in the year she receives the television set.

If instead, Ralph paid Jane by providing repair services for Jane's appliances, Jane would have income in the amount of the fair market value of the repairs in the year the services are provided.

for this method is somewhat deceiving, because income can be in the form of property or services in addition to cash, as demonstrated in Example 4.1.

So the term *cash method* is really just a timing rule that means income is recognized when actually or constructively received (in some form) rather than when it is earned or accrued.

This means that even though you have not actually received something, if it was credited to your account, set aside for you, or otherwise made available so you could get it at any time, it is still income.[13] This rule prevents cash method taxpayers from being able to manipulate their income to report it whenever they want. For example, maybe your bank calls on December 31, 2002 and says you have earned interest of $2.75 on your checking account that you can pick up at any time. You might say, "Let it ride." It doesn't matter—it's still income in 2002.

Deductions under the Cash Method

Deductions can generally be claimed in the year in which paid under the cash method.[14] Certain things that are not paid, like depreciation, depletion and losses can also be claimed.[15] Payments by check constitute a payment at the time of delivery even though actual receipt or deposit by the payee may occur at a later date. If a check is paid in the normal course of business, it is respected even though the maker can stop payment or issue the check when there are insufficient funds.[16] If you postdate a check, though, no deduction is allowed until the check is cashed.[17] If you charge something to your credit card, it is considered payment with third party debt and is deductible at the time the charge is made.[18]

PAYMENTS IN PROPERTY OR SERVICES

Similar to income under the cash method, payments do not have to be made in cash to be deductible. They can also be made in property or services. If payments are made in property or services, the amount of the deduction is the fair

---

Example 4.2

Bert and Ernie both have businesses they operate using the cash receipts and disbursements method of accounting. Bert provides services to Ernie in exchange for business property owned by Ernie. Both the services and the business property are worth $1,000, and Ernie's basis in the business property is $500.

Results to Bert: Bert must recognize income of $1,000, just as if he had received cash for his services. Bert also gets a $1,000 cost basis in the property received from Ernie.[19]

Results to Ernie: Ernie must report gain of $500 from the disposition of the business property, just as if he had received cash for the property. Ernie is also allowed a deduction under IRC § 162 attributable to the services received from Bert.[20]

---

market value of the property or services. In addition, paying for something with property or services usually gives rise to another taxable transaction. For example, if you pay for something with appreciated property, you will have to report gain from the disposition of the property. If you pay for something by providing services, you will have income in the amount of the value of the services. This is called bartering, and it is treated the same as if money had changed hands. See Example 4.2.

PREPAYMENTS

Everything you pay for as a cash method taxpayer cannot be deducted currently. If you buy a car for your business, for example, you cannot deduct the cost of the car just because you are using the cash method. According to the regulations, "if an expenditure results in the creation of an asset having a useful life which extends substantially beyond the close of the taxable year, such an expenditure may not be deductible, or may be deductible only in part, for the taxable year in which made."[21] The cost of a tangible asset, like a car, is a capital expenditure and can generally be deducted only through depreciation (discussed in Chapter 8) beginning in the year the asset is placed in service.

If you make an advance payment of a deductible item, you can deduct it when paid if you can show that it is actually a payment rather than merely a deposit, and that it does not have a useful life substantially beyond the taxable year. Whether a particular expenditure is a deposit or a payment depends on the facts of each case. According to the IRS, if you can show that the expenditure is not refundable and is made pursuant to an enforceable sales contract, it will be considered a payment.[22] The IRS adds, however, that to be deductible the payment must be made for a valid business purpose—not merely for tax avoidance. Also, the deduction must not cause a material distortion of income. Some courts have held that no distortion exists if the one-year rule (discussed next) applies.

THE ONE-YEAR RULE

The regulation that refers to "the creation of an asset having a useful life which extends substantially beyond the close of the taxable year"[23] does not tell us what "substantially beyond" means. For example, if you sign a lease in December of 2002, and are required to pay one year in advance, how much of the lease payment can you deduct in 2002? The Ninth Circuit Court of Appeals adopted the one-year rule in *Zaninovich v. Commissioner.*[24] Under the one-year rule, a payment is treated as a capital expenditure only if it creates an asset (or a like benefit to the taxpayer) having a useful life in excess of one year. That means all of the lease payment can be deducted in 2002. This one-year rule is nice and simple, and the Supreme Court has tacitly gone along with it.[25] The only problem is, the IRS has not formally agreed to it. If you use the one-year rule for expenses that are required to be prepaid, and an IRS agent questions you about it, simply repeat again and again Zaninovich, Zaninovich, Zaninovich . . .

Accrual Methods

The primary difference between the cash and accrual methods is that under accrual methods you deduct expenses when you incur them (not when you pay them) and you record income when you earn it (not when you receive it). Taxpayers who use accrual accounting for tax purposes have more flexibility than cash method taxpayers. There is not just one accrual method but many, depending on the industry you are in and your accounting practices. Accrual methods also have more complicated rules to follow.

Your banker and other creditors probably like to see accrual method financial statements for your business, so you might think you are required to use an accrual method on your tax return. *There is no such requirement.* There is a rule in the Code that says your method of accounting for tax purposes is supposed to be the same as it is for book purposes.[26] However, the IRS has held that you can use the cash method for tax purposes and an accrual method for book purposes as long as there are sufficient and accurate work papers to reconcile the two.[27] Additionally, there are many differences between the proper accrual rules for financial and accounting purposes and the proper accrual rules for tax purposes, so the two methods cannot possibly be the same.

Recall from the discussion of the cash method that certain taxpayers are required to use accrual accounting for tax purposes because they cannot use the cash method. They are the following:

- With some exceptions, C corporations and partnerships with C corporations as partners if, for any three-year period, average annual gross receipts are $5 million or more.[28]
- Any entity, other than a C corporation, that is classified as a "tax shelter."[29]
- Any taxpayer with average annual gross receipts of more than $1 million that is required to maintain inventory.[30]
- Certain farming corporations and partnerships with C corporations as partners, if annual gross receipts exceed $1 million.[31]

In the case of a taxpayer who is required to maintain an inventory, an accrual method is only required for income and deductions relating to the purchase and sale of the inventory. Although the IRS might not agree, the hybrid method (discussed later) could be an option here.

Income under Accrual Methods

Under an accrual method you generally report income when you earn it. The regulations say: "Generally, under an accrual method, income is to be included for the taxable year when all the events have occurred that fix the right to receive the income and the amount of the income can be determined with reasonable accuracy."[32]

FIXED RIGHT TO RECEIVE INCOME

The point at which a taxpayer has a fixed right to receive income is determined by the facts and circumstances of each case. Factors include (1) the agreement of the parties to the transaction, (2) the time when services are rendered or property delivered, (3) the existence of contingencies or prior

---

Example 4.3

Tess runs an interior decorating service as a sole proprietor. She uses an accrual method of accounting on Schedule C. Tess's standard billing rate is $50 per hour. Tess provided 10 hours of service to a client in December of 2002 and 30 hours in January of 2003, but did not bill the client until 2003 when all services were performed. Tess should accrue $500 of income ($50 x 10 hours) on Schedule C for 2002 for the services she performed in 2002.

conditions, and (4) whether the liability is acknowledged or disputed by the person who is paying.

In the view of the IRS, knowing when you have income as an accrual method taxpayer is fairly simple. It says generally, all the events that fix the right to receive income occur when (1) the required performance occurs, (2) payment therefor is due, or (3) payment therefor is made, whichever happens first.[33] The IRS position, in general, is that prepaid income is recognized when received by accrual method taxpayers.

AMOUNT DETERMINED WITH REASONABLE ACCURACY

If an amount is subject to conditions or contingencies, it is not possible to determine the amount with reasonable accuracy. However, if there is a fixed right to receive an amount that has not been computed at the end of the year, and information exists to make a reasonable estimate, it should be accrued.[34]

Treatment of Costs and Expense Items

Under an accrual method, a liability is incurred, and generally is taken into account for tax purposes, in the year in which (1) all the events have occurred that establish the fact of the liability, (2) the amount of the liability can be determined with reasonable accuracy, and (3) economic performance has occurred with respect to the liability.[35]

The first two parts of this test are pretty straightforward. The first requirement says a liability must exist on the basis of facts actually known or reasonably knowable as of the close of the year of deduction. The second part says that even though the exact amount of a liability that has been incurred cannot be determined, you can still accrue and deduct such part that can be computed with reasonable accuracy. But you can't do anything with a cost or expense item until *economic performance* occurs.

WHAT THE HECK IS ECONOMIC PERFORMANCE?

This is a fairly new requirement of accrual method taxpayers, and it is not a condition that applies in financial accounting. The basic requirements for economic performance are in the Internal Revenue Code,[36] but the detailed rules are laid out in a lengthy and complex set of Treasury regulations. The reason Congress enacted the economic performance rules was to prevent accrual method taxpayers from prematurely accruing deductions that are not paid until much later. Here are the general principles for determining when economic performance occurs:

- If a taxpayer receives services or property from another person, economic performance generally occurs as the other person provides the services or property. This means that even if you pay for these things in advance, you cannot deduct the cost until you actually receive the services or property.

- If a taxpayer leases or rents property, economic performance occurs as the taxpayer uses the property.

- If a taxpayer is required to provide services or property to another person, economic performance occurs as the taxpayer incurs costs to provide such services or property.

- There are several categories of liabilities for which payment constitutes economic performance. They are: (1) liabilities arising under a workers compensation act or out of any tort, breach of contract, or violation of law; (2) rebates and refunds; (3) awards, prizes and jackpots; (4) insurance, warranty and service contracts; and (5) taxes. For some of these things, the recurring item exception (discussed next) is available.

- For certain recurring items there is an exception to the general rule requiring economic performance to occur before an item may be treated as incurred. Under the recurring item exception, an item may be treated as incurred in the taxable year before economic performance occurs, as long as the other elements of the all events test have been met by the end of the prior year.

- In the case of any other liability of a taxpayer, economic performance occurs at the time determined under regulations.

Needless to say, these are the kinds of rules that make tax accountants drool, because they greatly complicate the determination of when something can be deducted under an accrual method.

The Hybrid Method

According to the Code,[37] a taxpayer may use a combination of the cash method and an accrual method, as long as the combination clearly reflects income and is consistently used. For income to be clearly reflected, all related items of revenue and expense must be reported under the same method. This is what it says in the regulations:

A taxpayer using an accrual method of accounting with respect to purchases and sales may use the cash method in computing all other items of income and expense. However, a taxpayer who uses the cash method of accounting in computing gross income from his trade or business shall use the cash method in computing expenses from such trade or business. Similarly, a taxpayer who uses an accrual method of accounting in computing business expenses shall use an accrual method in computing items affecting gross income from his trade or business.[38]

This means that if you are in the business of selling both goods and services, you might be allowed to use accrual accounting for income and deductions relating to the goods, and the cash method for income and deductions relating to the services. However, you will probably only be allowed to use this method if you properly adopt it when you first start doing business. If you are currently using the cash method or an accrual method, it is unlikely the IRS will allow you to change to the hybrid method. Remember that the IRS must approve any change of accounting you want to make, and it would much rather have you using an overall accrual method than the hybrid method.

Which Method Is Best for You?

This is a question that you can probably answer best, after having been introduced to the general principles of accounting methods. Keep in mind that if you purchase or manufacture products to sell, you are no longer required to use an accrual method for income and deductions relating to the purchase and sale of your inventory until your average gross receipts exceed $1 million. If you believe that $1 million of gross receipts is several years away, or if you run a service business, your best choice is probably the cash method. It's the easiest, and it usually allows you to defer income that would be reportable under an accrual method.

If you sell both goods and services and are soon to exceed $1 million in gross receipts, the hybrid method is an option if you choose it from the start. It is unlikely the IRS will allow you to change to the hybrid method if you are using another method.

Accounting Periods

An accounting period is the taxable year for which you report your income and deductions. A taxable year includes the calendar year, which is from January 1 to December 31. It also includes a *fiscal year*, which means a period of 12 months ending on the last day of any month other than December. Certain taxpayers are allowed to use a 52 to 53 week taxable year, which is a fiscal year that varies from 52 to 53 weeks and ends on a particular day of the week.[39]

The Code says the taxable year for a taxpayer who does not keep books must be the calendar year.[40] The regulations say that a new taxpayer may adopt, without permission from the IRS, any permitted taxable year on or before the due date of its first return. Once a taxable year is adopted, however, it must not be changed unless approved by the IRS, or unless permitted by the Code or regulations.[41] For these reasons, just about all individuals use the calendar year as their accounting period.

If you operate your business as a sole proprietorship, you must report your income and deductions on Schedule C, which is filed with your individual return. That means your business must also use the calendar year.

On the other hand, if you operate your business as a C corporation that is not a personal service corporation, the corporation can adopt any fiscal year it wants. A C corporation that meets the requirements under the regulations can also change its taxable year automatically by following the rules in the regulations.[42]

Required Years for PSCs, S Corporations, and Partnerships

A personal service corporation (PSC) is a C corporation that meets certain conditions, and has as its principal activity the performance of personal services. For this purpose, only services in the fields of health, law, engineering, architecture, accounting, actuarial science, performing arts, and consulting are considered personal services.[43]

PSCs and S corporations are required to use the calendar year for their taxable year, unless they come up with a really good business purpose to use a different taxable year, or they make a Section 444 election.[44] Partnerships must conform their tax years to the tax years of their owners unless a business purpose can be established, or the partnership makes a Section 444 election.[45]

Remember (from Chapter 3) that the income and deductions of S corporations and partnerships pass through to be reported on the owners' individual returns. If an S corporation or partnership is on a different taxable year than an owner, the owner reports income and deductions from the entity's taxable year that ends within the owner's taxable year. Therefore, if an individual on the calendar year owns an interest in a partnership that has a January 31 fiscal year, the owner can defer tax on 11 months of income from the partnership. The required taxable year rules were enacted to prevent this tax deferral potential.

Because of the required taxable year rules, it takes a very good business purpose to convince the IRS to allow a PSC, S corporation, or partnership to adopt a fiscal year. About the only business purpose that will satisfy the IRS is if the PSC, S corporation, or partnership has a seasonal business. Businesses that have insignificant income during part of the year, such as a golf course, ski resort, or professional sports franchise will qualify. If the PSC, S corporation, or partnership is already on the calendar year, it is unlikely the IRS will allow a change to a fiscal year, even with a business purpose.

The Section 444 Election

The required taxable year rules for PSCs, S corporations and partnerships were enacted as part of the Tax Reform Act of 1986, because Congress wanted to end the tax deferral that shareholders and partners of fiscal year entities were benefiting from. Before the law was changed, PSCs, S corporations, and partnerships could adopt a fiscal year to create a tax deferral of up to three months, even without a business purpose. The new rules created a large group of disgruntled taxpayers who were required to change their fiscal year entities to the calendar year. So, as part of the Revenue Act of 1987, Section 444 was enacted to provide limited relief.

Section 444 grants an option to PSCs, S corporations, and partnerships to adopt a fiscal year if they lack a business purpose. A Section 444 election can be made only if the deferral period of the taxable year to be elected is the shorter of three months or the deferral period of the taxable year that is being changed.[46] This means that a Section 444 election is only available to elect a September, October, or November year-end for a new entity whose required year is the calendar year. If an existing PSC, S corporation, or partnership has already adopted its required taxable year, it cannot make a Section 444 election, because the deferral period is zero.

THE DOWNSIDE

This might sound like a pretty good deal for a new entity, but here's the catch. Congress generated considerable revenue by enacting the required year rules, and it was not willing to give it back. So additional rules were enacted in concert with Section 444 in order to deny owners of PSCs, S corporations, and partnerships the benefit of tax deferral on the income generated during their deferral periods. S corporations and partnerships must make annual deposits of "required payments" representing the tax deferral to their owners attributable to the deferral period.[47] Since PSCs are not pass-through entities, they are required to make annual minimum distributions to their shareholders during the deferral period.[48] This prevents the shareholders from deferring the tax on these payments.

As you may have guessed, this is another one of those drool-inducing provisions for tax accountants. It is only for taxpayers who want a fiscal year bad enough to be willing to pay for it. If you think you might want to take the Section 444 road be advised that it is fraught with potholes, speed traps, and slick spots. You should find a CPA who has been that way before to do the driving for you.

Additional Resources

IRS Publication 538, *Accounting Periods and Methods,* gives more information on the topics discussed in this chapter, and includes a discussion on methods of valuing inventory. Publication 911, *Direct Sellers,* also might be of interest. It provides information on figuring income from direct sales and identifies deductible expenses. A direct seller is someone who sells merchandise to others on a person-to-person basis, such as door-to-door, at sales parties, or by appointment in someone's home.

You can get these publications free by calling the IRS at (800) TAX-FORM [(800) 829-3676]. If you have access to TTY/TDD equipment, you can call (800) 829-4059. To download them from the Internet, go to *www.irs.gov* (World Wide Web), or *ftp.irs.gov* (FTP). If you would like to get forms and instructions (not publications) by FAX, dial (703) 368-9694 to reach IRS Tax Fax.

As an alternative to downloading files from the Internet, you can order *IRS Federal Tax Products* on CD-ROM. This CD includes over 2,000 tax products, including all of the above publications and forms. It can be ordered by calling (800) 233-6767. Also, Publication 3207, *Small Business Resource Guide,* is an interactive CD-ROM that contains information important to small businesses. It is available in mid-February. You can get one free copy by calling (800) 829-3676.

Notes

[1] IRC § 454.

[2] IRC § 446(e).

[3] IRC § 481.

[4] IRC § 454(a).

[5] See Rev. Proc. 89-46, 1989-2 C.B. 597. This information is also in IRS Publication 17, *Your Income Tax.*

[6] Treas. Reg. § 1.446-1(c)(2)(i).

[7] Rev. Proc. 2001-10, 2001-2 IRB 272, superceding Rev. Proc. 2000-22, 2000-20 IRB.

[8] *J.P. Sheahan Associates, Inc. v. Commissioner,* T.C. Memo 1992-239; *Thompson Electric Inc. v. Commissioner,* T.C. Memo 1995-292.

[9] IRC § 448(a)(3).

[10] IRC § 448(d)(3), § 461(i)(3), and § 1256(e)(3)(B).

[11] IRC § 448. Also certain farming corporations and partnerships with C corporations as partners are denied use of the cash method if annual gross receipts exceed $1 million. IRC § 447.

[12] Treas. Reg. § 1.446-1(c)(1)(i).

[13] Treas. Reg. § 1.451-2.

[14] Treas. Reg. § 1.446-1(c)(1)(i).

[15] Treas. Reg. § 1.461-1(a).

[16] *Estate of Witt v. Fahs,* USTC ¶ 9534 (S.D. Fl. 1956); Estate of Spiegel, 12 T.C. 524 (1949), acq. 1949-2 C.B. 3.

[17] *Griffin v. Comm.,* 49 T.C. 253 (1967).

[18] Rev. Rul. 78-38, 1978-1 C.B. 67.

[19] Rev. Rul. 80-196, 1980-2 C.B. 32; *McDougal v. Comm.*, 62 T.C. 720, 728 (1974).

[20] Treas. Reg. § 1.83-6(a)(1).

[21] Treas. Reg. § 1.461-1(a)(1).

[22] Rev. Rul. 79-229, 1979-2 C.B. 210.

[23] Treas. Reg. § 1.461-1(a)(1).

[24] 616 F2d 429 (9th Cir. 1980).

[25] *Hillsboro National Bank v. Commissioner*, 457 U.S. 1103 n. 25 (1983).

[26] IRC § 446(a).

[27] LTR 9103001. See also S. Rep. No. 99-313, 99th Cong., 2d Sess. 118 (1986) ("This [book conformity] requirement is considered satisfied where the taxpayer maintains sufficient records to allow reconciliation of the results obtained under the method regularly used in keeping its books and the method used for Federal income tax purposes").

[28] IRC § 448.

[29] IRC § 448(d)(3).

[30] Treas. Reg. § 1.446-1(c)(2)(i); Rev. Proc. 2000-22, 2000-20 IRB.

[31] IRC § 447.

[32] Treas. Reg. § 1.446-1(c)(1)(ii).

[33] Rev. Rul. 74-607, 1974-2 C.B. 149.

[34] Treas. Reg. § 1.451-1(a).

[35] Treas. Reg. § 1.446-1(c)(1)(ii).

[36] IRC § 461(h).

[37] IRC § 446(c).

[38] Treas. Reg. § 1.446-1(c)(1)(iv).

[39] IRC § 441(f).

[40] IRC § 441.

[41] Treas. Reg. § 1.441-1T(b)(3).

[42] Treas. Reg. § 1.442-1(c).

[43] Treas. Reg. § 1.441-4T.

[44] IRC § 1378 and IRC § 441(i).

[45] IRC § 706(b).

[46] IRC § 444(b).

[47] IRC § 7519.

[48] IRC § 280H.

CHAPTER 5

Limitations on Use of Your Home

> The Court's contrary conclusion misreads ... the Internal Revenue Code, ... and unfairly denies an intended benefit to the growing number of self-employed taxpayers who manage their businesses from a home office.
>
> —Justice Stevens dissent to the Supreme Court's Soliman decision

The pursuit of tax breaks was probably not your primary reason for setting up your home office. Instead, like other home-based workers, you chose to work from home because of your personal needs and circumstances. However, if there are legitimate tax advantages to working from home, you owe it to yourself to take full advantage of them.

The problem is that Congress, the courts and the IRS have made it rather difficult for us to deduct home-based business expenses. There is a net income limitation on the amount of deductions that can be claimed, and allocations must be made (on Form 8829) between personal and business use.

Additionally, the Supreme Court placed severe restrictions on allowable deductions in a 1993 landmark decision. As a result, some tax preparers have advised against claiming home-based business deductions out of fear of red flagging a return for audit.

But guess what! Effective for 1999 and later years, the Supreme Court decision has effectively been overturned through legislation. The complexity of the net income limitation and business/personal use allocations remain, but home-office deductions are available to more people now than they have been for over two decades. Through proper tax planning, virtually anyone who runs a home-based business can legitimately claim home-office deductions without fear of triggering an IRS audit. Even those who maintain a permanent office outside the home but use a home office for administrative or management activities are eligible. Since the IRS conducts audits to generate revenue, properly claimed and documented deductions for the business use of your home should not be a principal target.

This chapter describes the various uses for which deductions for the business use of your home are allowable, including an in-depth discussion of the new rules. Chapter 6 describes the proper methods for allocating expenses, and shows how the net income limitation is applied.

Why Pick on Us?

Why are home-based business deductions treated differently than other business expenses? Well, they haven't always been. Before 1976, taxpayers could claim home-based business deductions under IRC Section 162 if their home office met the general requirements of Section 162, and was "appropriate and helpful" to them.[1] That loose standard was abused by some home-based workers. Congress became concerned that people were getting away with deducting living expenses by calling them business expenses. IRC Section 280A was therefore enacted in 1976 to prohibit deductions under Section 162 for the business use of a dwelling unit unless certain specific conditions are satisfied. Section 280A applies to individuals, partnerships, trusts, estates, and S corporations, but not to C corporations.[2]

Section 280A says that the first thing you need in order to have any hope of deducting expenses for the business use of your home is a trade or business, and not merely an investment activity. If you are not sure whether your activity qualifies as a trade or business, take another look at the qualifying factors in Chapter Two. If you discover that you do *not* meet the Section 280A requirements for deducting home-based business expenses, keep in mind that the limitations under Section 280A apply only to a specific category of expenses as discussed below. There are still a lot of expenses you can deduct that relate to the use of your home for business or investment activities that are *not* limited by Section 280A. Check out Chapters 7 and 8.

A Quick Summary of the Restrictions

Section 280A basically says that you cannot deduct expenses for the business use of your home unless you use a portion of your home on a *regular* and *exclusive* basis:

1. As the *principal* place of any business in which you are engaged; or
2. As a place of business where patients, clients or customers meet and deal with you; or
3. In the case of a separate structure (like a garage) which is not attached to your house, in a use that is *connected* with any business in which you engage.

These rules apply to employees as well as self-employed individuals. But if you are an employee, using a home office must be for the convenience of your employer and not simply for your own convenience.[3]

You also qualify to claim deductions for two additional uses that require *regular* use only (not *exclusive* use). They are:

4. The use of space in your home for the storage of inventory or (for 1996 and later) product samples, if your business is selling products at retail or wholesale, but only if your home is the sole fixed location of such business; and
5. The use of a portion of your home in your business of providing daycare for children, for individuals 65 or over, or for physically or mentally handicapped people.

If you satisfy one or more of the use tests discussed above, you must then determine what portion of the various expenses of maintaining your home can be allocated to business use. This is explained in Chapter 6.

The Net Income Limitation

Even if the use tests are met, deductions for the business portion of expenses for the business use of your home may not exceed net income derived from the business use. Expenses disallowed because of the income limitation may be carried forward and treated as home-based business expenses for next year. The carryover, as well as the expenses incurred next year, are subject to the income limitation for that year. This limitation is explained in detail in Chapter 6.

What Expenses Are Limited?

The only expenses that are limited by Section 280A are those related directly or indirectly to the use of your home office that are not otherwise deductible. Expenses that are deductible regardless of their business connection are not subject to the limitation. That means gas, sewer, water, heat, electricity, garbage pickup, homeowners insurance, and depreciation allocable to your home office are limited. Cleaning and any direct repairs to your home office are also limited. The portions of your property taxes, mortgage interest, and any casualty loss allocated to your home office, are specifically excluded from the limitation, because they are deductible regardless of their business connection.

Additionally, all of the other expenses you incur in your home-based business that are unrelated to the use of your home office are deductible without the limitations of Section 280A. However, they must qualify as ordinary and necessary business expenses, so any amount allocated to personal use must be excluded. For example, if you purchase a computer for use in your home office and use it 25 percent of the time for personal things and 75 percent of the time for business, you can only deduct 75 percent of the cost of the computer (see Chapter 8). As mentioned above, Chapters 7 and 8 are devoted to deductions that are not subject to the Section 280A limitations.

Is Your "Home" Where You Think It Is?

Section 280A limits the deductibility of home-business expenses, but what does the law consider to be your home? For example, if you have an office in your lake cabin, or in your winter condo in Tucson, would it be considered a "home office"? Well, Section 280A states that the home-office rules apply if you use for your office a "dwelling unit" that is also used by you during the taxable year as a "residence."[4]

Dwelling Unit

NOTE

Most of you can skip the next few paragraphs, because you are using your principal residence for your home office or daycare facility, which you already know constitutes your home.

The term *dwelling unit* means anything that provides basic living accommodations, including an apartment, condominium, mobile home, boat, or similar property.[5] Basic living accommodations means sleeping space, toilet and cooking facilities.[6] So if your lake cabin has running water and an outhouse out back, it's a dwelling unit. If you have a garage or a shed on the same property as the dwelling unit, it is considered part of the dwelling unit.[7] It doesn't matter whether you own or rent the dwelling unit.

Example 5.1

If you do not rent out your lake cabin during the year, but use it for more than 14 days during the year for personal purposes, it is your residence. That's because 14 days is greater than 10 percent of the number of days the unit was rented to someone else (zero days), and you used the unit for a period longer than 14 days.

Residence

Whether a dwelling unit constitutes your *residence* is a little more complicated. Section 280A says that if you, a member of your family, or anyone else who has an ownership interest in the dwelling unit uses it during the year for personal purposes for a period that exceeds the greater of (1) 14 days, or (2) 10 percent of the number of days during the year you rent the unit to someone else at a fair rental, then you are deemed to have used the unit as a residence.[8] See Examples 5.1, 5.2, and 5.3.

Your family for this purpose includes brothers and sisters (whether by whole or half blood), your spouse, ancestors (parents and grandparents), and lineal descendants (kids and grandkids).[9] So your kids (including adopted ones) and their kids, and your parents and grandparents are members of your family, but your aunt Sophie and cousin Bubba are not. Renting the unit to anyone at less than fair rental is deemed to be personal use by you. Renting the unit to a family member, even at fair rental, is deemed to be personal use by you, unless the dwelling unit constitutes the family member's *principal* residence.[10] Also, if you use the dwelling unit for personal purposes while it is also rented to someone else, it is not treated as rented on such days.

Example 5.2

If you use your condo in Tucson for 30 days in the winter and rent it out at fair rental for at least 300 days during the rest of the year, it is not considered to be your residence. That's because personal use must exceed 30 days, which is the greater of 14 days or 10 percent of the number of days the unit was rented to someone else. In this case, therefore, you don't need to meet the Section 280A business-use tests if you have an office in your condo because it is not your residence, but deductible expenses must still be allocated between business and personal use.

> **Example 5.3**
>
> Let's say you own a boat suitable for overnight use, and you use the boat for personal purposes for 16 days during the year. If you rent your boat at fair rental for 163 days during the year, and you do not use the boat for personal purposes on any of those 163 days, your boat is not your personal residence. That's because the number of days for which the boat is used for personal purposes (16) does not exceed 16.3, which is 10 percent of the number of days the boat is rented.

Regular Use of a Home Office

Any qualified business use of your personal residence requires *regular* use. Regular use means on a continuing basis.[11] This means that using a portion of your home only occasionally for business doesn't make it. The intent of this requirement is to disallow costs related to areas of your house that are primarily personal. If you have a seasonal business, you can still satisfy the regular use test even though the use is limited to the part of the year the business is active.

The determination of regular use is based on individual judgment rather than exact criteria. As a practical matter, if you have a business that requires both regular *and* exclusive use, it's the exclusive use test that you generally have to worry about. If you can show that an area of your home is used exclusively for business, an IRS agent will probably concede that you use it on a regular basis.

The regular use test becomes much more critical for activities that do *not* require exclusive use. As noted above, those include storing inventory and running a daycare facility. Congress recognized the unique nature of those activities in exempting them from the exclusive use requirement. For a home daycare business, space seized by the daycare kids during the day gets won back by the owner's family at night. The exclusive use test would seldom be met. However, taxpayers operating such a business incur expenses beyond those incurred if the house was used solely for personal purposes. Congress decided that to enforce the "exclusive use" test would effectively deny taxpayers a deduction for legitimate business expenses. The regular use test must still be satisfied, though.

A Daycare Example

Consider the following situation. A daycare is run out of a small one-story house with a finished basement, a detached garage, and a play area out back. In the basement is a playroom, a laundry room, a bathroom, and a storage area.

Daycare activities occupy virtually the whole house during the day, but the children are not allowed to play in the garage, the basement storage area, or the laundry room. The question is: Do the garage, the storage area, and the laundry room satisfy the regular use test along with the rest of the house? The Tax Court answered these questions in a recent case.[12]

The garage contains the owner's car and other personal items, but also is the storage place for most of the toys that the kids play with outside. Some of the personal items stored in the garage are also used for daycare purposes. There are tools for fixing bikes, lawn equipment for caring for the yard, and a snow blower for keeping the walk clear for the kids and their parents in the winter. The daycare owner makes numerous excursions in and out of the garage daily to retrieve or return toys, or to round up a stray kid. The Tax Court said the regular use test is satisfied for the garage.

The laundry room is used for the owner's personal laundry, and to do laundry for the daycare children. On average, the owner does two loads for each purpose daily. The owner makes numerous trips into the laundry room each day to load or unload laundry from the washer or dryer, fold the laundry, or put the laundry away. The laundry room also contains a freezer for storing food for the daycare children. The freezer is accessed about once a day. The Tax Court said the laundry room satisfies the regular use test as well.

The storage area is an open space adjacent to the laundry room that is used to store toys for the daycare kids as well as personal items. The owner enters the area several times a day, and kids wander in and out on occasion. The Tax Court said this area also satisfies the regular use test.

This case demonstrates situations in which the regular use test is met for a daycare business, even when business use is not the most important purpose of the particular area. Keep in mind, however, that unless your business use relates to the storage of inventory or the running of a daycare facility, you must also satisfy the exclusive use test.

Exclusive Means *Exclusive!*

"Exclusive use" means that the portion of your home used for business cannot be used for any other purpose.[13] According to the Tax Court and the legislative history of Section 280A, this requirement is to be taken quite literally; meaning "the taxpayer must use a specific part of a dwelling unit solely for the purpose of carrying on his trade or business."[14] That means you don't qualify if your home office is a space you have cleared off on the dining room table. Congress wants you to have an area set up just for doing business. You flunk the test if you do investment-related work, balance your personal checkbook, or let the kids play games on the computer.[15]

This is a higher standard than you would have to maintain for an office outside the home. Admittedly it is harsh, ruthless and downright unkind. It's there because Congress, in enacting Section 280A, wanted to prevent deductions for personal expenses and to allow deductions only for the business use of a residence. It would seem, however, that negligible nonbusiness use of your office would not violate the spirit of Section 280A. In fact, in at least one case the Tax Court ruled that a space satisfied the exclusive use test even though there was evidence of minimal personal use.[16]

For purposes of the regular and exclusive use tests, the "portion of your home" in which your home office is occupied does not have to constitute an entire room. You must have a separately identifiable space, but it is not necessary that it be marked off by a permanent partition.[17] A separately identifiable space means you should not have personal use items mixed with business use items. To convince the IRS that the use is exclusive, you should take special care to show that your only activities in the business space are business activities.

Where Is the Evidence?

You might be thinking, "Hey, who's going to know if I let the kids play games on my business computer? What if I just pull the blinds and do a little personal book work in my home office?" Well, just remember that the burden of proof for any deductions you claim is on you.[18] The best way to support your claim is with evidence indicating strict business use. For example, kid games on your computer and a joy stick attached will look pretty suspicious. Even a program on your computer for your personal checking account will not help your cause. (Buy a used computer for the personal stuff and put it someplace else.) It goes without saying that a television and an easy chair should not be in your office, unless watching television is an integral part of your business.[19] If you have only one phone in the house it should not be located in your office, because it is obvious that personal calls must be made and received at that location. (Get yourself a second phone for the kitchen or the family room.)

How About Two Businesses?

There is no rule that says exclusive business use of your home office must be limited to one business, or even to your principal business.[20] Therefore, you can manage more than one business from your home office and still satisfy the exclusivity test; but if one of your businesses does not satisfy any of the business-use requirements, the exclusivity test is failed for all of your business activities.[21] This rule applies to two people conducting business in the same space, such as you and your spouse. If one person fails the business use tests, the other person's deductions are also denied.

What Is Your Principal Place of Business?

This is the test most people rely on to qualify (so don't doze off—this is the important part!). The question is, "What is a principal place of business?" Unfortunately, Congress did not bother to define the term when it enacted Section 280A. Consequently, the IRS and the courts have struggled with a definition over the years. The Supreme Court finally took up the issue in the 1993 case of *Commissioner of Internal Revenue v. Soliman.*[22] The Court's definition in *Soliman* was so restrictive that it put home-office deductions out of reach for most home-based business owners. Congress finally eased up on the restrictions as part of the Taxpayer Relief Act of 1997, but the new rules did not take effect until 1999. Because the *Soliman* standards still apply for 1998 and earlier years, and might be relevant even under the new rules, a brief explanation is included here.

The Soliman Case

In 1983, Nader Soliman was a self-employed anesthesiologist who practiced at three hospitals in the Washington, DC, area. He spent 30 to 35 hours per week providing care to patients at the hospitals during the year, 80 percent of that time being at one of the hospitals. None of the hospitals provided him with an office. Soliman's only office was in one of the three bedrooms in his condominium, which he used regularly and exclusively in his business of being an anesthesiologist. From his home office he contacted surgeons, patients and hospitals by telephone; maintained his billing records and patient logs; read medical journals to keep abreast of advances in anesthesiology; and performed other tasks essential to being an anesthesiologist. Dr. Soliman spent 10 to 15 hours per week in his home office.

On his tax return, Dr. Soliman claimed deductions relating to his home office. On audit, the IRS disallowed the deductions, claiming his home office was not his "principal place of business" within the meaning of Section 280A. Soliman took the issue to the Tax Court, where he won. Through IRS appeals, the Supreme Court eventually heard the case and ruled in favor of the IRS.

THE SUPREME COURT'S RATIONALIZATION

The Court said that "principal" means the "most important, consequential, or influential" (referring to *Webster's Third New International Dictionary*). A taxpayer's "principal place of business," therefore, should be determined through a comparison of all of the places where business is transacted.

The Court stated that there are two primary considerations in deciding whether a home office is the principal place of business:

1. The relative importance of the activities performed at each business location, and

2. The amount of time spent at the home office compared to the time spent at each of the other places where the business is transacted.

In determining the relative importance of activities, the place where a person is required to meet with clients or deliver goods or perform services is generally the principal place of business, especially if that place has unique or special characteristics like a hospital. The Court determined that a home office might be legitimate, it might even be essential because no other office space is available to the taxpayer, but that doesn't necessarily make it the taxpayer's principal place of business. Based upon the two primary criteria it established, the Court concluded that Dr. Soliman's home office was not his principal place of business. The Doctor's most important activities were conducted outside his home office. Furthermore, the 10 to 15 hours per week he spent in his home office were less than the 30 to 35 hours per week he spent at the hospitals.

These tests are obviously subject to the interpretation and judgement of the IRS, making it difficult to be assured of a hassle-free return. The good news is that the tests have been rendered generally irrelevant, for years after 1998, by the new rules to be discussed next.

New Law Overrides Soliman for Years after 1998

Congress has finally ridden to the rescue of home-office workers to reverse the *Soliman* decision—albeit on a slow horse. Effective for years after 1998, the Taxpayer Relief Act of 1997 amended Section 280A to provide that the term "principal place of business" includes a place of business which is used by the taxpayer for the administrative or management activities of any trade or business. To apply, however, there must be no other fixed location where the taxpayer conducts substantial administrative or management activities of that trade or business. Although not defined in the Code, activities that are administrative or managerial in character include billing customers or clients, keeping books and records, ordering supplies, setting up appointments, and forwarding orders or writing reports.[23] Mostly anything that is not directly related to generating revenue could be considered administrative or managerial.

The new law does not change the regular and exclusive use requirements, or the condition that employee use must be for the convenience of the employer. Furthermore, the new law does not otherwise displace *Soliman's* two-part test for determining whether a home office is a principal place of business if the new conditions are not met.

Under the new rule, a home office used for administrative or management activities will qualify as a principal place of business, regardless of whether such activities connected with the same trade or business are performed by others at other locations (such as billing activities). The fact that a taxpayer also carries out administrative or management activities at sites that are not fixed locations of the business, such as a car or hotel room, will not affect the taxpayer's ability to claim home-office deductions. In addition, if a taxpayer conducts some administrative or management activities at a fixed location outside the home, the taxpayer will still be able to claim home-office deductions, as long as the administrative or management activities conducted at the other location are not substantial. A taxpayer's ability to claim home-office deductions under the new rule will not be affected by the fact that the taxpayer conducts substantial nonadministrative or nonmanagement business activities at a fixed location of the business outside the home.[24]

Therefore, under the new rule you could have an outside office in which you meet with or provide services to clients, but choose not to use for administrative or management activities. If you use your home office regularly and exclusively for the administrative and management activities, it will qualify as your principal place of business. If you are conducting business as an employee, however, the convenience-of-the-employer test must still be satisfied.

Congress revised the definition of principal place of business because it believed the *Soliman* decision unfairly denied home-office deductions to a growing number of entrepreneurs who manage their business from their homes. It also believed that the new rule will enable more taxpayers to work efficiently at home, save commuting time and expenses, and spend additional time with their families.

The new rule permits virtually all home-based business owners to structure their affairs so that they qualify for the deduction. Examples 5.4 to 5.8 on pages 92 to 95 compare how the old and new rules work. Most of the examples are borrowed from IRS Publication 587, "Business Use of Your Home."

The Separate Business Issue

Keep in mind that the principal place of business test does not dictate that expenses must relate to your principal business. In other words, the business conducted at home could be a secondary or sideline business. It might even be related to your main business that is not conducted in your home. See Example 5.9 on page 95.

The initial question to consider in this example is whether Robert works in his home laboratory as part of his business of being a physician, or whether Robert's specialized biopsy practice can be considered a separate business. The Tax Court has ruled that a taxpayer may have two or more trades or businesses, or be engaged in a profession and a business at the same time, and that the office in the home may be the "principal place" of that second trade or business.[25]

Example 5.4

Jake is a self-employed anesthesiologist. He spends the majority of his time administering anesthesia and postoperative care in three local hospitals. One of the hospitals provides him with an office where he could conduct administrative or management activities.

Jake does not use the office the hospital provides. He uses a room in his home that he has converted to an office. He uses this room exclusively and regularly for all of the following activities.

- Contacting patients, surgeons and hospitals regarding scheduling
- Preparing for treatments and presentations
- Maintaining billing records and patient logs
- Satisfying continuing medical education requirements
- Reading medical journals and books.

In 1998, Jake's home office would not have qualified as his principal place of business. The home office activities are less important to Jake's business than the services he performs in the hospitals.

Under the new rules, however, Jake's home office qualifies as his principal place of business. He conducts administrative or management activities for his business there and has no other fixed location where he conducts such activities. His choice to use his home office instead of one provided by the hospital does not disqualify his home office as his principal place of business. His performance of substantial nonadministrative or nonmanagement activities at fixed locations outside his home also does not disqualify his home office as his principal place of business. Because he meets all of the qualifications, he can deduct expenses, subject to the deduction limit, for the business use of his home for the years 1999 and beyond.

In a case identical to Robert's, the Tax Court ruled that a home laboratory constituted the principal place of business for the taxpayer's specialized biopsy practice.[26] However, in the case of another doctor, the Tax Court refused to allow the taxpayer to divide a single practice into separate activities for the purpose of claiming home office deductions.[27]

A Place to Meet Patients, Clients, or Customers

If your home office does not meet the principal place of business test referred to above, your home-business expenses might still be deductible (subject to the net income limitation explained in Chapter 6). If you use your home office to

---

Example 5.5

Julie is a self-employed sales representative for several different product lines. Her only office is a room in her house used regularly and exclusively to set up appointments, store product samples, and write up orders and other reports for the companies whose products she sells. She occasionally writes up orders and sets up appointments from her hotel room when she is away on business overnight.

Julie's business is selling products to customers at various locations within the metropolitan area where she lives. To make these sales, she regularly visits the customers to explain the available products and to take orders. Julie makes only a few sales from her home office.

In 1998, Julie's home office would not have qualified as her principal place of business. The essence of her business as a salesperson requires her to meet with customers primarily at the customer's place of business. The home-office activities are less important to Julie's business than the sales activities she performs when visiting customers.

Under the new rules, however, Julie's home office qualifies as her principal place of business. She conducts administrative or management activities there and she has no other fixed location where she conducts administrative or management activities. The fact that she conducts some administrative or management activities in her hotel room (not a fixed location) does not disqualify her home office as her principal place of business. She can deduct her expenses, to the extent of the deduction limit, for the business use of her home for the years 1999 and beyond.

---

meet or deal with patients, clients or customers, the office does not need to be your principal place of business.[28] To qualify, you must meet or deal with your patients or customers in the home office, not just talk with them on the phone or through fax or e-mail communications.[29] In today's cyberspace environment this strict focus on face-to-face communication seems archaic, but that's the way the law is written.

The office must still be used exclusively and regularly for your business. If you only meet with patients, clients, or customers occasionally in your home office, it will not qualify.[30] Such meetings must be "substantial and integral" to the conduct of your business.[31] Also, if you are an employee, the use of your home office must be for the convenience of your employer (discussed later in this chapter).

Example 5.6

Albert is a self-employed plumber who installs and repairs plumbing in customers' homes and offices. Albert spends about 40 hours of his work time per week at these customer locations. He has a small office in his home that he uses regularly and exclusively, for about 10 hours per week, talking with customers on the telephone, deciding what supplies to order, and reviewing the books of his business.

Albert does not do his own billing. He uses a local bookkeeping service to bill his customers.

In 1998, Albert's home office would not have qualified as his principal place of business. The essence of Albert's trade or business as a plumber requires him to perform services and deliver goods at the homes or offices of his customers. The administrative tasks that Albert performs at his home office are less important and take less time than his service calls to customers.

Under the new rules, however, Albert's home office qualifies as his principal place of business. He uses the home office for the administrative or managerial activities of his plumbing business and he has no other fixed location where he conducts these activities. His choice to have his billing done by another company does not disqualify his home office as his principal place of business. He can deduct his expenses, to the extent of the deduction limit, for the business use of his home for the years 1999 and beyond.

Example 5.7

Barbara is employed as a teacher. Barbara is required to teach and meet with students at the school, and to grade papers and tests. The school provides her with a small office where she can work on her lesson plans, grade papers and tests, and meet with parents and students. The school does not require her to work at home.

Barbara prefers to use the office she has set up in her home and does not use the one provided by the school. She uses her home office exclusively and regularly for the administrative activities of her teaching job.

In 1998, Barbara's home office would not have qualified as her principal place of business because administrative activities are less important than her actual teaching duties at the school.

In 2000, Barbara still must meet the convenience-of-the-employer requirement, even if her home office qualifies as her principal place of business. Because the school provides her with an office and does not require her to work at home, she does not meet the convenience-of-the-employer test and cannot claim home-office deductions.

Example 5.8

Carl is a self-employed author who uses his home office regularly and exclusively in which to write. Carl is engaged in writing 30 to 35 hours per week in the home office. Carl also spends another 10 to 15 hours per week at other locations conducting research, meeting with his publishers, and attending promotional events.

In 1998, Carl's home office would have qualified as his principal place of business. The essence of Carl's trade or business as an author is writing. Carl's research, meetings with publishers, and attendance at promotional events, although essential, are less important and take less time than Carl's writing, which is conducted in his home office. Therefore, Carl could have deducted his expenses, to the extent of the deduction limit, for the business use of his home in 1998.

For the years 1999 and beyond, Carl's home office remains his principal place of business, so his home-office expenses are deductible, to the extent of the deduction limit.

Example 5.9

Robert is a physician. He maintains a medical office (not in his home), and is on the staffs of two hospitals where he specializes in thoracic surgery and surgical oncology. In addition to his medical practice, he set up a laboratory in the basement of his home for a specialized biopsy practice. The laboratory is equipped with a table area with running water for staining and preparing slides, a desk, and a microscope. There is an area for dictating and typing reports, as well as for slide storage. Half of the lab work comes from his office patients and half comes from hospital consultations, and the lab work generates several thousand dollars of income per year. Robert spends approximately 5 hours per week in his home laboratory and 45 hours per week at his other places of business.

The essence of Robert's business as a physician is the treatment of patients, and he does not do that in his home office laboratory. If Robert's activities all constitute the single business of being a physician, then his laboratory will not qualify as his principal place of business under the *Soliman* standards. However, the activities of Robert's medical practice are substantially different from that of his laboratory work. Income generated by the work that he does in the laboratory is a supplemental source of income that complements his medical practice income. If substantial differences exist in the tasks and activities of two occupations, then each occupation constitutes a separate trade or business. Since Robert's specialized biopsy practice constitutes a separate business, his laboratory constitutes its principal place of business, and Robert may deduct home-business expenses related to the laboratory.

This Can Be Your Second Office

As noted above, your home office does not have to be your main office to qualify for this rule. Therefore, doctors, dentists, attorneys, and other self-employed professionals can have an office downtown that they work at two or three days a week, and also maintain a home office for meeting with patients or clients the rest of the time. In this case, it's a good idea to have an appointment calendar showing your home appointments. To further support your home-business deductions, your advertising literature and business cards should show your home address and phone number.[32]

Who Is a Patient, Client, or Customer?

Keep in mind that you must have regular meetings with "patients, clients, or customers." Meetings with people who do not fall into one of these categories don't count. For example, if you are a member of the city council, meeting with your "constituents" in your home office doesn't make it according to the IRS.[33] The IRS has not expressed an opinion on other relationships that might fail this test, nor have the courts. For instance, if you are a pastor who meets with parishioners in your home office, it is uncertain whether the IRS or the courts would consider the rule satisfied.

The Use of Separate Structures

The third way to qualify for home-business deductions is to have a separate, freestanding structure on your residential property that you use regularly and exclusively in connection with your trade or business. A separate structure does not have to qualify as your principal place of business or a place for meeting patients, clients, or customers. Expenses connected with the use of this structure are deductible, subject to the income limitation.

Example 5.10

John operates a floral shop in town. He grows the plants for his shop in a greenhouse behind his home. Since he uses the greenhouse exclusively and regularly in his business, he can deduct the expenses for its use, subject to the net income limitations.

Use as Storage Space

If you have a home office that is the sole fixed location of a retail or wholesale business, you can claim household expenses allocable to the area of your residence in which inventory or product samples are stored on a regular basis.[34] These deductions qualify, subject to the net income limitations, even if the expenses allocable to your home office do not. Note that there is no requirement that the area be used exclusively for inventory or product samples. That means if the kids happen to play there, the dog sleeps there, and you can't find anyplace else to store your golf clubs, no problem. However, the space allocated for this purpose must be a separately identifiable space suitable for storage.[35]

Daycare Services

If your business is providing daycare in your home for children, for the elderly, or for physically or mentally disabled people, you can deduct the household expenses allocated to the part of your home used for that purpose.[36] The rooms used do not have to be used exclusively, but the use must be regular. If the use is not exclusive, you must figure what part of available time is devoted to business use, and allocate the expenses accordingly. See the example in Chapter 6. These deductions are also subject to the net income limitation, which is explained in Chapter 6.

Here is how the IRS defines "daycare":

Daycare services are services which are primarily custodial in nature and which, unlike foster care, are provided for only certain hours during the day. Daycare services may include educational, developmental, or enrichment activities which are incidental to the primary custodial services. If the services performed in the home are primarily educational or instructional in nature, however, they do not qualify as daycare services. The determination whether particular activities are incidental to the primary custodial services generally depends upon all the facts and circumstances of the case. Educational instruction to children of nursery school age shall be considered incidental to the custodial services. Further, educational instruction to children of kindergarten age would ordinarily be considered incidental to the custodial services if the instruction is not in lieu of public instruction under a State compulsory education requirement. In addition, enrichment instruction in arts and crafts to children, handicapped individuals, or the elderly would ordinarily be considered incidental to the custodial services rendered.[37]

If the services you provide qualify as daycare, you must be in compliance with the applicable state law relating to the licensing, certification, registration, or approval of daycare centers or family or group daycare homes. That is, you must have applied for, been granted, or be exempt from having a license, certification, registration, or approval as a daycare center or as a family or group daycare home under applicable state law. You do not meet this requirement if your application was rejected or your license or other authorization was revoked.[38]

Application of Section 280A Business-Use Tests to Partnerships and Corporations

Read this part if you are (or are considering) conducting your business as a partnership, an S corporation, or a C corporation rather than as a sole proprietor. As noted at the beginning of this chapter, the Section 280A limitations apply directly to partnerships and S corporations, but do not apply to C corporations.

Partnership Expenses Incurred by You

If your business is in the form of a partnership, any expenses paid or incurred by the partnership are reported on the partnership return (Form 1065). Your share of all income and deductions from the partnership are reported by the partnership to you on Schedule K-1, and are then shown on your personal Form 1040. Any business expenses you pay on behalf of the partnership for which you are reimbursed cannot be deducted by you directly on your personal return, but are reported on the partnership return. Consequently, you do not include the reimbursement in your Gross Income.[39]

UNREIMBURSED HOME-BUSINESS EXPENSES

If "under the partnership agreement or practice," you are required to pay certain partnership expenses out of your own funds, then you are entitled to a deduction for the amount of such expenses.[40] You should make sure there is an agreement between you and your partners in the partnership agreement detailing the specific expenses you are required to pay. If you cannot show evidence of an agreement, your deductions will be disallowed.[41] If there is an agreement, and you can establish that the expenses are not personal but partnership related, you can deduct them above the line (that is, from Gross Income on Schedule E). That means they do not go on Schedule A and are not reduced by two percent of your Adjusted Gross Income (AGI).[42] Both the Tax Court and the IRS have agreed to this.[43]

For example, if the headquarters of your partnership is in your home office, unreimbursed home-business deductions and other deductions you pay that are applicable to the operation of the partnership go in Part II of Schedule E (Form 1040), along with your share of income and deductions from the partnership shown on your Schedule K-1. The net income limitation applies to your home-business expenses just as if you were filing Schedule C. The income limitation is based on the partnership Gross Income allocable to your home office, minus all the other allowable deductions of the partnership.[44] You should attach a schedule to your return for Part II of Schedule E indicating in detail the expenses you are claiming.

Corporation Expenses Incurred by You

If you have set up a corporation, you are an employee of your corporation, whether it is a C or S corporation. Any expenses paid or incurred by your corporation are reported on the corporate tax return (Form 1120 or 1120S), not your personal Form 1040. If your residence is owned or leased by you rather than your corporation, any unreimbursed home-business expenses you incur are reportable on your Form 1040 as employee business expenses on Schedule A. They are not deductible on the return of your corporation, because the corporation does not own the house, and has not incurred the expenses. Any home-business expenses you incur that are reimbursed by your corporation are deductible by the corporation. Section 280A requires that home-business expenses incurred by employees must meet one of the business-use requirements, and must be for the convenience of the employee's employer.

HOME-BUSINESS DEDUCTIONS AND C CORPORATIONS

The limitations on home-business deductions do not apply to a C corporation (that is, a tax-paying corporation). Therefore, you could set up your business as a C corporation, have the corporation own your residence and rent it to you as your personal residence (charging fair rent). Then the corporation could provide an office in the residence for you to use as corporate headquarters. All of the expenses of maintaining the residence would be deductible by the corporation.

Wait a minute—bad idea! Here's why. Regular corporations are taxed separately, and do not pass their income and deductions through to their shareholders. That means your rental payments to the corporation must be reported as income by the corporation, but are not deductible on your personal return. (By the way, if you don't pay fair market rent to the corporation, the IRS will consider the underpayment a dividend or additional compensation from the corporation to you.) Also, you get no advantage on your personal return from the deductions relating to the residence that the corporation deducts. You can see that this is not a good idea.

Partnership or S Corporation Expenses

If your business is in the form of a partnership or S corporation, and your residence is actually owned by the business entity, any deductions relating to the use of the residence are reported on the return of the partnership or S corporation. These deductions are then passed through to the partners or shareholders to be reported on their personal returns. When a pass-through entity, such as a partnership or S corporation, owns a dwelling unit, the entity itself is considered the taxpayer for purposes of Section 280A—not the partners or shareholders.[45]

Aha! You might be thinking that since a partnership or S corporation doesn't use a dwelling unit as a residence, you will transfer your home to the partnership or S corporation and the home office restrictions won't apply. Sorry! Since this would be an easy way to avoid the limitations on home-business deductions, personal use of the dwelling unit by you or any other owner of the partnership or S corporation is deemed to be personal use by the entity.[46] Therefore, if the partnership or S corporation rents the dwelling unit to you for your personal residence, it will be considered the residence of the entity. If the partnership or S corporation maintains an office in the residence (which you occupy), all the limitations on home-business deductions will apply. Additionally, you might end up paying more tax by transferring your property because the tax on the rent you pay to the pass-through entity will show up on your Schedule K-1 as income. Therefore, don't consider making your partnership or S corporation the owner of your personal residence.

Employee Expenses

If you are an employee who satisfies either the principal place of business test, the place to meet patients or customers test or the separate structure test, you can deduct your home-business expenses if they are incurred for the "convenience" of your employer. They are generally Miscellaneous Itemized Deductions (Schedule A, line 20) if you do not receive reimbursement. That means they are subject to the two percent of AGI reduction. If you are a "statutory employee," you can deduct your allowable business expenses above the line and avoid the two-percent of AGI reduction. Use Schedule C to claim the expenses. The Statutory Employee box within box 15 on your Form W-2 will be checked if you are a statutory employee.

Convenience of the Employer

As noted above, any home-business deductions claimed by employees must be incurred "for the convenience of their employer."[47] This term is pretty vague, and the Code does not provide a definition. In a case of a university professor who claimed home-office deductions, the Seventh Circuit Court of Appeals said:

> If . . . the university failed to supply him with adequate office facilities, this would imply that it expected him to equip his home with a suitable office. If he did so,

and used the home office exclusively and on a regular basis for his scholarly research and writing, then he would be entitled to the home-office deduction. But if he is given adequate facilities on the campus to conduct the major part of his scholarly research and writing there, the fact that he chooses to work at home instead does not entitle him to a deduction. It is then not the convenience of the employer but the professor's own convenience, and perhaps his tax planning, that induces him to maintain a home office.[48]

So according to this court, if you can show that your facilities at work are inadequate for the work that you are required to do, your home office will meet the convenience of the employer test.

TOUGHER IRS STANDARDS

Unfortunately, the IRS takes a more rigid view of this requirement. It says that the convenience of the employer requirement is only met if the employer:

1. Views the home office as the expected principal place of the employee's activities,
2. Requires the employee to maintain it, and
3. Compensates the employee for his or her activities there.[49]

If you are claiming home-business deductions as an employee, you should try to get a statement to that effect from your employer, and attach it to your return. This might avoid a hassle with your friendly neighborhood IRS agent.

Reimbursed Employee Expenses

You might be able to arrange to have your employer reimburse you directly for your home-business expenses. If you are the sole shareholder of your corporate employer you simply have to get yourself to agree to this. Any expenses you are reimbursed for are deductible above the line (on Form 2106) rather than as Miscellaneous Itemized Deductions on Schedule A.[50] That means you avoid the 2 percent of AGI reduction, and the deduction offsets income from the reimbursement in full. The corporate employer is allowed to deduct the reimbursed amount.

In order to qualify for this, you still must satisfy the above requirements for employee expenses, and the reimbursement arrangement must be part of an accountable plan. That means: (1) you are required to account, and do account to your employer for the expenses, and (2) you are required to return, and do return, any payments in excess of the reimbursed business expenses.[51] If you fail to comply with either of these requirements, the deductions become itemized (subject to the two percent of AGI reduction) and the reimbursement is treated as additional compensation.[52] For more on how to report reimbursed employee expenses, see Chapter 7 under "How To Report Travel and Transportation Deductions on Your Return" on page 160.

Treatment of Rental to Your Employer

A few years ago, a taxpayer cooked up a plan to avoid the Section 280A business-use requirements by renting his home office to his employer. The business-use requirements don't have to be met if you rent part of your home to a tenant (a roommate, for example).[53] The taxpayer reported the rent as income, and deducted the portion of his insurance, utilities, city charges, pest control, repairs, maid service and depreciation allocable to the rented room. The taxpayer used the rented room as his home office, but this arrangement was not for the convenience of his employer. The IRS contended that this was simply a phony tactic to avoid the business-use requirements, and disallowed the deductions. The Tax Court, however, sided with the taxpayer, and said that in this situation the business-use requirements did not have to be met.[54] That prompted Congress to step in to put a stop to this scheme. As part of the Tax Reform Act of 1986, Congress amended Section 280A with a provision that denies a home-business deduction to employees who rent or lease a portion of their homes to their employers.[55]

HERE IS A PLAN

Although Congress disallowed rental deductions to employees, it did not actually prohibit the renting of a home office by an employee to an employer. There are situations in which this might still be advantageous. For example, let's say you have a wholly owned C corporation. The corporation has no other office space, so you operate it out of your home. As an employee of your corporation, assume your home office fails all of the business-use tests, so you cannot deduct home-business expenses on your personal return. If the corporation were to compensate you for the use of the office in the form of rent, the corporation's rental expense would be deductible on its corporate tax return as long as the rent was an ordinary and necessary business expense under Code Section 162 (the home-business limitations don't apply to the corporation). That would certainly be the case if it had no other office facility. You would report the rent paid to you from the corporation as income, but could claim no related home-business deductions. This arrangement might be advantageous if you were going to take the rent money out of the corporation anyway.

To illustrate, if you withdrew the money in the form of wages, the income tax consequences to you and the corporation would be the same as if you were paid rent. However, wages are subject to Social Security tax—7.65 percent paid by the corporation and 7.65 percent withheld from your paycheck. If you withdrew the money in the form of dividends, there would be no Social Security tax liability, but you would have to pay income tax on the amount received and the corporation could not deduct the payment. Therefore, the cheapest way tax-wise to withdraw the money is in the form of rent.

If you do this, be sure that the rent is fair and not excessive. Also, the corporation's rental deduction might be challenged if there isn't a legitimate business purpose for this arrangement. By the way, this doesn't work for a partnership or S corporation because the business-use tests apply directly to those entities. The effect would be rental income to you and no rental deduction to the partnership or S corporation.

Additional Resources

The IRS publication that addresses home office rules is Publication 587, *Business Use of Your Home.* You can get this publication free by calling the IRS at (800) TAX-FORM [(800) 829-3676]. If you have access to TTY/TDD equipment, you can call (800) 829-4059. To download them from the Internet, go to *www.irs.gov* (World Wide Web), or *ftp.irs.gov* (FTP). If you would like to get forms and instructions (not publications) by FAX, dial (703) 368-9694 to reach IRS Tax Fax.

As an alternative to downloading files from the Internet, you can order *IRS Federal Tax Products* on CD-ROM. This CD includes over 2,000 tax products, including all of the above publications and forms. It can be ordered by calling (800) 233-6767. Also, Publication 3207, *Small Business Resource Guide,* is an interactive CD-ROM that contains information important to small businesses. It is available in mid-February. You can get one free copy by calling (800) 829-3676.

Notes

[1] See *Commissioner v. Tellier,* 383 US 687, 689 (1966); *Newi v. Commissioner,* 432 F2d 998 (Second Cir. 1970).

[2] § 280A(a); Prop. Reg. § 1.280A-1(a).

[3] IRC § 280A(c)(1).

[4] IRC § 280A(a).

[5] IRC § 280A(f)(1).

[6] Prop. Treas. Reg. § 1.280A-1(c)(1). A proposed regulation is the IRS interpretation of a Code section that has been drafted and published, but is not yet approved for use by taxpayers or IRS agents. Nevertheless, absent alternative guidance from the IRS, or a different interpretation by a court, we rely on proposed regulations when they contain reasonable explanations of the statute.

[7] Prop. Treas. Reg. § 1.280A-1(c)(1).

[8] IRC § 280A(d).

[9] IRC § 267(c)(4).

[10] Proposed Reg. § 1.280A-1(e)(1) and (2).

[11] IRS Publication 587.

[12] *Uphus v. Commissioner,* T.C. Memo 1994-71.

[13] Prop. Treas. Reg. § 1.280A-2(g).

[14] *Goldberger, Inc. v. Commissioner,* 88 T.C. 1532, 1557 (1987), quoting S. Rept. 94-938 (1976), 1976-3 C.B. (Vol. 3) 49, 186; H. Rept. 94-658 (1975), 1976-3 C.B. (Vol. 2) 695, 853.

[15] Necessary repair or maintenance does not constitute non-business use for purposes of this rule. Prop. Treas. Reg. § 1.280A-2(g)(1).

[16] *Culp v. Commissioner,* T.C. Memo 1993-270.

[17] Prop. Treas. Reg. § 1.280A-2(g)(1).

[18] *Welch v. Helvering,* 290 U.S. 111 (1933).

[19] See *Steinberg v. Commissioner,* T.C. Memo 1995-116 where, in the case of a financial consultant, the Court allowed a deduction for cable service to the taxpayer's home office to bring in the Financial News Network.

[20] The language of § 280A was changed in 1981 to indicate that the business use need *not* relate to the taxpayer's *principal* business. See § 280A(c)(1)(A).

[21] *Hamacher v. Commissioner,* 94 T.C. 348 (1990).

[22] *Commissioner v. Soliman,* 113 S. Ct. 701 (1993).

[23] IRS Pub No. 587, (2001), pp. 3–4.

[24] House Ways and Means Committee Rept. accompanying the Taxpayer Relief Act of 1997, H.R. 2014, ¶ 932.

[25] *Curphey v. Commissioner,* 73 T.C. 766, 775 (1980).

[26] *Hoye v. Commissioner,* T.C. Memo 1990-57.

[27] *Chong v. Commissioner,* T.C. Memo 1996-232.

[28] IRC § 280A(c)(1)(B).

[29] Prop. Reg. § 1.280A-2(c); *Green v. Commissioner,* 707 F2d 404 (9th Cir. 1983); *Frankel v. Commissioner,* 82 T.C. 318 (1984).

[30] S. Rept. 94-938, p. 148-149 (1976), 1976-3 C.B. (Vol. 3) 186-187; H. Rept. 94-658, at 161 (1975), 1976-3 C.B.; *Crawford v. Commissioner,* ¶ 93,192 RIA Memo. T.C. (1993) (emergency room physician who saw some patients at home office did not qualify because "incidental or occasional meetings with patients are not enough to qualify the home office for this exception").

[31] Prop. Reg. § 1.280A-2(c).

[32] See *Jackson v. Commissioner,* 76 T.C. 696 (1981) (Real estate agent's claim that her home office was used to meet with clients rejected in part because her home address and phone number were not printed on her business cards).

[33] LTR 8048014.

[34] IRC § 280A(c)(2), as amended by the Small Business Job Protection Act of 1996.

[35] Prop. Reg. § 1.280A-2(e)(2).

[36] IRC § 280A(c)(4).

[37] Prop. Reg. § 1.280A-2(f)(2).

[38] IRC § 280A(c)(4).

[39] See LTR 9330001(July 30, 1993).

[40] *Cropland v. Commissioner,* 75 T.C. 288, 295 (1980); *Lewis v. Commissioner,* 65 T.C. 625 (1975).

[41] See *Jessie Mae Dollard, et ux. v. Commissioner,* T.C. Memo 1987-346.

[42] LTR 9330001(July 30, 1993).

[43] *Klein v. Commissioner,* 25 T.C. 1045 (1956); Accord, Rev. Rul. 70-253, 1970-1 C.B. 31; LTR 9330001 (July 30, 1993).

[44] IRC § 280A(c)(5).

[45] Section 280A applies to partnerships, trusts, estates, and S corporations as well as to individuals. § 280A(a) and Prop. Reg. § 1.280A-1(a).

[46] Prop. Treas. Reg. § 1.280A-1(e)(5)(ii).

[47] IRC § 280A(c)(1).

[48] *Cadwallader v. Commissioner,* 919 F.2d 1273, 1275 (7th Cir. 1990).

[49] IRS Action on Decision, cc-1986-035 (June 23, 1986).

[50] IRC § 62(a)(2)(A).

[51] IRC § 62(c).

[52] Reg. § 1.62-2(c)(5).

[53] IRC § 280A(c)(3).

[54] *Feldman v. Commissioner,* 84 T.C. 1 (1985).

[55] IRC § 280A(c)(6).

CHAPTER 6

Form 8829 Line by Line

An income tax form is like a laundry list—either way you lose your shirt.

—Fred Allen

This chapter explains how your home-business expenses are allocated between business and nonbusiness use, how the income limitation is applied to your allowable deductions, and how to compute depreciation on your home office. This is shown by guiding you through the completion of Form 8829, "Expenses for Business Use of Your Home," line by line. An example showing a completed Form 8829 is at the end of the chapter.

Form 8829, which is filed with Form 1040, is the form self-employed individuals use to compute their home-business deductions. The amount computed on Form 8829 is carried over as a deduction to Schedule C (line 30). If you are a farmer and file Schedule F, you report home-business deductions directly on line 34 of Schedule F, and do not file Form 8829. If you are an employee claiming home-business deductions, you report the deductions as "Miscellaneous Itemized Deductions" on Schedule A (if unreimbursed), and do not file Form 8829. If you are an employee and are reimbursed for your home-business expenses, file Form 2106 if your deductible expenses are more than your reimbursements, but do not file Form 8829. If you are a statutory employee, file Schedule C and Form 8829 to claim your expenses, the same as a self-employed individual. (The Statutory Employee box within box 15 on your Form W-2 will be checked if you are a statutory employee.)

Since you still have to figure out how to compute your home-business deductions if you are a farmer or an employee, IRS Publication 587 provides a worksheet you can use. The worksheet computation is about the same as for Schedule C filers, so you might as well follow the instructions below for filling out Form 8829, and I'll point out the differences. Then, instead of filing the completed Form 8829, just report the deductible amount and keep the form with your records.

Before completing Form 8829, you should complete Schedule C (or Schedule F), and include all deductions other than the direct and indirect expenses relating to the use of your home office. Also, review the business use requirements explained in Chapter 5 to make sure you qualify. If you're ready, get Form 8829 (or open it in your tax software program) and let's get started.

Determining the Part of Your Home Used for Business

The purpose of Part I of Form 8829 is to isolate the portion of your home that is used for business. You must arrive at a percentage of the total, which you will use in Parts II and III to compute the business portion of expenses that pertain to the whole house. If you use your home as a daycare facility, don't do anything on the form yet—just keep reading.

Lines 1 through 3

The square footage of your office space goes on line 1, and the square footage of your entire house goes on line 2. To determine square footage, you should include all functional space, both finished and unfinished.[1] If you use a separate, unattached structure as your office, put the square footage of the office on line 1, and the combined square footage of the house and the office on line 2.

The instructions to Form 8829 say you can use square footage "or any other reasonable method" that accurately represents your business percentage. Another method is to put the number of rooms you use for business on line 1, and the total number of rooms in your house on line 2. You might not be allowed to use this method though, if the percentage you arrive at is greater than what you would get using the square-footage method. In one Tax Court case, the taxpayer used the rooms method and arrived at a business-use percentage of 15 percent. The IRS said the square-footage method would have given the taxpayer a business-use percentage of only nine percent. The court held that the square-footage method was more precise, and was therefore the most reasonable method to use.[2] Only use the rooms method if all the rooms in your house are approximately the same size.

To determine square footage you will probably have to do some measuring. You can just step it off—it doesn't have to be exact. Now divide line 1 by line 2, and enter the amount as a percentage (move the decimal 2 places to the right) on line 3. (*Note:* If the percentage on line 3 is greater than 100, you did something wrong—try it again.)

Example 6.1

Ed has a home office that is 200 square feet. Ed's whole house is 3,000 square feet. Ed puts 200 on line 1 and 3,000 on line 2. On line 3 Ed puts 6.67 percent (200 divided by 3,000). See Figure 6.1.

Form **8829**	**Expenses for Business Use of Your Home**	OMB No. 1545-1266
Department of the Treasury Internal Revenue Service (99)	File only with Schedule C (Form 1040). Use a separate Form 8829 for each home you used for business during the year. See separate instructions.	**2002** Attachment Sequence No. **66**
Name(s) of proprietor(s) Ed Smith		Your social security number 123 : 45 : 6789

Part I   **Part of Your Home Used for Business**

1 Area used regularly and exclusively for business, regularly for day care, or for storage of inventory or product samples (see instructions) **1**   200
2 Total area of home **2**   3,000
3 Divide line 1 by line 2. Enter the result as a percentage . . . . **3**   6.67 %

For day-care facilities not used exclusively for business, also complete lines 4–6. All others, skip lines 4–6 and enter the amount from line 3 on line 7.

4 Multiply days used for day care during year by hours used per day . **4**   hr.
5 Total hours available for use during the year (365 days   24 hours) (see instructions) **5**   8,760 hr.
6 Divide line 4 by line 5. Enter the result as a decimal amount . . **6** .
7 Business percentage. For day-care facilities not used exclusively for business, multiply line 6 by line 3 (enter the result as a percentage). All others, enter the amount from line 3 . . .▶ **7**   6.67 %

FIGURE 6.1

If you began using your residence for business during the year, you cannot deduct any costs as home-business expenses that were incurred before you established your home office. You should reduce the expenses shown in Part II of Form 8829 to reflect the partial year.

If the business use of your home is anything other than having a daycare facility, take the percentage on line 3 and put it on line 7. This is the business percentage you will use in the rest of the form to determine the deductible portion of your indirect business expenses.

Example 6.2

If Ed, in the previous example, first became eligible to deduct home-business expenses in April of 2003, he would have only nine months of business use. Ed should include only three-fourths of applicable expenses in Part II of Form 8829.

DAYCARE

If you use your home for daycare, and the rooms used are used exclusively for daycare, complete lines 1 through 3, copy the percentage from line 3 to line 7 and go on to Part II. If you have a daycare facility and you do not use any of the rooms exclusively for business, complete lines 1, 2, and 3, then proceed to line 4.

Line 4

On this line they want the total number of hours during the year you regularly used the area listed on line 1 for daycare.

So if your hours of operation are 12 hours per day, count the days during the year you were open for business and multiply that number by 12. Be sure to include in your hours of operation the time spent for preparation and clean-up, not just the hours it is open.

Line 5

The number on this line should be 24 hours times the number of days during the year your home daycare facility was available for use. The printed number (8,760 hours) is 24 hours times 365 days. If you began or ended your daycare operation during the year, or if you bought or sold your house during the year, you should cross out 8,760 and write in the correct number of hours. The correct number is the number of days the daycare facility was in the house times 24 hours.

Line 6

This line shows the percentage of the time the portion of the house that was regularly used for daycare was actually used for daycare. This is the percentage you can claim of direct expenses related to your daycare activities. Show this number as a decimal amount rather than a percentage. Be careful with the math when you multiply this number by the number on line 3 to enter on line 7 (make sure the decimal is in the right place).

Example 6.3

Laura operated a daycare facility out of her home for all of 2000, and the portion of her home used regularly for daycare was 25 percent (shown on line 3). The rooms were used 12 hours per day for 255 days during the year, so the amount she puts on line 4 is 3,060. This amount is divided by the number of hours on line 5, which equals .3493 (or 34.93%). The amount that goes on line 7 is 8.73 percent (25% × .3493). See Figure 6.2.

Form **8829**	**Expenses for Business Use of Your Home**	OMB No. 1545-1266
Department of the Treasury Internal Revenue Service (99)	File only with Schedule C (Form 1040). Use a separate Form 8829 for each home you used for business during the year. See separate instructions.	**2002** Attachment Sequence No. **66**

Name(s) of proprietor(s)	Your social security number
Laura White	234 : 56 :7890

Part I — Part of Your Home Used for Business

1	Area used regularly and exclusively for business, regularly for day care, or for storage of inventory or product samples (see instructions)	1	750
2	Total area of home	2	3,000
3	Divide line 1 by line 2. Enter the result as a percentage	3	25 %
	For day-care facilities not used exclusively for business, also complete lines 4–6. All others, skip lines 4–6 and enter the amount from line 3 on line 7.		
4	Multiply days used for day care during year by hours used per day .	4	3,060 hr.
5	Total hours available for use during the year (365 days 24 hours) (see instructions)	5	8,760 hr.
6	Divide line 4 by line 5. Enter the result as a decimal amount . .	6	. 3,493
7	Business percentage. For day-care facilities not used exclusively for business, multiply line 6 by line 3 (enter the result as a percentage). All others, enter the amount from line 3 . . . ▶	7	8.73 %

FIGURE 6.2

Special Computation for Certain Daycare Facilities

If you have a daycare facility and you use some of the rooms exclusively for business and other rooms regularly but not exclusively, you should have made it to this point without having written anything on the form. (Go ahead and erase what you've got—I'll wait.) Now you need to complete a schedule on your own paper that you will attach to your return, because you need to compute two separate percentages and add them together. As shown above, one percentage is computed for the exclusively used areas, and another percentage is computed for the nonexclusively used areas. Follow the instructions for lines 1 through 6 above. The only line in Part I of Form 8829 that you will put a number on is line 7. You will then write above line 7 "See Attached Computation." Use the format in Figure 6.3 as a guide for your schedule.

The percentage on the last line of Figure 6.3 is what you put on line 7 of Form 8829. This is the percentage of the indirect expenses you can deduct, shown on lines 9(b) through 20(b). You are now ready to move on to Part II of the form.

Figuring Your Allowable Deduction

Part II of the form is where the net income limitations are applied. Here is a general overview of what's going on. Your net income from using your home office, before adding in any home-business deductions, goes on line 8. Then there are three tiers of deductions you subtract from this amount.

Tier One Deductions

You are allowed to deduct the business portion of deductions that would be allowed on Schedule A, even if you did not have a home office (that is, personal

A. Business Percentage of Exclusively Used Area:

   1. Area used exclusively for daycare   _____

   2. Total area of home   _____

   3. Business percentage of exclusive
     use area (A1 ÷ A2)   _____%

B. Business Percentage of Nonexclusively Used Area:

   1. Area used regularly but not exclusively
     for daycare   _____

   2. Total area of home   _____

   3. Percentage of non-exclusive use area (B1 ÷ B2)   _____%

   4. Total hours used for daycare   _____ hrs.

   5. Total hours available during the year   8,760 hrs.

   6. Proportion of hours used (B4 ÷ B5)   _____

   7. Business percentage of nonexclusive use
     area (B3 × B6)   _____%

C. Combined Business Percentage: A3 + B7
   (enter on Line 7, Form 8829)   _____%

FIGURE 6.3 Computation of Exclusive and Nonexclusive Use Percentage for Daycare Facility

casualty losses affecting the residence, deductible mortgage interest and real estate taxes). The business portion of these deductions is computed on lines 9 through 11 of Form 8829. These deductions are allowed on Schedule C (the nonbusiness portion is deductible on Schedule A) even if they exceed your net business income on line 8.

Tier Two Deductions

If you still have net income after subtracting the tier one expenses from the amount on line 8 (see line 15 of Form 8829), you can deduct operating expenses for your home office. These are expenses that would not be deductible if your home office did not qualify under one of the business-use requirements. These deductions are limited to the amount shown on line 15 (line 8 minus the tier one deductions), and are shown on lines 16 through 20 of Form 8829. If your home office operating expenses exceed the amount on line 15, you can carry the excess over and use it as a deduction next year. (This is done in Part IV of the form.)

Tier Three Deductions

If you still have net income left after subtracting the tier one and tier two expenses from the amount on line 8, you can subtract depreciation allocable to your home office, and the business portion of any casualty loss allocable to your home office. These deductions are limited to the amount on line 8 minus the tier one and tier two deductions, which is shown on line 26 of the form. If depreciation and casualty loss deductions exceed the amount on line 26, you can carry the excess over and use it as a deduction next year.

Line 8

SCHEDULE C

If you file Schedule C, generally you should put on this line the amount from line 29 of Schedule C. This is your net income from business before deducting home-business expenses. If you have more than one business, and you file more than one Schedule C, only use the Schedule Cs that relate to your home office. If your home office was used for more than one qualifying business, combine the amounts on line 29 of those Schedule Cs to report on line 8. If you sold any assets used in your business and reported the gain or loss on Schedule D or Form 4797, also include the net gain or loss on line 8.

FARMERS AND EMPLOYEES

If you are a farmer filing Schedule F, put on line 8 your income from farming minus total expenses from Schedule F (before home-business expenses). Include any net gain or loss from selling farm assets reported on Schedule D or Form 4797. If you are an employee, enter total wages on line 8 that were from business use of the home, minus any unreimbursed business expenses that are not attributable to business use of the home. Examples include travel, supplies, and business telephone expenses.

GROSS INCOME ALLOCATION

If your business is conducted in your home and at one or more other locations, Section 280A requires you to allocate the gross income to the different locations on a reasonable basis.[3] Gross income is the amount reported on line 7 of Schedule C. The income allocated to the home office is then reduced by the total Schedule C deductions (before home-business expenses) on line 28 of Schedule C, and the net amount is what goes on line 8 of Form 8829.

Although there is no precise rule on how to allocate income between the home office and other locations, here is what the IRS says about how to come up with a reasonable method of allocation:

> In making this determination, the taxpayer shall take into account the amount of time that the taxpayer engages in activity related to the business at each location, the capital investment related to the business at each location, and any other facts and circumstances that may be relevant.[4]

This appears to mean that you should not have to worry about allocating income, even if you work outside your home office, unless you have another permanent place of business that generates revenue. But if your home office meets the principal place of business test, and you do not have another permanent place of business that you can attribute revenue to, don't worry about the allocation.

Direct and Indirect Expenses

Note that there are two columns for the tier one and tier two deductions on lines 9 through 11 and 16 through 20. Column (a) is for direct expenses and column (b) is for indirect expenses.

Direct expenses benefit only the business portion of your home. For example, if you paint your home office, it is a direct expense. Because you use your home office regularly and exclusively for business, you can deduct 100 percent of the cost of the paint job on line 18, column (a) (Repairs and maintenance). If you run a daycare facility, and you do not use the space exclusively for business, you can only deduct the portion of the direct expenses allocable to business use, which is the percentage from line 6 of Form 8829, or line B7 of Figure 6.3. Direct expenses relating to any space used exclusively in your daycare business are deductible in full.

Indirect expenses are those that cannot be attributed to a particular area of the house, so they benefit both the business and personal areas. Examples are real estate taxes, home mortgage interest, certain casualty losses, rent, utilities, insurance, repairs, and security systems. These costs are reported in full in column (b). The total of these indirect costs is then multiplied by the business percentage from line 7.

Line 9

CASUALTY LOSSES

If your house suffered a casualty during the year (it blew up, burned down, or got flooded) you can claim a personal casualty loss deduction regardless of whether you have a home office. Casualty losses are computed on Form 4684, "Casualties and Thefts." If the instructions to Form 4684 do not tell you what you need to know, call the IRS at (800) TAX-FORM [(800) 829-3676)] and ask for Publication 547, *Nonbusiness Disasters, Casualties and Thefts.*

If you suffered a casualty or theft of business property that is not attached to your house, you can claim a business casualty loss whether or not you qualify for home-business deductions, so do not put those losses on line 9. Put those losses in Section B of Form 4684, and follow the instructions to the form.

FORM 4684

You can allocate a portion of any casualty loss attributable to your house (the business percentage on line 7) to your home office. To do this, fill out Form 4684, Section A, by including only casualties that pertain to the residence in which your home office is located. You have to reduce the loss by $100 for each casualty, then by 10 percent of your Adjusted Gross Income (AGI). When you get to line 17 of Form 4684, use 10 percent of the amount on line 32 of Form 1040 (Adjusted Gross Income), before including the net income from your business (the amount on line 8, Form 8829).

If you end up with a positive amount on line 18 of Form 4684, and the casualty affected your entire residence, transfer it to column (b), line 9, of Form 8829. This is an indirect expense, so on line 13 we will apply the business percentage from line 7 to determine the business portion. If the casualty affected only an area of your home that you use exclusively for business it is a direct expense, so put the amount from line 18 of Form 4684 in column (a) of line 9. If you run a daycare facility, and you do not use the space exclusively for business, you can only deduct the portion of the casualty loss allocable to business use, which is the percentage from line 6 of Form 8829.

Do not send in the Form 4684 you just filled out. Wait until you are done figuring your home-business deductions, and have finished completing Schedule C. When you get the final amount that goes on line 32 of Form 1040, complete another Form 4684, including *all* casualties and thefts that occurred during the year. If you have a positive amount on line 18 of Form 4684, subtract from it the business percentage of the amount you reported on line 9(b) of Form 8829, or the full amount from line 9(a), and enter the rest on Schedule A, line 19.

Line 10

HOME MORTGAGE INTEREST

Home mortgage interest is deductible on Schedule A, whether or not you have a home office. The portion of this deduction that is allocable to your home office is deductible as a business expense. Generally, there are two types of deductible home mortgage interest. The first is interest on "acquisition indebtedness,"[5] which is any indebtedness incurred in acquiring, constructing or substantially improving your residence, including refinanced debt, up to $1 million ($500,000 if you are married and filing separately). The second is interest on "home equity indebtedness."[6] This is debt (other than acquisition indebtedness) secured by your residence, which does not exceed the lesser of your equity in the residence, or $100,000 ($50,000 if you are married filing separately). Home equity indebtedness is generally interest on a second loan that you took out to buy a car, take a trip or pay off your credit cards. You could also have used your home equity indebtedness for business purchases.

ACQUISITION DEBT

The amount you should put on line 10, column (b), is the interest you paid on acquisition indebtedness (on the residence your home office is in) up to the $1 million debt limit, if the loan was to purchase your house or make general improvements. This is an indirect expense, so on line 13 we will apply the business percentage from line 7 to determine the business portion. The non-business portion is deductible on Schedule A as home mortgage interest. If any of the loan proceeds were used to make improvements to your home office, the interest on that portion of the loan is a direct expense, and should go in column (a) of line 10.

EQUITY DEBT

Do not put any interest you paid on home equity indebtedness on line 10. If you used the proceeds from a home equity loan on anything other than your home, it is neither a direct nor an indirect expense. If you used any of your proceeds from home equity indebtedness for business purposes, and you are filing Schedule C, you can deduct that interest on Schedule C, line 16(a), without showing it on Form 8829.[7] If you are filing Schedule F, deduct the business portion of your home equity interest on line 23(a). If you are claiming home-business deductions as an employee, report all of your home equity interest on Schedule A, along with your other home mortgage interest, regardless of how you used the loan proceeds.[8] For Schedule C and Schedule F filers, remember to claim interest on home equity indebtedness (up to the $100,000 debt limit) that was not used for business purposes on Schedule A as home mortgage interest.

Line 11

Real estate taxes, like personal casualty losses and home mortgage interest (the other tier one deductions), are deductible whether or not you have a home-based business. The amount that is attributable to your home office is deductible as a business expense. Put the entire amount in column (b) of line

11, unless you can allocate a definite amount to your home office. For instance, if your home office is a separate structure, and you have the information to determine the portion of your property taxes that are attributable to it, put that amount in column (a) of line 11, and don't put anything in column (b). Otherwise, put the entire amount in column (b), and on line 13 you will reduce it to the business percentage from line 7. The amount of your real estate taxes that are not allocated to your home's business use are deductible on Schedule A.

Lines 12 Through 14

Add columns (a) and (b) separately for lines 9, 10, and 11, and put the totals on line 12 (you probably only have numbers in column (b)). Then multiply the amount in column (b) of line 12 by the business percentage on line 7, and put that amount in column (b) of line 13. If you have anything in column (a) of line 12, add that to the amount in column (b) of line 13 and put the total on line 14. The amount on line 14 is the business portion of your deductions for personal casualty losses, home mortgage interest, and real estate taxes. These amounts are not limited by Section 280A, so they are deductible regardless of your net business income on line 8. Remember to deduct the non-business portion of these expenses, as described above under lines 9 through 11, on Schedule A.

Line 15

All the rest of your home-business deductions are limited to the amount on this line. So if it is zero, you cannot claim any additional home-business deductions for the current year. Don't stop here though; finish computing the rest of your home-business deductions. Those that are not deductible will be available to deduct on next year's return. This is the purpose of Part IV of the form.

Line 16

If your home mortgage acquisition indebtedness exceeded $1 million in 2000 then the amount you could report on line 10 was limited. On this line put the interest attributable to acquisition indebtedness in excess of $1 million ($500,000 if married filing separately) that was paid on the residence your home office is in. This is an indirect expense, so put the amount in column (b). You will take the business percentage of this amount on line 22. The rest of it is not deductible. If you're still reading this, you would probably like more information on how the limits on home mortgage interest are applied. Call the IRS at (800) TAX-FORM [(800) 829-3676] and ask for Publication 936, *Home Mortgage Interest Deduction.* The publication can also be downloaded from the IRS Web site at *www.irs.gov.*

Line 17

Insurance that covers the residence in which your home office is located goes on this line. Unless you can allocate an actual amount to your home office, it is an indirect expense, so put the amount in column (b); you will apply the business percentage from line 7 when we get to line 22. The rest of it is not deductible.

If you have business insurance separate from the amount that covers your dwelling unit, such as coverage for professional liability, or damage to business property and inventory, do not put the premium amount on line 17. This is an expense that does not relate to the dwelling unit, so it is not limited under Section 280A. Deduct this amount on line 15 of Schedule C (line 22 of Schedule F).[9] If you have prepaid insurance, the IRS says you can only deduct one year of the prepaid premium.[10] However, the Eighth Circuit Court of Appeals says that a cash method taxpayer can deduct the amount paid for during the year, even if it related to future years.[11] See the discussion on page 189 under "Business Liability Insurance" in Chapter 8.

Line 18

REPAIRS AND MAINTENANCE

If you spent money on cleaning or pest control services for your whole house, the amount goes in column (b) as an indirect expense. The IRS considers amounts spent for lawn care and landscaping to be unrelated to your home office, and therefore nondeductible.[12] The Tax Court, on the other hand, has held that when a taxpayer had clients visiting on a regular basis, and the appearance of the residence and grounds was of significance to the taxpayer's business operation, an allocable portion of lawn-care expenses was deductible.[13] If you are in this situation, you can put your lawn-care expenses in column (b). You might get an argument from your friendly neighborhood IRS agent, but you have support from the Tax Court for claiming this deduction. If you do not have patients, clients, or customers visiting your home office on a regular basis, you should not claim this deduction.

Think of all the repairs you made to the house that benefited the entire home. For example, if you had your furnace repaired, put that amount in column (b). You will apply the business percentage from line 7 to the amount in column (b) when we get to line 22. If you had any repair or maintenance costs that related directly to your home office, put those amounts in column (a). If you run a daycare facility, and you do not use the space exclusively for business, you can only deduct the portion of the repairs and maintenance allocable to business use, which is the percentage from line 6 of Form 8829. Repairs that benefited only personal areas of your home are not deductible.

WAGES

You can only put down amounts that you actually spent on repair work during the year. The cost of your own labor is not deductible, but the amount you paid someone else is. Wages paid for work that is not related to the location of your office are reported directly on Schedule C, and are not shown on Form 8829.[14]

REPAIR VERSUS CAPITAL IMPROVEMENT

Maintenance and repair expenses are not treated in the same way as costs incurred for improvements and replacements. You can deduct repairs and maintenance in their entirety, but you cannot deduct capital improvements. Only repairs and maintenance go on line 18; capital improvements do not. You can depreciate the portion of capital improvements that relate directly or indirectly to your home office (see "Depreciation of the Business Portion of Your Home," page 123).

The difference between repairs and maintenance and capital improvements relates to the substance of the work performed. Repairs and maintenance keep your home in good working order, whereas capital improvements increase the value of the property, add to its life or give it a new or different use. For example, repairing the furnace is a repair; replacing the furnace is a capital improvement. Fixing the roof is a repair; replacing the roof is a capital improvement. Painting the exterior of the house is maintenance; installing steel siding is a capital improvement. Cleaning the office carpet is maintenance; replacing the carpet is a capital improvement. Choosing the proper category is a judgment call that is not always easy to make. What would normally be considered repairs are considered part of a capital improvement if they are part of an extensive remodeling or restoration of your home.

Example 6.4

You buy an older home and fix up two rooms as a hairdressing shop. You patch the plaster on the ceilings and walls, paint, repair the floor, put in an outside door and install new wiring and plumbing. The plaster patching, painting and floor work are repairs. However, since this work is done as part of a general plan to alter your home for business use, the amount you pay for this work is a capital expenditure. You cannot deduct it as a repair expense.[15]

Line 19

UTILITIES

Utilities include amounts you spent on heat, lights, water, sewer, and garbage pickup. If none of these costs relate specifically to the area of your home office, put the total amount in column (b). You will apply the business percentage from line 7 to the amount in column (b) when we get to line 22. The rest of the amount in column (b) is not deductible. If you can identify a specific amount of any of these costs that benefit only your home office, put that portion in column (a) and do not include the rest in column (b). If you run a daycare facility, and you do not use the space exclusively for business, you can only deduct the portion of the repairs and maintenance allocable to business use, which is the percentage from line 6 of Form 8829.

THE PHONE BILL

Your telephone expense does not go on this line. The Code denies a deduction for any charge required to be paid by a taxpayer to obtain local telephone service for the first residential phone line.[16] You can deduct, as a business expense, your long distance business calls and the cost of a second phone line dedicated to business.[17] The deductible telephone costs are not considered related to your home office, so they do not go on Form 8829.[18] If you are self-employed, deduct your business phone expense on line 18 of Schedule C, or line 34 of Schedule F (label it "business phone"). If you are an employee and have not been reimbursed by your employer, your business phone deduction goes on line 20 of Schedule A.

Line 20

If you rent rather than own your home, put the rent you paid in column (b). If you own your home, and have installed a security system that protects your whole house, put the amount you spent during the year to maintain and monitor the system in column (b). You will apply the business percentage from line 7 to the amount in column (b) when we get to line 22. The rest of the amount in column (b) is not deductible. You can also take a depreciation deduction for the installation cost of the security system allocated to your home office. We'll do depreciation when we get to Part III of the form.

Lines 21 through 24

The portion of the amount in column (b) on line 21 that is deductible is the business percentage from line 7. This amount is shown on line 22. Any amount you put in column (a) should not have been put in column (b), and vice versa. The amount in column (a) on line 21 represents your direct home-business expenses, and is fully deductible (subject to the income limitation). If you filed Form 8829 for 2001 (or used a worksheet in the case of a farmer or employee) and were limited in the amount of operating expenses you could deduct, the amount that was disallowed (from 2001 Form 8829, line 41) goes on line 23. Line 24 is the total of this year's direct operating expenses, the business portion of this year's indirect operating expenses, and the operating expenses that were disallowed in 2001.

Line 25

This is the amount of operating expenses you can deduct for 2002. If the amount on line 24 is greater than this amount, the excess can be carried over and deducted next year. Subtract line 25 from line 24 and enter the difference on line 41.

Line 26

This shows the maximum amount of excess casualty losses and depreciation you can deduct for 2002. If the amount on line 24 is greater than the amount on line 25, the amount on this line must be zero. That means you cannot deduct excess casualty losses or depreciation. Don't stop here though; compute the excess casualty losses and depreciation so you can carry it over to next year.

Line 27

(You only have to read this if you suffered a casualty relating to your home office—see line 9.) This is kind of a difficult one to explain, but I'll give it a try. There are two types of casualty losses you can deduct: losses that pertain to personal use property; and losses that pertain to business or investment property. Losses that pertain to personal use property are itemized deductions on Schedule A, and are reduced by $100 per casualty and 10 percent of your Adjusted Gross Income. Losses that pertain to business or investment property are *not* reduced by $100 or 10 percent of AGI, and are deductible as a business expense on Schedule C. The amount you computed on line 9 is fully deductible, because it represents your personal casualty loss after the $100 and 10 percent of AGI reduction. The business percentage of the amount in column (b) of line 9, or the full amount in column (a) of line 9, represents the part of your personal casualty loss you can treat as a business deduction relating to your home office. This amount is not limited by Section 280A, so it is deductible in full (the instructions for line 33 below tell you where to put it).

At this point we have accounted only for the part of your casualty loss that is in excess of $100 and 10 percent of your AGI. As noted, a business casualty loss is not reduced by these amounts—it is deductible in full. On line 27 we can account for the amount of the casualty loss allocable to your home office that you were not allowed to deduct on line 9—the home-office portion of the $100 and 10 percent of AGI reduction. So get out the Form 4684 that you filled out for line 9 (the one you are not going to send in) and add the amounts on line 11 and line 17 of that form. Take the business percentage of this amount, and put it on line 27 of Form 8829. If your casualty was indirect (in column (b) of line 9), use the percentage on line 7; if your casualty directly affected office space you used exclusively in your home business, use the entire amount. If you run a daycare facility, and you do not use the space exclusively for business, you can only deduct the portion of the casualty allocable to business use, which is the percentage from line 6 of Form 8829.

If you are completely confused at this point, don't worry—you're normal. Take a look at Example 6.5, then go back and read the instructions for this line again.

If you suffered a casualty or theft of business property that is not attached to your house, you can claim a business casualty loss whether or not you qualify for home-business deductions, so do not put those losses on line 27. Put those losses in Section B of Form 4684, and follow the instructions to the form.

Example 6.5

Bob Johnson's house was damaged by a flood and the loss was not covered by insurance. Bob's house contains a home office that qualifies for home-business deductions, and takes up 20 percent of the house. Bob computed the loss pertaining to the flood on Form 4684, Section A, and arrived at $30,000 on line 10 of that form.

Bob's Adjusted Gross Income (before considering his Schedule C income) was $100,000, so the amount Bob put on line 17 of Form 4684 was $10,000. Bob reduced the $30,000 loss by $100 plus $10,000 and arrived at $19,900 on line 18 of Form 4684. See Figure 6.4. Bob put that amount on line 9(b) of Form 8829. On line 27 of Form 8829, Bob took the amount of the loss that was excluded on line 9 ($100 + $10,000 = $10,100), multiplied it by the business percentage (20%) and arrived at $2,020.

		A					
8	Enter the **smaller** of line 2 or line 7 . . .	8 30,000					
9	Subtract line 3 from line 8. If zero or less, enter -0-	9 30,000					
10	Casualty or theft loss. Add the amounts on line 9 in columns A through D					10	30,000
11	Enter the **smaller** of line 10 or $100					11	100
12	Subtract line 11 from line 10					12	29,900
13	**Caution:** Use only one Form 4684 for lines 13 through 18. Add the amounts on line 12 of all Forms 4684					13	29,900
14	Add the amounts from line 4 of all Forms 4684					14	—
15	If line 14 is **more** than line 13, enter the difference here and on Schedule D. **Do not** complete the rest of this section (see instructions). If line 14 is **less** than line 13, enter -0- here and go to line 16. If line 14 is **equal** to line 13, enter -0- here. **Do not** complete the rest of this section.					15	—
16	If line 14 is **less** than line 13, enter the difference					16	29,900
17	Enter 10% of your adjusted gross income from Form 1040, line 36. Estates and trusts, see instructions . .					17	10,000
18	Subtract line 17 from line 16. If zero or less, enter -0-. Also enter the result on Schedule A (Form 1040), line 19. Estates and trusts, enter the result on the "Other deductions" line of your tax return					18	19,900

For Paperwork Reduction Act Notice, see page 4 of the instructions.　　Cat. No. 129970　　Form **4684** (2002)

FIGURE 6.4

Depreciation of the Business Portion of Your Home

Before we get into how to compute depreciation on your home office, a little background on the concept of depreciation might be helpful. When you buy (or convert from personal use) an asset that has a useful life substantially longer than a year, you generally cannot deduct its entire cost in the year it is first used for business. (There is an exception to this rule that you will learn about in Chapter 8, which is the Section 179 election.) But if the asset you purchased will eventually wear out, get used up, or become obsolete, a portion of its cost is deductible each year until the entire cost has been deducted. The allocation of an asset's cost over its useful life is called—you guessed it—depreciation. Depreciation deductions may be claimed only for property used in your business or other income-producing activity. Depreciation may not be claimed on property held for personal purposes such as a personal residence or pleasure car. If property, such as a car, is used both for business and pleasure, only the business portion may be depreciated. MACRS is a term you will see in other books referring to the cost recovery of tangible assets. It stands for "modified accelerated cost recovery system," which is derived from the heading of IRC Section 168—the Code section that deals with depreciation. If the asset is intangible, its cost recovery is called amortization. If the asset does not wear out (land, for example) then its cost cannot be depreciated.

Computing Basis

The portion of your residence used as a home office is a depreciable business asset. To determine the depreciable amount, you must first determine your home's adjusted basis. If you filed Form 8829 for 2001, go to Part III of that form, and use the same amounts from lines 35 to 37 on this year's form. If you are filing Form 8829 for the first time, you'll need to do some calculating. To compute basis you generally start with the original cost of the property, including closing costs and any amount you borrowed to buy the property. But if you filed Form 2119, "Sale of Your Home," when you bought your house to postpone being taxed on the gain from your previous house, start with the amount from the last line of that form (hopefully you saved it). Then add the cost of any special tax assessments you have paid for local improvements (such as streets and sidewalks), and any capital improvements you have made prior to the time you began using your home office. Also, if you have ever deducted a casualty loss relating to your house, reduce the basis by this amount. The result is your home's adjusted basis.

Lines 28 and 35 through 40

Go to Part III of Form 8829 and on line 35, put down the lesser of your home's adjusted basis at the time your home office first became qualified for deductions, or its fair market value at that time. If there is no documented evidence that your house was worth less than its adjusted basis when you first began using your home office, put down the adjusted basis. Estimate the value of the lot your house sits on, and put that on line 36 (land is not depreciable). The amount that is depreciable is the business percentage (from line 7) of the basis of your house without the land (from line 37). This is the amount you put on line 38.

Do not put on line 38 the cost of any capital improvements or additions to the property after your home office first became qualified for deductions. You will compute depreciation for these on a separate schedule, and the amount will go on line 40. Also, do not include the cost of any furniture, books, or office equipment in Part III. Depreciation for these things is not reported on Form 8829 (see Chapter 8).

THE DEPRECIATION PERCENTAGE

You are now ready to compute the "depreciation percentage" for the current year on line 39, which is the percentage of the amount on line 38 you can claim as a deduction. It used to be that taxpayers were allowed to estimate the useful lives of tangible assets to compute depreciation, as long as the useful lives they estimated were reasonable. This issue created a lot of disputes between taxpayers and the IRS, so Congress enacted statutory useful lives for various categories of depreciable assets that everyone must use. These statutory useful lives, first enacted in 1981, have been changed from time to time—and each time they get longer. For example, in 1981 nonresidential real property, such as your home office, could be depreciated over 15 years. This was increased to 18 years in 1984, to 19 years in 1985, to 31.5 years in 1987, and to 39 years in 1993.

So if your home office first became depreciable in 2002, it is depreciable over 39 years, using the straight-line method, beginning in the middle of the month your business use began. Table 6.1 shows the depreciation percentage to put on line 39, depending on the month your home office first became depreciable.

If your home office first became depreciable after May 12, 1993, but before 2002, its useful life is also 39 years. In this case though, you can claim a whole year's worth of depreciation in 2002, so the percentage you put on line 39 is 2.564 percent (which is $1 \div 39$). If your home office first became depreciable after 1986 and before May 13, 1993, its useful life is 31.5 years. Put 3.175 percent (which is $1 \div 31.5$) on line 39. (This should be the same as on your 2001 Form 8829.)

TABLE 6.1

January	2.461%	May	1.605%	September	0.749%
February	2.247	June	1.391	October	0.535
March	2.033	July	1.177	November	0.321
April	1.819	August	0.963	December	0.107

Example 6.6

In April 2002, Brad White began to use one room in his home regularly and exclusively to meet clients. This room is 8 percent of the square footage of his house. He bought the house in 1981 for $100,000. He determined that his adjusted basis in the house (exclusive of land) is $90,000. The house had a fair market value of $165,000 in April. He multiplies his adjusted basis (which is less than the fair market value) by 8 percent. The result of $7,200 is his depreciable basis for the business part of his house. Brad multiplies his depreciable basis of $7,200 by 1.819 percent (.01819), the percentage from Table 6.1 for April. The result is $130.97 (round to $131), which is his depreciation deduction for 2002.[19] Brad reports his calculations in Part III of Form 8829 and on Form 4562.

If you began depreciating your home office prior to 1987, you are allowed accelerated depreciation, which permits you to claim more depreciation in the early years than in later years. That means you must refer to Tables 6.2 to 6.4[20] below to determine the depreciation percentage to put on line 39. Count the number of years the office has been depreciated, including 2002, and find that

TABLE 6.2   18-Year Real Property (First used after March 15, 1984 and before June 23, 1984)

| | MONTH OFFICE WAS FIRST USED FOR BUSINESS | | | | | | | | | | | |
YEAR	JAN	FEB	MAR	APR	MAY	JUN	JUL	AUG	SEP	OCT	NOV	DEC
8th–12th	5.0	5.0	5.0	5.0	5.0	5.0	5.0	5.0	5.0	5.0	5.0	5.0
13th	4.0	4.0	4.0	5.0	5.0	4.0	4.0	5.0	4.0	4.0	4.0	4.0
14th–18th	4.0	4.0	4.0	4.0	4.0	4.0	4.0	4.0	4.0	4.0	4.0	4.0
19th	-	-	1.0	1.0	1.0	2.0	2.0	2.0	3.0	3.0	3.0	4.0

TABLE 6.3   18-Year Real Property (First used after June 22, 1984 and before May 9, 1985)

| | MONTH OFFICE WAS FIRST USED FOR BUSINESS | | | | | | | | | | | |
YEAR	JAN	FEB	MAR	APR	MAY	JUN	JUL	AUG	SEP	OCT	NOV	DEC
8th–12th	5.0	5.0	5.0	5.0	5.0	5.0	5.0	5.0	5.0	5.0	5.0	5.0
13th	4.0	4.0	4.0	5.0	4.0	4.0	5.0	4.0	4.0	4.0	5.0	5.0
14th–17th	4.0	4.0	4.0	4.0	4.0	4.0	4.0	4.0	4.0	4.0	4.0	4.0
18th	4.0	3.0	4.0	4.0	4.0	4.0	4.0	4.0	4.0	4.0	4.0	4.0
19th	-	1.0	1.0	1.0	2.0	2.0	2.0	3.0	3.0	3.0	3.0	3.6

TABLE 6.4   19-Year Real Property (First used after May 8, 1985 and before 1987)

| | MONTH OFFICE WAS FIRST USED FOR BUSINESS | | | | | | | | | | | |
YEAR	JAN	FEB	MAR	APR	MAY	JUN	JUL	AUG	SEP	OCT	NOV	DEC
10th–19th	4.2	4.2	4.2	4.2	4.2	4.2	4.2	4.2	4.2	4.2	4.2	4.2
20th	0.2	0.5	0.9	1.2	1.6	1.9	2.3	2.6	3.0	3.3	3.7	4.0

year in the left column of the appropriate table. Move along that row to the column for the month you first began to use your home office. The number in that cell is the depreciation percentage for line 39.

If you have made no capital improvements to your house after you first began depreciating your home office, multiply the amount on line 38 by the percentage on line 39 and put that amount on lines 40 and 28. (Be sure to move the decimal on line 39 two places to the left before multiplying.)

Form 4562

If you first began depreciating your home office in 2002, you are also supposed to file Form 4562, "Depreciation and Amortization." You simply need to copy the information from Part III of Form 8829 to line 15(i) of Form 4562. The amount from line 38 of Form 8829 goes in column (c) of line 15(i) of Form 4562, and the amount from line 40 of Form 8829 goes in column (g) of line 15(i) of Form 4562. Include the amount on line 15(i), column (g) of Form 4562 in the total on line 21 of that form, but do not put it on line 13 of Schedule C.

TREATMENT OF CAPITAL IMPROVEMENTS

If you made capital improvements to your house after you began using your home office for business, and the capital improvements either benefit the entire house or directly benefit your home office, the business portion of each capital improvement is treated as a separate asset, depreciated as nonresidential real property. You must attach your own schedule showing your depreciation calculated for these improvements, and include the amount in the total on line 40 of Form 8829. Write "See attached schedule" next to line 40. For each capital improvement, simply follow the above instructions for computing the yearly depreciation, depending on when the capital improvement was made. See Example 6.7.

Line 29

If you filed Form 8829 for 2001 (or used a worksheet in the case of a farmer or employee) and were limited in the amount of excess casualty losses and depreciation you could deduct, the amount that was disallowed (from 2001 Form 8829, line 42) goes here.

Line 31

This is the amount of excess casualty losses and depreciation you can deduct. If the amount on line 30 is greater than this amount, the excess can be carried over and deducted next year. Subtract line 31 from line 30 and enter the difference on line 42.

> ## Example 6.7
>
> Sue began using her home office for business in 2001. The business basis of her house (amount from line 38 of Form 8829) at the time she began using it was $5,000. Sue had a home security system installed in June of 2002, and the business portion of its cost was $1,000. The depreciation percentage of Sue's home office for 2002 is 2.564 percent. The depreciation percentage of the security system for 2002 is 1.391 percent (from Table 6.1). Sue computes the depreciation allowable for 2002 on line 40 of Form 8829 by attaching the following schedule:
>
> | PROPERTY | PLACED IN SERVICE | BASIS FOR DEPRECIATION | % | DEDUCTION |
> |---|---|---|---|---|
> | Home Office | 2001 | $5,000 | 2.564 | $128 |
> | Security System | 6/02 | $1,000 | 1.391 | $14 |
> | Total | | | | $142 |

Lines 32 through 34

Subtract from the amount on line 32 any casualty losses you had for the year (that is, the business portion of line 9 and the amount on 27). Put the casualty losses on line 33, and the balance of the amount from line 32 on line 34. Any casualty losses on line 33 are supposed to be reported in Section B of Form 4684, "Casualties and Thefts." Fill out lines 19 through 28 of that form, then follow the instructions to the form.

SCHEDULE C

If you are self-employed, and your home-business deductions relate to a Schedule C activity, transfer the amount from line 34 to line 30 of Schedule C. If your home office was used for more than one qualifying business, the instructions to Form 8829 say to "allocate the amount shown on line 34 to each business using any method that is reasonable under the circumstances." The easiest way to do this, and one that is as reasonable as any, is to use the percentage of the net income on line 8 that pertains to each Schedule C.

SCHEDULE F

If you file Schedule F, report the amount from line 34 of Form 8829 on line 34 of Schedule F, and write "Business use of home" on the line beside the entry. Do not include these expenses on any of the other lines in Part II of Schedule F. You are not required to file Form 8829 with your return if you file Schedule F. Keep it, along with supporting documents, with your tax records for as long as your home office and improvements are depreciable.

EMPLOYEES

If you are an employee, and you were not reimbursed by your employer for any of your home-office expenses, your home-office expenses are only deductible as itemized deductions on Schedule A. Subtract from the amount on line 34 the amount from line 14 that is attributable to mortgage interest and real estate taxes. Deduct both the business and nonbusiness portion of your mortgage interest on line 10 or 11 of Schedule A. Deduct both the business and nonbusiness portion of your real estate taxes on line 6 of Schedule A. In other words, report your home mortgage interest and real estate taxes the same as if you did not have a home office. The balance of the amount on line 34 goes on line 20 of Schedule A, along with any other employee business expenses. You are not required to file Form 8829 with your return. Keep it, along with supporting documents, with your tax records for as long as your home office and improvements are depreciable. You do not have to attach Form 2106 or Form 2106-EZ unless

1. You claim travel, transportation, meal or entertainment expenses, or
2. Your employer reimbursed you for some of your employee business expenses. (Amounts your employer included in box 1 of your Form W-2 are not considered reimbursements.)

Any employee business expenses listed on lines 20 to 22 of Schedule A are subject to the 2 percent of AGI reduction. If your employee business expenses were reimbursed by your employer, you effectively avoid the 2 percent reduction because the expense simply offsets the reimbursement. Your expenses are considered reimbursed only when

1. You adequately account to your employer for the expenses, and
2. You are required to return, and do return, any payments not spent for business expenses.[21]

If you meet these reimbursement arrangement requirements, and your employer reimbursed you for the exact amount of your deductible employee business expenses, you do not report the reimbursement as income, and you do not report the expenses at all on your return. This saves you the hassle of filing Form 2106 and reporting the income and deductions on your return, because they are simply a wash. However, your home-office deductions still must meet the requirements of Section 280A to be considered reimbursable employee business expenses.

Carrying Over Unallowed Expenses to 2003

If the amount on line 24 is greater than the amount on line 25, you should have already filled in line 41; refer to the explanation of line 25 above. If the amount on line 30 is greater than the amount on line 31, you should have already filled in line 42; refer to the explanation of line 31 above. The amounts on lines 41 and 42 can be used as deductible expenses on next year's Form 8829.

An Example Using Form 8829 and Form 4562

The Business

On May 1, 2002, Paula Carlson began operations as a consultant in computer software applications. She runs her business as a sole proprietorship. Her only office is a converted spare bedroom in her home, which she uses exclusively for business. Her clients call on her for troubleshooting, and for special projects that require sophisticated software techniques. Although she spends several hours a week visiting clients and prospective clients, she spends most of her time working at the computer in her office and communicating with clients via phone or e-mail. Paula also performs administrative and management activities in her home office, and has no other fixed place of business where she performs such activities. Paula's home office meets the principal place of business test for 2002.

The House

Paula and her husband Rich purchased their house in 1991 for $165,000. The house is now valued at about $200,000. Paula estimates that the land value at the time of purchase was $25,000. The Carlsons have made capital improvements in the amount of $15,000 over the years, all before 2002. The house has 2,800 square feet of useable living space. Paula's office measures about 300 square feet.

Income and Deductions

Paula and Rich file a joint return. Paula has computed net income from her business on line 29 of Schedule C, prior to home-office deductions, of $1,400. The small amount is due to the fact that she spent the first few months in business mainly prospecting for clients. She now has a solid client base, which promises a good year in 2003. Household expenses for the entire year that relate indirectly to her home office are as follows:

- Home mortgage interest on acquisition indebtedness $12,500
- Real estate taxes   3,500
- Homeowner's insurance (exclusive of business liability)   650
- Heat and electricity   1,200
- Security monitoring system   875

Paula's completed Form 8829 is shown in Figure 6.5. Figure 6.6 shows what must be included on Form 4562.

Form 8829

Note the following regarding Paula's completed Form 8829 in Figure 6.5:

1. Only two-thirds of Paula's indirect expenses are shown on Form 8829 because she began her business on May 1.

2. The portion of the home mortgage interest on line 10 and real estate taxes on line 11 that is not allowed on Form 8829 is deductible on Schedule A. Therefore $11,608 [($12,500 − 8,333) + 8,333 × 89.3%] of mortgage interest is deductible on Schedule A, as is $3,250 [($3,500 − 2,333) + 2,333 × 89.3%) of the real estate taxes.

3. On line 35, the home's adjusted basis is $180,000 ($165,000 + $15,000), which is less than the $200,000 fair market value.

4. The depreciation percentage for line 39 is the amount for May, taken from Table 6.1.

5. Note that only $65 of the $266 of depreciation is deductible in 2002 because of the income limitation. The balance of $201 is carried to next year on line 42. This amount will be reported on line 29 of Paula's Form 8829 for 2003.

6. Line 34 shows Paula's total deductible home-business expenses, which are reported on line 30 of Schedule C.

Form **8829**	**Expenses for Business Use of Your Home**	OMB No. 1545-1266
Department of the Treasury Internal Revenue Service (99)	File only with Schedule C (Form 1040). Use a separate Form 8829 for each home you used for business during the year. **See separate instructions.**	**2002** Attachment Sequence No. **66**

Name(s) of proprietor(s) Paula Carlson	Your social security number 999 ; 00 ; 0000

Part I — Part of Your Home Used for Business

1	Area used regularly and exclusively for business, regularly for day care, or for storage of inventory or product samples (see instructions)	1	300
2	Total area of home	2	2,800
3	Divide line 1 by line 2. Enter the result as a percentage	3	10.7 %

For day-care facilities not used exclusively for business, also complete lines 4–6.
All others, skip lines 4–6 and enter the amount from line 3 on line 7.

4	Multiply days used for day care during year by hours used per day .	4	hr.
5	Total hours available for use during the year (365 days 24 hours) (see instructions)	5	8,760 hr.
6	Divide line 4 by line 5. Enter the result as a decimal amount . .	6	.
7	Business percentage. For day-care facilities not used exclusively for business, multiply line 6 by line 3 (enter the result as a percentage). All others, enter the amount from line 3 . . . ▶	7	10.7 %

Part II — Figure Your Allowable Deduction

		(a) Direct expenses	(b) Indirect expenses		
8	Enter the amount from Schedule C, line 29, **plus** any net gain or (loss) derived from the business use of your home and shown on Schedule D or Form 4797. If more than one place of business, see instructions			8	1,400
	See instructions for columns (a) and (b) before completing lines 9–20.				
9	Casualty losses (see instructions) . . .				
10	Deductible mortgage interest (see instructions) .		8,333		
11	Real estate taxes (see instructions) . . .		2,333		
12	Add lines 9, 10, and 11.		10,666		
13	Multiply line 12, column (b) by line 7 . .	13	1,141		
14	Add line 12, column (a) and line 13. . .			14	1,141
15	Subtract line 14 from line 8. If zero or less, enter -0- .			15	259
16	Excess mortgage interest (see instructions) .	16			
17	Insurance	17	433		
18	Repairs and maintenance	18			
19	Utilities	19	800		
20	Other expenses (see instructions) . . .	20	583		
21	Add lines 16 through 20	21	1,816		
22	Multiply line 21, column (b) by line 7 . . .	22	194		
23	Carryover of operating expenses from 2001 Form 8829, line 41 .	23			
24	Add line 21 in column (a), line 22, and line 23			24	194
25	Allowable operating expenses. Enter the **smaller** of line 15 or line 24			25	194
26	Limit on excess casualty losses and depreciation. Subtract line 25 from line 15 . .			26	65
27	Excess casualty losses (see instructions)	27			
28	Depreciation of your home from Part III below	28	266		
29	Carryover of excess casualty losses and depreciation from 2001 Form 8829, line 42	29			
30	Add lines 27 through 29			30	266
31	Allowable excess casualty losses and depreciation. Enter the **smaller** of line 26 or line 30 .			31	65
32	Add lines 14, 25, and 31			32	1,400
33	Casualty loss portion, if any, from lines 14 and 31. Carry amount to **Form 4684**, Section B .			33	
34	Allowable expenses for business use of your home. Subtract line 33 from line 32. Enter here and on Schedule C, line 30. If your home was used for more than one business, see instructions ▶			34	1,400

Part III — Depreciation of Your Home

35	Enter the **smaller** of your home's adjusted basis or its fair market value (see instructions) .	35	180,000
36	Value of land included on line 35	36	25,000
37	Basis of building. Subtract line 36 from line 35	37	155,000
38	Business basis of building. Multiply line 37 by line 7	38	16,585
39	Depreciation percentage (see instructions)	39	1.605 %
40	Depreciation allowable (see instructions). Multiply line 38 by line 39. Enter here and on line 28 above	40	266

Part IV — Carryover of Unallowed Expenses to 2003

41	Operating expenses. Subtract line 25 from line 24. If less than zero, enter -0-	41	
42	Excess casualty losses and depreciation. Subtract line 31 from line 30. If less than zero, enter -0- .	42	201

For Paperwork Reduction Act Notice, see page 4 of separate instructions.   Cat. No. 13232M   Form **8829** (2002)

FIGURE 6.5

Form **4562**	**Depreciation and Amortization**	OMB No. 1545-0172
	(Including Information on Listed Property)	**2002**
Department of the Treasury Internal Revenue Service	▶ See separate instructions. ▶ Attach to your tax return.	Attachment Sequence No. **67**

Name(s) shown on return	Business or activity to which this form relates	Identifying number
Paula Carlson	Computer Software Consultant	999-00-0000

Part I **Election To Expense Certain Tangible Property Under Section 179**

Note: *If you have any listed property, complete Part V before you complete Part I.*

1	Maximum amount. See page 2 of the instructions for a higher limit for certain businesses	**1**	$24,000
2	Total cost of section 179 property placed in service (see page 3 of the instructions)	**2**	
3	Threshold cost of section 179 property before reduction in limitation	**3**	$200,000
4	Reduction in limitation. Subtract line 3 from line 2. If zero or less, enter -0-	**4**	
5	Dollar limitation for tax year. Subtract line 4 from line 1. If zero or less, enter -0-. If married filing separately, see page 2 of the instructions	**5**	

(a) Description of property	(b) Cost (business use only)	(c) Elected cost
6		

7	Listed property. Enter the amount from line 29	**7**	
8	Total elected cost of section 179 property. Add amounts in column (c), lines 6 and 7	**8**	
9	Tentative deduction. Enter the **smaller** of line 5 or line 8	**9**	
10	Carryover of disallowed deduction from line 13 of your 2001 Form 4562	**10**	
11	Business income limitation. Enter the smaller of business income (not less than zero) or line 5 (see instructions)	**11**	
12	Section 179 expense deduction. Add lines 9 and 10, but do not enter more than line 11	**12**	
13	Carryover of disallowed deduction to 2003. Add lines 9 and 10, less line 12 ▶	**13**	

Note: *Do not use Part II or Part III below for listed property. Instead, use Part V.*

Part II **Special Depreciation Allowance and Other Depreciation (Do not** include listed property.)

14	Special depreciation allowance for qualified property (other than listed property) placed in service during the tax year (see page 3 of the instructions)	**14**	
15	Property subject to section 168(f)(1) election (see page 4 of the instructions)	**15**	
16	Other depreciation (including ACRS) (see page 4 of the instructions)	**16**	

Part III **MACRS Depreciation (Do not** include listed property.) (See page 4 of the instructions.)

Section A

17	MACRS deductions for assets placed in service in tax years beginning before 2002	**17**	
18	If you are electing under section 168(i)(4) to group any assets placed in service during the tax year into one or more general asset accounts, check here ▶ ☐		

Section B—Assets Placed in Service During 2002 Tax Year Using the General Depreciation System

(a) Classification of property	(b) Month and year placed in service	(c) Basis for depreciation (business/investment use only—see instructions)	(d) Recovery period	(e) Convention	(f) Method	(g) Depreciation deduction
19a 3-year property						
b 5-year property		1,800	5 yr	HY	DDB	
c 7-year property						
d 10-year property						
e 15-year property						
f 20-year property						
g 25-year property			25 yrs.		S/L	
h Residential rental property			27.5 yrs.	MM	S/L	
			27.5 yrs.	MM	S/L	
i Nonresidential real property			39 yrs.	MM	S/L	266
				MM	S/L	

Section C—Assets Placed in Service During 2002 Tax Year Using the Alternative Depreciation System

20a Class life					S/L	
b 12-year			12 yrs.		S/L	
c 40-year			40 yrs.	MM	S/L	

Part IV **Summary** (see page 6 of the instructions)

21	Listed property. Enter amount from line 28.	**21**	
22	**Total.** Add amounts from line 12, lines 14 through 17, lines 19 and 20 in column (g), and line 21. Enter here and on the appropriate lines of your return. Partnerships and S corporations—see instr.	**22**	266
23	For assets shown above and placed in service during the current year, enter the portion of the basis attributable to section 263A costs	**23**	

For Paperwork Reduction Act Notice, see separate instructions.   Cat. No. 12906N   Form **4562** (2002)

FIGURE 6.6

Additional Resources

IRS publications that might be helpful with respect to issues discussed in this chapter are Publication 587, *Business Use of Your Home;* Publication 547, *Nonbusiness Disasters, Casualties and Thefts;* and Publication 936, *Home Mortgage Interest Deduction.* You can get these publications free by calling the IRS at (800) TAX-FORM [(800) 829-3676]. If you have access to TTY/TDD equipment, you can call (800) 829-4059. To download them from the Internet, go to *www.irs.gov* (World Wide Web), or *ftp.irs.gov* (FTP). If you would like to get forms and instructions (not publications) by FAX, dial (703) 368-9694 to reach IRS Tax Fax.

As an alternative to downloading files from the Internet, you can order *IRS Federal Tax Products* on CD-ROM. This CD includes over 2,000 tax products, including all of the above publications and forms. It can be ordered by calling (800) 233-6767. Also, Publication 3207, *Small Business Resource Guide,* is an interactive CD-ROM that contains information important to small businesses. It is available in mid-February. You can get one free copy by calling (800) 829-3676.

Notes

[1] *Hefti v. Commissioner,* T.C. Memo. 1988-22, affd. 894 F.2d 1340 (8th Cir. 1989), cert. denied 495 U.S. 933 (1990); *Ronald Culp and Rosemarie Trenjan v. Commissioner,* T.C. Memo 1993-270.

[2] *Feldman v. Commissioner,* 84 T.C. 1, 8 (1985).

[3] IRC § 280A(c)(5)(A); Prop. Reg. § 1.280A-2(i)(2)(ii).

[4] Prop. Reg. § 1.280A-2(i)(2)(ii).

[5] IRC § 163(h)(3)(B).

[6] IRC § 163(h)(3)(C).

[7] This is interest that is not allocable to your home office, and is deductible as a business expense under IRC § 162.

[8] Interest paid by an employee for business purposes is considered personal interest (under IRC § 163(h)(2)(A)), so it is only deductible as home mortgage interest.

[9] This deduction is authorized under IRC § 162.

[10] Rev. Rul. 70-413, 1970-2 C.B. 103.

[11] *Waldheim Realty & Investment Co. v. Commissioner,* 245 F2d 823, 51 AFTR 801, (8th Cir. 1957).

[12] Prop. Reg. § 1.280A-2(i)(3); IRS Publication 587, p. 3.

[13] *Hefti v. Commissioner,* T.C. Memo 1988-22.

[14] *Dollard v. Commissioner*, T.C. Memo 1987[nd]346.

[15] IRS Publication 587, p. 5.

[16] IRC § 262(b).

[17] *Shepherd v. Commissioner*, T.C. Memo 1976-48; *Barry v. Commissioner*, T.C. Memo 1978-250.

[18] Prop. Reg. § 1.280A-2(i)(7).

[19] From IRS Publication 578, p. 5-6.

[20] From IRS Publication 534, "Depreciation," Appendix C.

[21] IRC § 62(c).

CHAPTER 7

Planes, Trains, and (Especially) Automobiles

The taxpayer—
that's someone who
works for the
federal government
but doesn't have to
take a civil service
examination.

—Ronald Reagan

If you discovered in Chapter 5 that you are now eligible to claim home-office deductions under the newly liberalized principal-place-of-business rule, prepare yourself for another pleasant surprise—you can now deduct more of your car expenses! This is an important collateral benefit of claiming home-office deductions. In this chapter you will learn how to get the best tax advantages from being on the road.

First, there are two main categories of deductions for being on the road for business. One is "travel away from home" and the other is "transportation." Travel away from home in tax talk means you are out of town long enough to require a rest—generally overnight. Allowable deductions while you are in the travel mode generally include all of your out-of-town expenses for meals, lodging, and other living expenses, and all of your transportation costs for getting there and back. Transportation in tax talk (when not referring to part of your travel expenses) means local excursions around town, or trips out of town that are completed within one day. Transportation includes only the expenses directly related to getting from one place to another, such as car expenses, but not meals or lodging.

Travel Away from Home

Under IRC Section 162, you can deduct "traveling expenses . . . while away from home in the pursuit of a trade or business. . . ."[1] Such expenses include virtually all of your reasonable living expenses while away from home, including laundry and incidental expenses.

Away from Home

As noted above, being away from home doesn't simply mean being out of the house. It means the following:

1. Your business requires you to be away from your "tax home" (defined below) for longer than an ordinary day's work (but not necessarily 24 hours), and

2. You need time for sleep (not just to eat or rest before returning home).[2]

You do not have to be gone overnight to satisfy this requirement.

Example 7.1

On Monday morning Harold flies out of town for business meetings and is scheduled to fly back 14 hours later. During a break in the meetings, Harold has five hours to grab a meal and rent a hotel room to get some rest. Harold is considered to be away from home and can deduct his travel expenses.

What Is Your Tax Home?

For travel expense purposes, your tax home is the place where you regularly derive your principal source of income, regardless of where your family resides.[3] It includes the entire city or general area in which your work is located. Therefore, if you commute to a different city to work, your tax home is where your work rather than where your home is. The idea here is that you should not be allowed to deduct away from home expenses while performing duties at your principal place of business just because you choose to live somewhere else.

TEMPORARY WORK ASSIGNMENTS

As a home-based worker, your tax home is probably the city in which you live, even if your home office is not your principal place of business. On the other hand, you may be required to work or conduct business at another location outside your metropolitan area. It might not be practical to return home from this other location at the end of each day's work. If the other location is "temporary," you can deduct away from home expenses incurred at the other location. If the other location is not temporary, your tax home will change to the other location and you cannot deduct away from home expenses.

A temporary assignment is one that is expected to last, and in fact does last, for one year or less.[4] An assignment might initially be expected to last for one year or less, then circumstances change to make it last for a longer period. In this case, the assignment is temporary (away from home expenses are deductible) until the point at which it is known that the assignment will last beyond a year. When it is known the assignment will last longer than a year, away-from-home expenses are no longer deductible.

Combined Business and Pleasure Travel

If you take a business trip, you don't have to be engaged in business activities for the entire time for the trip to be deductible. However, taking a pleasure trip and doing a little business on the side doesn't make it. The regulations say travel expenses to and from your destination are deductible only if the trip is related primarily to your trade or business.[5] This test is generally met if you spend more days on business activities than on personal activities. This is an all or nothing test for travel to and from your destination. Once at your destination, you can only deduct expenses for the days you conduct business. Your expenses that are allocable to business are deductible even if your travel expenses to and from your destination are not.

Example 7.2

Tess travels from Minneapolis to Dallas for a business convention. She spends three days attending the convention and two days sightseeing. Her plane and taxi fare to get to and from the convention hotel amounts to $1,200. Her meals cost $50 per day, and lodging and incidental expenses are $150 per day.

Tess can deduct all of the $1,200 relating to her transportation, because her trip is primarily for business (three days business and two days sightseeing). She can deduct meals and lodging for only three out of the five days.

If your spouse or another family member goes along on a business trip, expenses attributable to that person's travel are not deductible unless you can show that their presence has a bona fide business purpose.[6] They must actually be involved in the business for this test to be met. Simply having them do some clerical duties is not enough.

What Are Deductible Travel Expenses?

When you are in the travel mode you can generally deduct all normal living expenses during the days you are conducting business, and any expenses necessary to take the trip. For example, you can deduct your transportation, regardless of the mode, between your house and your business destination. You can also deduct the cost of sending baggage and display items. If you take your car you can either use the standard mileage rate or deduct the actual costs (discussed under *Car Expenses* later). You can also deduct the cost of leasing a car for business purposes. If you travel by ship, the amount you can deduct may be limited. (See *Luxury Water Travel* in Publication 463.)

You can deduct taxi, limousine, and bus fares between the airport and the hotel, and between the hotel and your work locations. You can also deduct tips to the drivers. You can deduct lodging for the nights you are required to stay for business, but lodging for additional nights you stay over for sightseeing is not deductible. The same rule applies to meals. Other deductible items include cleaning and laundry expenses, telephone and fax bills, and computer rental fees. Be sure to read Chapter 11, where the substantiation requirements for these expenses are discussed.

Per Diem Allowances

You usually have better things to do on a trip than write down all the food you eat. So the government allows you to deduct a standard amount per day for meals and incidental expenses in lieu of what you actually spend. The amount is computed at the Federal meal and incidental expense (M&IE) rate for your locality of travel for each calendar day (or part thereof) that you are away from home. The Federal M&IE rate includes an allowance for "incidental expenses," which include expenses for laundry, cleaning and pressing of clothing, and fees and tips for services, such as for porters and baggage carriers. It does not cover taxi fares or telephone calls. The daily amount is deemed a substantiated deduction, regardless of what you actually spend, as long as you can verify that you were traveling away from home on business that day.[7]

You can use the standard meal allowance whether you are an employee or self-employed. You cannot use it, though, if you are related to an employer who is reimbursing you.[8] You are related to your employer if it is a corporation that you own more than 10 percent of, or you are employed by a sibling, spouse, ancestor or lineal descendant.[9]

If you are an employee and are being reimbursed for your out-of-town expenses, an employer has the option of using the applicable per diem lodging rate as well as the M&IE rate. If you are self-employed, or an employee who is not reimbursed, however, you cannot use the Federal lodging rate.

WHERE TO FIND THE RATES

The General Services Administration (GSA) establishes the per diem rates that are deemed substantiated for areas in the continental United States (CONUS). These rates are reviewed annually. The maximum rates vary for specific areas of the country and particular times of the year. The per diem rate for lodging ranges from a minimum of $59 to over $200 is certain parts of the country in 2002. The per diem rate for meals goes from $30 to $46. The Standard CONUS Per Diem Rate for areas not specified in the rate listing is $55 for Lodging (excluding taxes) and $30 for Meals and Incidentals, effective October 1, 2001.

The Secretary of State establishes maximum rates of per diem allowances for travel in foreign areas and updates these rates at the beginning of every month. The Per Diem Travel and Transportation Committee of the Department of Defense provides rates for overseas US areas such as Alaska, Hawaii, Guam, etc. at the beginning of every month, or as necessary.

You can get all of the current rates by going to *www.policyworks.gov /perdiem* on the Internet. This is a well designed site and will quickly guide you to the information you need for both domestic and foreign travel. The rates are also listed in IRS Publication 1542, *Per Diem Rates*.

THE HIGH-LOW SUBSTANTIATION METHOD

Rather than searching for the applicable rates for each area of travel within the continental United States, you can use a simplified method where only two rates apply for the combined meals and lodging rates. Specific high-cost localities are assigned one rate for lodging, meals and incidental expenses, and all other areas within CONUS are assigned a lower rate. For 2002, the high-cost rate is $204 and the low cost rate is $125. The meals component of the high-cost rate is $42, and is $34 for the low cost rate. However, the high-low method can only be used as a substitute for both meals and lodging per diem—it cannot be used to substantiate meals only. Table 7.1 shows the high-cost localities for all of the calendar year 2002 or the portion of the calendar year specified in parenthesis under the key city name.

TABLE 7.1 High-Cost Areas for 2002

KEY CITY	COUNTY OR OTHER DEFINED LOCATION
California	
Napa (April 1–November 15)	Napa
Palm Springs (January 1–May 31)	Riverside
San Francisco	San Francisco
San Mateo/Redwood City	San Mateo
Sunnyvale/Palo Alto/San Jose	Santa Clara
Tahoe City	Placer
Colorado	
Aspen (December 1–June 30)	Pitkin
Silverthorne/Keystone	Summit
Telluride (November 1–March 31)	San Miguel
Vail (December 1–March 31)	Eagle
District of Columbia	Washington, DC; the cities of
Washington, DC	Alexandria, Fairfax, and Falls Church, and the counties of Arlington, Fairfax, and Loudoun, in Virginia; and the counties of Montgomery and Prince George's in Maryland
Florida	
Key West (December 15–April 30)	Monroe
Palm Beach (also the cities of Boca Raton, Delray Beach, Jupiter, Palm Beach Gardens, Palm Beach Shores, Singer Island, and West Palm Beach	Palm Beach
Idaho	
Sun Valley (June 1–September 30)	City limits of Sun Valley
Illinois	
Chicago	Cook and Lake
Lousiana	
New Orleans/St. Bernard (January 1–May 31)	Orleans, St. Bernard, Plaquemine, and Jefferson Parishes
Maine	
Kennebunk/Kittery/Sandord (June 15–October 31)	York
Maryland	
Counties of Montgomery and Prince George's	
Ocean City	Worcester
Massachusetts	
Boston	Suffolk
Cambridge	Middlesex County (except Lowell)
Martha's Vineyard (June 1–October 15)	Dukes
Nantucket (June 1–October 15)	Nantucket

TABLE 7.1 (Continued)

KEY CITY	COUNTY OR OTHER DEFINED LOCATION
Michigan	
Mackinac Island	Mackinac
Traverse City	Grand Traverse
Montana	
Big Sky	Gallatin (except West Yellowstone Park)
Nevada	
Stateline	Douglas
New Jersey	
Atlantic City (June 1–November 30)	Atlantic
Cape May (June 1–September 30)	Cape May (except Ocean City)
Edison	Middlesex (except Piscataway)
Newark	Bergen, Essex, Hudson, and Passaic
Ocean City (June 15–September 15)	City limits of Ocean City
Piscataway/Bellemead	Somerset and Middlesex
Princeton	City limits of Princeton
New York	
The Bronx/Brooklyn/Queens	The boroughs of The Bronx, Brooklyn, and Queens
Manhattan	Manhattan
Nassau County/Great Neck	Nassau County
Suffolk County	Suffolk County
White Plains	City limits of White Plains
Pennsylvania	
Hershey (June 1–September 15)	City limits of Hershey
Utah	
Ogden/Layton/Davis County (January 1–February 28)	Weber, Davis
Park City (December 20–March 31)	Summit
Provo (January 15–February 28)	Utah
Salt Lake City (January 15–February 28	Salt Lake; Dugway Proving Ground, Tooele Army Depot
Virginia (For the cities of Alexandria, Fairfax, and Falls Church, and the counties of Arlington, Fairfax, and Loudoun, see District of Columbia)	
Wintergreen	Nelson

THE 50 PERCENT REDUCTION FOR MEALS

Whether you are self-employed or an employee, you can generally only deduct 50 percent of your meal expenses.[10] This rule applies to the standard meal allowance as well as actual costs. There is an exception if your meal expenses are reimbursed by your employer. In such case you can deduct the full amount, but the deduction allowable to your employer is reduced by 50 percent.

Transportation

Transportation refers to business trips that are concluded without having to stop for sleep. Transportation deductions include only the costs of getting you and your equipment from one place to another. Such costs include automobile expenses, tolls, parking, and taxi and bus fares. They could also include airfare if you take a day trip out of town. If you get hungry while in the transportation mode and stop off at the *Happy Chef,* you had better order a sandwich instead of the 16-ounce sirloin, because your meal is not deductible.

Generally, transportation from one place of business to another place of business is deductible,[11] while commuting between your home and your place of work is considered personal and nondeductible.[12] The fact that commuting is not deductible shouldn't concern you if your only workplace is just down the hall from your bedroom. If, on the other hand, your home office is not your only place of business you will want to read the next few paragraphs about when commuting is deductible.

When Is Commuting Deductible?

WHEN YOUR HOME OFFICE IS YOUR PRINCIPAL PLACE OF BUSINESS

If your home office qualifies as your principal place of business (see Chapter 5), you can deduct daily transportation expenses incurred in going between your home and another work location in the same trade or business. It doesn't matter where the other work location is or if it is regular or temporary.[13] This is a great

Example 7.3

Bubba is an insurancagent who maintains a home office as his principal place of business. On Monday he went to the office supply store to buy some things for his business. On Tuesday he went to the post office to mail some business letters. On Wednesday he visited a couple of clients in the metropolitan area. On Thursday he went to a business seminar in a nearby town, but was back by evening. On Friday he went bowling. His transportation on Monday, Tuesday, Wednesday, and Thursday is deductible. On Friday his transportation did not have a business purpose so it is not deductible.

extra benefit for the legion of home-based business owners who can take advantage of the new easier home-office deduction rules discussed in Chapter 5.

WHEN YOUR HOME OFFICE IS NOT YOUR PRINCIPAL PLACE OF BUSINESS

If your home office does not qualify as your principal place of business, and you have one or more *regular* work locations outside of your home, transportation between your residence and the regular work locations is considered nondeductible personal commuting. Nevertheless, when you have a regular work location outside the home, the IRS allows you to deduct daily transportation expenses in going between your home and *temporary* work locations in the same trade or business, regardless of the distance.[14]

If your home office is not your principal place of business, and if you have no regular work location outside your home, then you cannot deduct the cost of transportation between your home and any temporary work locations within the metropolitan area. However, you can deduct daily transportation expenses incurred in going between your home and a temporary work location *outside* the metropolitan area where you live and normally work.[15]

If your home office is not your principal place of business, then, you have to determine the difference between a "regular" work location and a "temporary" one—something that is not always easy to do. According to the IRS, "a regular place of business is any location at which the taxpayer works or performs services on a regular basis."[16] (Pretty insightful, huh?) The IRS goes on to say:

> [A] taxpayer may be considered as working or performing services at a particular location on a regular basis whether or not the taxpayer works or performs services at that location every week or on a set schedule. Thus, for example, daily transportation expenses incurred by a doctor in going between the doctor's residence and one or more offices, clinics, or hospitals at which the doctor works or performs services on a regular basis are nondeductible commuting expenses.[17]

While the doctor in the above example cannot deduct the transportation between his residence and any of his regular work locations, he could deduct transportation expenses in going from one work location to another, whether they are temporary or regular locations.

A temporary place of business, according to the IRS, is any location where employment is expected to last (and in fact does last) for one year or less.[18] If employment is realistically expected to last longer than one year, it is not considered temporary even if it does not exceed a year. Also, if employment is expected to last one year or less, but actually lasts longer than a year, it is considered temporary up to the day the taxpayer's realistic expectation changes, after which it will not be treated as temporary. Therefore, if a doctor pays daily visits to a patient at the patient's residence for a period of up to a year while the patient is sick, the transportation would be deductible.

Example 7.4

Assume the same facts as in Example 7.3, except Bubba is employed by a large insurance agency. Bubba maintains an office in his home but it does not qualify as his principal place of business. His employer is located in a building downtown, where Bubba is provided an office that he uses regularly. His transportation from his home on Monday and Tuesday to the office supply store and the post office is not deductible if Bubba visits these locations regularly for business. His transportation on Wednesday to visit clients and on Thursday to the seminar is deductible. Any transportation between business locations after he arrives at his downtown office is also deductible. However, Bubba's commute from his home directly to his downtown office is not deductible.

Before you get too creative with these rules concerning temporary work locations, you should read this warning from the IRS:

> If it is determined upon examination that there is a clear pattern of abuse by the taxpayer in claiming a business expense deduction for daily transportation expenses paid or incurred in going between the taxpayer's residence and asserted temporary work locations without proof of a valid business purpose, the Service will disallow any deduction for such expenses and impose appropriate penalties.[19]

Since places such as the office supply store and the post office are commonly paid regular visits, it's best to be cautious here.

Example 7.5

Assume Bubba from Example 7.3 maintains a home office that is not his principal place of business. Also, his employer does not provide him office space. Only his transportation to the out-of-town business seminar on Thursday is deductible. None of his transportation within the metropolitan area is deductible.

Your Car: Standard Mileage Rate versus Actual Expenses

If you started to use your car for business in 2002, you have a choice of either deducting the actual business operating costs of your car (including depreciation) or deducting a flat IRS allowance (the standard mileage rate) for business mileage traveled. Before seeing the details of these methods, you should know that using the standard mileage allowance is a lot easier and less time consuming than using the actual cost method. Also, because of the depreciation limitations for "luxury automobiles," the actual cost method might not produce significantly higher deductions than the standard mileage allowance. Sometimes trying to squeeze out the last penny of a deduction is not the wisest course when you consider the time and frustration involved. If you choose to claim actual costs for the year you begin to use your car for business, then later decide that it isn't worth it, you cannot switch to the standard mileage allowance method for later years. I would therefore recommend the standard mileage allowance if you are eligible, but only if your car does not qualify for the special 30 percent first year depreciation allowance, described later in this chapter. If your car does qualify for the special allowance, the actual expense method might provide a significantly higher deduction.

The Standard Mileage Allowance Method

The standard mileage allowance is generally available to both employees and the self-employed, and is used in lieu of claiming actual costs of operating your car, van, pickup or panel truck for business. The business mileage rate for 2002 is 36.5 cents per mile. The business standard mileage allowance is also available for leased cars beginning in 1998. If you use the standard mileage allowance you cannot deduct depreciation, maintenance and repairs, gasoline (including gasoline taxes), oil, insurance and vehicle registration fees.[20]

ADDITIONAL ALLOWABLE EXPENSES

There are a few expenses you can deduct in addition to using the standard mileage allowance. Parking and tolls are deductible when the transportation costs of getting to your destination are deductible.[21] The part of your annual auto license fee based on the value of the vehicle is deductible.[22] But if you use your car less than 100 percent for business, an allocation is required to determine the business and non-business portion. The business portion goes on Schedule C if you are self-employed, and the non-business portion goes on Schedule A. If you are using your car as an employee, it should all go on Schedule A in the section for taxes.

If you are self-employed and paying interest on a car loan, the part allocable to business use of the car is deductible; the part allocable to personal use is not deductible.[23] If you use your car as an employee, all of the interest on your car loan is considered personal interest and is not deductible. If you have a cellular phone in your car, the expenses attributable to its business use are deductible. A cellular phone is generally depreciable over seven years, but you might be able to deduct its cost all in the first year with a Section 179 election. Cellular phones are categorized as listed property, which is subject to special limitations and restrictions (see Chapter 8).

MAKING THE CHOICE THE FIRST YEAR

As noted, if you want to use the standard mileage rate for a car, you must choose to use it in the first year the car is available for use in your business.[24] When you use the actual cost method for a particular car for the first year, you cannot use the standard mileage allowance for that car in any later year. If you begin with the standard mileage allowance the first year, then decide to use the actual cost method, you can change methods, but you are limited to claiming straight-line depreciation for the car's remaining estimated useful life. To compute depreciation you will have to determine the car's remaining basis after using the standard mileage allowance. See page 149 under Depreciation adjustments when you used the standard mileage allowance.

WHEN YOU CANNOT USE THE STANDARD MILEAGE ALLOWANCE

There are a few instances in which you cannot use the standard mileage allowance, and are therefore forced to use the actual cost method. These are when you:[25]

- Use the car for hire (such as a taxi cab),
- Use two or more vehicles simultaneously (as in a fleet operation),
- Have claimed a Section 179 deduction,
- Have claimed depreciation for the car in an earlier year using the Accelerated Cost Recovery System (ACRS) under former IRC Section 168, the Modified Accelerated Cost Recovery System (MACRS) under current IRC Section 168, or any other method of depreciation besides straight-line, or
- Have deducted actual operating costs in the first year you used the car for business.

The requirement that you cannot use two or more vehicles simultaneously means that you cannot actually use them at the same time. That means if there is only one of you, you cannot possibly violate this rule regardless of how many vehicles you own. On the other hand, if you have an employee who uses your van for business at the same time you are using your car for business, you have to use the actual cost method for both of them.

DEPRECIATION ADJUSTMENTS WHEN YOU USED THE STANDARD MILEAGE ALLOWANCE

If you use the standard mileage rate, a portion of it is considered an allowance for depreciation, which reduces your car's basis. Even so, you can use the standard mileage rate for as long as you own your car, even if it would be totally depreciated if you used the actual cost method. However, if you later switch to the actual cost method, or sell or trade in your car, you need to determine the car's new adjusted basis in order to figure additional depreciation or to compute gain or loss.

The IRS says depreciation will be considered to have been allowed at the rate of 11.5 cents per business mile for 1992 and 1993; 12 cents per business mile for 1994 through 1999; and 14 cents per business mile for 2000 and 15 cents per mile for 2001 and 2002.[26] For years before 1990, the depreciation rates applied only to the first 15,000 of business miles. From 1990 on, the depreciation rates apply to

Example 7.6

In 1995, Buford bought a car for $14,000, and has used it for business each year claiming the standard mileage rate. Buford's business mileage was 18,000 miles for 1995, 16,300 miles for 1996, 17,600 miles for 1997, 15,000 miles for 1998, 6,000 miles for 1999, 10,000 for 2000 and 4,000 for 2001. In 2001 Buford sold the car for $8,000. The basis of the car when it was sold is computed as follows:

When the car was sold in 2001 its basis was $3,252 ($14,000 − $10,748). That means Buford must report a gain on the sale of $4,748 ($8,000 − $3,252). This gain is ordinary income rather than capital gain because it is considered "recapture" of the depreciation claimed.

YEAR	MILES × RATE	DEPRECIATION
1995	18,000 × .12	$2,160
1996	16,300 × .12	1,956
1997	17,600 × .12	2,112
1998	15,000 × .12	1,800
1999	6,000 × .12	720
2000	10,000 × .14	1,400
2001	4,000 × .15	600
Total depreciation		10,748

all business miles. These amounts will reduce your car's basis, but not below zero. If you switched to the actual cost method for one or more years, you need to compute actual depreciation; the above rates will not apply to those years.

The Actual Cost Method

If you choose not to use the standard mileage allowance, or are not allowed to, you can deduct the actual expenses of using your car for business. These deductible costs include depreciation, lease or rental fees, garage rent, licenses, repairs, gas, oil, tires, insurance, parking fees, and tolls. If you use your car for personal use, you only get to deduct the business portion of these expenses. So you must separate your business and personal mileage, and deduct only the percentage of your expenses that represents business use. For example, let's say you drive your car a total of 20,000 miles during the year, and 15,000 miles were for business. You can deduct 75 percent (15,000/20,000) of your operating expenses as business expenses, including 75 percent of the car's depreciation for the year.

There are some things that you cannot deduct, such as traffic tickets, parking tickets and any other fines or penalties.[27] Luxury or sales taxes are considered part of the cost of the car and are added to the car's basis for depreciation.[28]

DEPRECIATION AND THE SECTION 179 DEDUCTION

You will find a detailed explanation of depreciation of personal property, including the Section 179 deduction, in Chapter 8, *Other Common Business Deductions.* The explanation applies to a car, truck, or van used for business, as well as other business property. Keep in mind that a business vehicle is one type of "listed property." That means if you do not use it more than 50 percent of the time in a qualified business use during every year of its recovery period, you must use straight-line depreciation. Also, you cannot use the Section 179 allowance if your business vehicle is not used over 50 percent of the time in a qualified business. Before you read about the rules for luxury automobiles, this might be a good time to take a look at "Depreciation of Personal Property" on page 168 in Chapter 8.

DEPRECIATION AND SECTION 179 LIMITS FOR LUXURY AUTOMOBILES

There are ceilings on the amount you can deduct each year for depreciation of certain passenger automobiles.[29] A passenger automobile is defined as any four-wheeled vehicle made primarily for use on public streets, roads and highways, and rated at 6,000 pounds or less of unloaded gross vehicle weight (6,000 pounds or less of gross vehicle weight for trucks and vans).[30] Note that if you are in the market for an SUV for business use, be sure to consider its weight. If you get one that weighs more than 6,000 pounds it will greatly accelerate your depreciation deductions, as shown below. Vehicles that are not considered passenger automobiles for this purpose are ambulances, hearses and any vehicle used in the business of transporting people or property for compensation.[31]

The ceilings apply for both the year the car is placed in service and for each succeeding year. The Section 179 deduction is treated as depreciation for this purpose, so you may not exceed the ceiling by claiming first-year expensing. The maximum amount you can deduct each year depends on the year you begin to use your car for business. As a result of the ceilings, the actual write-off period for your car may be several years longer than the normal recovery period of five years.

The reason Congress enacted this provision was supposedly to prevent business owners from writing off the cost of high-priced luxury cars. That being the case, you might think you can just skip over this part because you don't drive a Porsche, a Mercedes, or even a Lexus. Not so fast, Sport. Maybe you don't consider yourself to be in the lap of luxury when you're driving your beater—but the government might. For example, if you first started to use your car for business in 2002, and its depreciable basis at the time was over $15,300, then you have a luxury automobile that is subject to the limitations. So congratulations! You have finally "arrived" and you were not even aware of it.

The ceilings will apply for gas vehicles that cost more than the following amounts:

- $15,300 for business use beginning in 1999, 2000, 2001, or 2002,
- $15,800 for business use beginning in 1997 or 1998,
- $15,300 for business use beginning in 1995 or 1996, and
- $14,800 for business use beginning in 1994.

If you buy an electric car, you can pay three times as much as the above amounts before the depreciation limits apply. The depreciation limits for gas cars are shown in Table 7.2.

As explained in Chapter 8, your business car, truck, or van is five-year property. The usual percentages for depreciating five-year property using the 200 percent declining balance method and the half-year convention are shown in Table 7.3. If you have what the government considers a luxury car, each year you must compare the depreciation allowable under Table 7.3 with the limitations under Table 7.2 and deduct the lesser amount.

NEW 30 PERCENT ALLOWANCE FOR QUALIFIED VEHICLES

The Job Creation and Worker Assistance Act of 2002 allows you to claim a special depreciation allowance equal to 30 percent of the depreciable basis of qualified property.[32] You can claim the special depreciation deduction only for

TABLE 7.2 Depreciation Deduction Limits for Passenger Automobiles

YEAR PLACED IN SERVICE	FIRST YEAR	SECOND YEAR	THIRD YEAR	FOURTH AND LATER YEARS
2000–2002	$3,060	$4,900	$2,950	$1,775
1999	3,060	5,000	2,950	1,775
1998	3,160	5,000	2,950	1,775
1997	3,160	5,000	3,050	1,775
1995–1996	3,060	4,900	2,950	1,775
1994	2,960	4,700	2,850	1,675
1993	2,860	4,600	2,750	1,675
1992	2,760	4,400	2,650	1,575

TABLE 7.3 200% Declining Balance Method Half-Year Convention

YEAR	5-YEAR PROPERTY
1	20.00%
2	32.00
3	19.20
4	11.52
5	11.52
6	5.76

the year the qualified property is placed in service. Here is what it takes for your car to be qualified:

1. You must have bought it new. Used cars don't qualify.
2. You must have bought it at any time after September 10, 2001 and before September 11, 2004.
3. Over 50 percent of the car's use must be qualified business use.

The 2001 and 2002 limits on your depreciation deduction for the first year only, shown in Table 7.2, is increased to $7,660 (from $3,060) for a car that qualifies and for which you claim the special depreciation allowance.[33] The limit is increased to $23,080 if the car is an electric car. The Section 179 deduction (explained below) is treated as depreciation for purposes of the limit.

Example 7.7

Bob bought a new car on October 15, 2002, for $20,000 and placed it in service immediately, using it 100 percent for business. Bob's car is qualified property. Bob chooses not to take a Section 179 deduction for the car. He does claim the new special depreciation allowance. Bob first must figure the special depreciation allowance of $6,000 ($20,000×30%). The remaining depreciable basis of $14,000 ($20,000−$6,000) is depreciated using the 200 percent declining balance method, half-year convention, and results in a deduction of $2,800 ($14,000×20%). The total depreciation for 2002 is $8,800 ($6,000+ $2,800). However, Bob's depreciation deduction is limited to $7,660.

You can elect not to use the additional 30 percent allowance if you want to. Also, since the law was signed after most people filed their 2001 return, you are allowed to file an amended return for 2001 to claim the special deduction.

Example 7.8

Lena purchased a new car in April 2002 for $18,000 to use 75 percent of the time in her business. Lena's car is qualified property for the special 30 percent depreciation allowance. Lena chooses not to take a Section 179 deduction for the car. Lena must first figure the car's depreciable basis, which is $13,500 ($18,000 × 75%). She then figures the special depreciation allowance of $4,050 ($13,500 × 30%). The remaining depreciable basis of $9,450 ($13,500 − $4,050) is depreciated using the 200 percent declining balance method, half-year convention, and results in a deduction of $1,890 ($9,450 × 20%). The total depreciation for 2002 is $5,940 ($4,050 + $1,890). However, Lena's depreciation deduction is limited to $5,745 ($7,660 × 75%).

REDUCTION FOR PERSONAL USE

The maximum amounts allowable in Table 7.2 including the special 30 percent allowance must be reduced by the percentage of the time you use your car for nonbusiness or noninvestment activities.[34]

THE SECTION 179 LIMITATION

The Section 179 deduction (see page 168 in Chapter 8 under "Depreciation of Personal Property") is treated as a depreciation deduction when applying the

Example 7.9

In October 2002 Carmon bought a used car for $8,000. She used it 60 percent for her business in 2002, and elected to take a Section 179 deduction for the car. The car did not qualify for the special 30 percent depreciation allowance. Before applying the limit, Carmon figures her maximum deduction to be $4,800. This is the amount of her qualifying property multiplied by her business use ($8,000 × 60%), and is less than the limit under Section 179 for 2002 of $24,000. Referring to Table 7.2, Carmon computes the limitation on her Section 179 deduction to be $1,836 ($3,060 × 60%). She then has a remaining basis of $2,964 [($8,000 × 60%) − $1,836] for determining her depreciation deduction. Since she has already reached the maximum depreciation limit for her car for 2002, Carmon will use the remaining basis to figure her depreciation deduction for 2003.

Carmon can elect to take an additional Section 179 deduction with respect to other Section 179 property up to the remainder of the maximum amount for 2002 (see Chapter 8).

luxury auto limitations.[35] So even if your car is not considered a luxury automobile, you will still be limited in the amount that you can deduct. Just like for regular depreciation, the maximum amounts in Table 7.2 are reduced by the percentage of the time you use your car for nonbusiness or noninvestment activities. See Example 7.9.

DEPRECIATION OF UNRECOVERED BASIS

If you look at Table 7.2 and add up the amounts your deductions are limited to over the normal six year recovery period for a car placed in service in 2002, you get $16,235 ($3,060 + $4,900 + $2,950 + $1,775 + $1,775 + $1,775). That means regardless of the cost of your car, you cannot deduct more than $16,235 during the normal recovery period. If your car cost more than that, you will have unrecovered basis at the end of the recovery period. They let you continue to depreciate your unrecovered basis in the car after the recovery period ends if you continue to use your car for business.[36] Unrecovered basis is the car's original basis, reduced by depreciation and the Section 179 deduction that would have been allowable if you had used the car 100 percent for business and investment activities. For cars placed in service in 1995 through 2002, the maximum amount of unrecovered basis you can claim per year is $1,775 (see column 5 of Table 7.2), until you recover your full basis in the car. This limit is reduced by the percentage of the car's personal use during the year. See Example 7.10.

Example 7.10

In June of 1997 Elroy bought a car for $29,000. Each year Elroy uses the car 75 percent of the time for his business. Elroy did not elect to use the Section 179 deduction, and he chose the 200 percent declining balance method to figure his depreciation deductions. Allowable depreciation deductions for the car's six-year recovery period are limited as follows (see Table 7.2):

1997: $2,370 ($3,160 × 75%)
1998: $3,750 ($5,000 × 75%)
1999: $2,288 ($3,050 × 75%)
2000: $1,331 ($1,775 × 75%)
2001: $1,331 ($1,775 × 75%)
*2002: $1,253 ($29,000 × 5.76% × 75%)

*Note that allowable depreciation in the sixth year of the recovery period (see Table 7.3) is less than the limitation from Table 7.2 of $1,331 ($1,775 × 75%).

The depreciation Elroy would have been allowed to claim during the six year recovery period if he had used the car 100 percent in business is:

1997: $3,160
1998: $5,000
1999: $3,050
2000: $1,775
2001: $1,775
2002: $1,670 ($29,000 × 5.76%)

Total: $16,430

Therefore, at the beginning of the year 2003 Elroy has unrecovered basis in the car of $12,570, which is the purchase price of $29,000 minus $16,430. If Elroy continues to use the car 75 percent for business in 2003 and later years, each year he can deduct the lesser of $1,331 ($1,775 × 75%) or his remaining unrecovered basis.

Depreciation Limits for Employees

If you are using your car as an employee, you cannot deduct depreciation, the Section 179 allowance or lease payments, unless your car is

1. Used for the convenience of your employer, and

2. Required by your employer as a condition of employment.[37]

The first requirement means that the use of your car is not merely for your own convenience, but is primarily for your employer's convenience. In order to satisfy

> **Example 7.11**
>
> Bertha is an inspector for Dirty Movers, Inc., a construction company with many construction sites in the local area. Bertha is required to travel to the various construction sites on a regular basis, and she uses her car to make the trips. Although the company does not furnish Bertha a car, it does not explicitly require her to use her own car. However, the company reimburses Bertha for any costs she incurs in traveling to the various job sites. Bertha's use of her car in her employment is for the convenience of her employer and is required as a condition of employment.

the second requirement, use of your car must be required in order for you to perform your duties as an employee properly. This is a facts and circumstances test, so it does not matter that your employer does not explicitly require you to use your car. See Chapter 8 under "Depreciation of Personal Property" on page 168.

Inclusion Amounts for Leased Cars

If you lease a car to use for your business, and use the actual cost method rather than the standard mileage rate, the lease payments are deductible in lieu of depreciation. If you use your car only partly for business, you can deduct only the business portion of the lease payments, just like your other car expenses. You cannot deduct any part of a lease payment that is related to your personal use of the car.

If you could deduct the total business portion of the lease payments on a big fat luxury car, then the depreciation limitations on luxury cars would be easy to avoid by simply leasing a luxury car rather than buying one. You probably guessed that Congress figured out a way to put the kibosh on that. The Code says that your annual deductions for lease payments on a luxury car leased for 30 days or more are reduced to substantially equal the depreciation limitations you would have on the car if you bought it.[38] The regulations refer to these lease payment reductions as "inclusion amounts," which means you add them to your gross income. The way they are treated on your tax form, however, is to simply reduce your lease payment deductions.

These lease payment inclusion amounts apply to each tax year that you lease the car if the fair market value of the car when the lease began was more than:

- $15,500 for business use beginning in 2000, 2001, or 2002,
- $15,300 for business use beginning in 1999,
- $15,800 for business use beginning in 1997 or 1998,

- $15,300 for business use beginning in 1995 or 1996,
- $14,800 for business use beginning in 1994,
- $14,300 for business use beginning in 1993,
- $13,800 for business use beginning in 1992, and
- 13,300 for business use beginning in 1991.

These are the same prices as for cars that are subject to the depreciation limitations.

HOW TO FIGURE THE INCLUSION AMOUNT

You must use tables published by the IRS for this. The proper table to use depends on when you first placed the car in service. Table 7.4 is partially reproduced on pages 158 to 160. Use this table if you leased your car in 2002.[39] The tables for cars leased in prior years are in IRS Publication 463, *Travel, Entertainment, Gift, and Car Expenses.*

The inclusion amount for each year of a car's lease is determined as follows:[40]

1. For the appropriate range of fair market values, select the dollar amount from the column for the corresponding year of the lease, except for the last year. If the last year of the lease does not begin and end in the same taxable year, use the dollar amount for the preceding taxable year.

2. In the first and last year of the lease, prorate the dollar amount for the number of days during the year the lease was in effect.

3. Multiply the prorated dollar amount by the business/investment use for the taxable year.

4. This is the inclusion amount that must reduce your deductible lease payments. If you file Schedule C, this amount is reported as a reduction of the lease payments shown on line 20. If you are an employee and file Form 2106, there is a line specified as "Inclusion amount" under "Vehicle rentals" in Section C.

Example 7.12

On April 1, 2002, Allen, a calendar year taxpayer, leased and placed in service a car with a fair market value of $35,000. The lease is to be for a period of three years. During 2002 Allen used the car 45 percent for business. From Table 7.4, the appropriate dollar amount is $89. Allen's inclusion amount for 2002 is: $89 × [275/365] days × 45% business use = $30.

TABLE 7.4 Dollar Amounts for Automobiles with a Lease Term Beginning in Calendar Year 2002

FAIR MARKET VALUE		TAX YEAR OF LEASE				
OVER	NOT OVER	1ST 2002	2ND 2003	3RD 2004	4TH 2005	5TH 2006 AND LATER
$15,500	$15,800	2	3	5	6	6
15,800	16,100	3	7	9	11	13
16,100	16,400	4	10	14	17	19
16,400	16,700	6	13	18	22	26
16,700	17,000	7	16	23	28	31
17,000	17,500	9	20	29	35	40
17,500	18,000	11	25	37	44	50
18,000	18,500	14	30	44	53	61
18,500	19,000	16	35	52	62	72
19,000	19,500	18	40	60	71	82
19,500	20,000	21	45	67	80	93
20,000	20,500	23	50	75	89	103
20,500	21,000	25	56	82	98	114
21,000	21,500	28	60	90	108	123
21,500	22,000	30	66	97	117	134
22,000	23,000	33	74	108	130	150
23,000	24,000	38	84	123	149	171
24,000	25,000	43	94	139	166	192
25,000	26,000	47	104	154	185	213
26,000	27,000	52	114	169	203	234
27,000	28,000	57	124	185	220	255
28,000	29,000	61	135	199	239	276
29,000	30,000	66	145	214	258	296
30,000	31,000	71	155	230	275	318

TABLE 7.4 (Continued)

FAIR MARKET VALUE		TAX YEAR OF LEASE				
OVER	NOT OVER	1ST 2002	2ND 2003	3RD 2004	4TH 2005	5TH 2006 AND LATER
31,000	32,000	75	165	245	294	338
32,000	33,000	80	175	260	312	360
33,000	34,000	85	185	276	329	381
34,000	35,000	89	196	290	348	402
35,000	36,000	94	206	305	367	422
36,000	37,000	99	216	321	384	443
37,000	38,000	103	226	336	403	464
38,000	39,000	108	236	351	421	485
39,000	40,000	112	247	366	439	506
40,000	41,000	117	257	381	457	527
41,000	42,000	122	267	396	475	549
42,000	43,000	126	278	411	493	570
43,000	44,000	131	288	426	512	590
44,000	45,000	136	298	441	530	611
45,000	46,000	140	308	457	548	632
46,000	47,000	145	318	472	566	653
47,000	48,000	150	328	489	584	674
48,000	49,000	154	339	502	602	675
49,000	50,000	159	349	517	620	717
50,000	51,000	164	359	532	639	737
51,000	52,000	168	369	548	657	758
52,000	53,000	173	379	563	675	779
53,000	54,000	177	390	578	693	800
54,000	55,000	182	400	593	711	821

(continued)

TABLE 7.4 (Continued)

FAIR MARKET VALUE		TAX YEAR OF LEASE				
OVER	NOT OVER	1ST 2002	2ND 2003	3RD 2004	4TH 2005	5TH 2006 AND LATER
55,000	56,000	187	410	608	729	842
56,000	57,000	191	420	624	747	863
57,000	58,000	196	430	639	766	883
58,000	59,000	201	440	654	784	905
59,000	60,000	205	451	669	802	925
60,000	62,000	212	466	692	829	957
62,000	64,000	222	486	722	866	999
64,000	66,000	231	507	752	902	1,041

How to Report Travel and Transportation Deductions on Your Return

You can deduct the expenses described in this chapter only if you can prove certain elements of the expense. Read Chapter 11 where the substantiation requirements are described in detail.

If You Are Self-Employed

As a sole proprietor you should use Schedule C or C-EZ (Form 1040) to report your business income and deductions. File Schedule F (Form 1040) if you are a farmer. Use Part I of Schedule E (Form 1040) if you receive rental or royalty income. Do not use Form 2106 or Form 2106-EZ.

SCHEDULE C

1. Report on line 10 the actual costs of operating your car, or the standard mileage allowance, whichever method you are using. There are some questions you should answer in Part IV of the form, unless you are required to file Form 4562 for depreciation or amortization. See more on Form 4562 below. Do not report on line 10 depreciation or the Section 179 allowance, or lease payments on you car.

2. Report depreciation and the Section 179 allowance on line 13, and lease payments (reduced by the inclusion amount, if any) on line 20a.

3. Report your other travel expenses, except for meals, on line 24a.

4. Report your meals and entertainment on line 24b.

5. Report local transportation expenses, other than car expenses, on line 27.

SCHEDULE C-EZ

If your deductions are $2,500 or less you can use this form. Put all travel and transportation expenses on line 2. If you include car expenses, you must also complete Part III of the form.

SCHEDULE F

1. Report on line 12 the actual costs of operating your car, or the standard mileage allowance, including deductions allocable to traveling away from home.

2. Report depreciation and the Section 179 allowance on line 16, and lease payments (reduced by the inclusion amount, if any) on line 26a.

3. If you claim any car or truck expenses (actual or the standard mileage rate) you must provide the information requested in Part V of Form 4562, "Depreciation and Amortization." Be sure to attach Form 4562 to your return.

SCHEDULE E, PART I

1. Report on line 6 the actual costs of operating your car, or the standard mileage allowance, including deductions allocable to traveling away from home.

2. Report depreciation and the Section 179 allowance on line 20, and lease payments on line 18.

3. If you claim any car or truck expenses you must provide the information requested in Part V of Form 4562, "Depreciation and Amortization," and attach Form 4562 to your return.

FORM 4562

You are required to fill out and send in Form 4562, "Depreciation and Amortization," only under the following circumstances:

1. You are claiming depreciation for property placed in service during the year.

2. You are making a Section 179 election, or have a Section 179 deduction carryover.

3. You are claiming depreciation on listed property, regardless of when it was placed in service.

4. You are claiming amortization costs that began during the current year.

5. You are claiming a deduction for any vehicle on any form other than Schedule C (Form 1040) or Schedule C-EZ (Form 1040).

6. You are claiming any depreciation on a corporate income tax return (other than Form 1120S).

If You Are an Employee

UNREIMBURSED EXPENSES

Generally, an employee must report unreimbursed job related deductions on Schedule A (Form 1040) as Miscellaneous Itemized Deductions on line 20. These deductions, along with your other Miscellaneous Itemized Deductions, must be reduced by two percent of your Adjusted Gross Income. You also must complete Form 2106 if you have travel, transportation, meal or entertainment expenses. The total from Form 2106 flows to line 20 of Schedule A. You can use Form 2106-EZ instead of Form 2106 if you meet the following conditions:

1. You do not get reimbursed by your employer for any expenses (amounts your employer included in Box 1 of your Form W-2 are not considered reimbursements), and

2. If you claim car expenses, you own the vehicle and are using the standard mileage rate.

REIMBURSED EXPENSES

An employee who receives reimbursed employee business expenses under an accountable plan can offset the reimbursement with the expenses. That means the reimbursement is not included in your income and the expenses are not reported on Schedule A. An accountable plan is generally an arrangement that meets two requirements:[41]

1. You must be required to substantiate, or adequately account to your employer for your reimbursed business expenses within a reasonable period of time, and

2. You must not be allowed to keep any advances or reimbursements in excess of the substantiated expenses.

You could be in one of four situations when receiving reimbursements from your employer for business expenses:

1. You are reimbursed under an accountable plan, and the reimbursement is in the exact amount of the claimed expenses.

2. You adequately account to your employer for the reimbursed expenses, but the reimbursement is in excess of the reimbursed expenses. Generally, the excess must be returned to your employer, or you will be required to include the entire reimbursement in income and must claim the related deductions on Schedule A (subject to the two percent of AGI reduction). An exception to this rule is if you get a per diem allowance of more than the federal rate. In this case, the reimbursement up to the federal per diem rate is not included in your income, but the excess should be shown as additional wages. You are not required to file Form 2106.

3. You are reimbursed under an accountable plan, and the reimbursement is less than the reimbursed expenses. In this case, you must show all of your reimbursement and expenses on Form 2106. The deductions allocable to the reimbursement can be deducted against the reimbursement on Form 2106. The excess deductions are reported on Schedule A (subject to the two percent of AGI reduction).

4. You are reimbursed by an employer who does not require an adequate accounting. In this case the plan is not an accountable plan, so the reimbursement is included in your income as wages, and the deductions are deductible on Schedule A (subject to the two percent of AGI reduction).

PARTNERSHIPS AND S CORPORATIONS

If you are a partner in a partnership, or a shareholder in an S corporation, you will be issued Schedule K-1 (Form 1065 or Form 1120S) showing your share of income and deductions. You generally report active business income or loss from these entities in Part II of Schedule E (see Schedule K-1 instructions). If you incurred unreimbursed travel or transportation expenses on behalf of a partnership, and you were required to pay these expenses under the partnership agreement, you can claim them in Part II of Schedule E (see instructions). If you incurred unreimbursed travel or transportation expenses on behalf of an S corporation, they are treated the same as unreimbursed employee business expenses.

Additional Resources

For the rules on how to document travel and transportation expenses, as well as other types of business expenses, see Chapter 11. For more information on most of the topics in this chapter, including specific examples of how an employee completes Form 2106, see IRS Publication 463, *Travel, Entertainment, Gift, and Car Expenses*. IRS Publication 535, *Business Expenses*, also contains information on travel and transportation deductions, including how to report per diem reimbursements. IRS Publication 1339, *Highlights of the Job Creation and Worker Assistance Act of 2002,* provides information on how the special 30 percent first year depreciation deduction applies to cars. This information is not included in the 2002 version of Publication 463.

IRS Publication 1542, *Per Diem Rates,* contains the current domestic per diem rates. Domestic per diem rates are also available at *www.policy-works.gov/perdiem.* The federal per diem rates for locations outside the continental U.S. are published monthly in the Maximum Travel Per Diem Allowances for Foreign Areas. You can purchase this supplement from: Superintendent of Documents, U.S. Government Printing Office, P.O. Box 371954, Pittsburgh, PA 15250-7954. Or you can order it by calling the Government Printing Office at (202) 512-1800 (not toll-free). Foreign per diem rates are also available at http://www.state.gov/www/perdiems.

You can get IRS publications free by calling the IRS at (800) TAX-FORM [(800) 829-3676]. If you have access to TTY/TDD equipment, you can call (800) 829-4059. To download them from the Internet, go to *www.irs.gov* (World Wide Web), or *ftp.irs.gov* (FTP). If you would like to get forms and instructions (not publications) by FAX, dial (703) 368-9694 to reach IRS Tax Fax.

As an alternative to downloading files from the Internet, you can order *IRS Federal Tax Products* on CD-ROM. This CD includes over 2,000 tax products, including all of the above publications and forms. It can be ordered by calling (800) 233-6767. Also, Publication 3207, *Small Business Resource Guide,* is an interactive CD-ROM that contains information important to small businesses. It is available in mid-February. You can get one free copy by calling (800) 829-3676.

Notes

[1] IRC § 162(a)(2).
[2] *US v. Correll,* 88 Sp. Ct. 445 (1967).
[3] Rev. Rul. 75-432, 1975-2 C.B. 60.
[4] IRC § 162(a).
[5] Treas. Reg. § 1.162-2(b).
[6] Treas. Reg. § 1.162-2(c).
[7] Rev. Proc. 2000-9, 2000-2 IRB.
[8] Rev. Proc. 2000-9, Sec. 6.
[9] IRC § 267(b)(2).
[10] IRC § 274(n).

[11] Rev. Rul. 94-47, 1994-2 C.B. 18; Rev. Rul. 55-109, 1955-1 C.B. 261.

[12] Section 262 of the Code provides that no deduction is allowed for personal, living, or family expenses. Commuting expenses are specifically treated as nondeductible personal expenses under Reg. § 1.162-2(e) and Reg. § 1.262-1(b)(5).

[13] Rev. Rul. 94-47.

[14] Ibid.

[15] Ibid.

[16] Rev. Rul. 90-23, 1990-1 C.B. 28.

[17] Rev. Rul. 90-23.

[18] Rev. Rul. 99-7, 1999-5 IRB.

[19] Rev. Rul. 90-23.

[20] Rev. Proc. 2001-54, 2001-48 IRB 530.

[21] Rev. Proc. 2001-54.

[22] IRC § 164(b)(1).

[23] IRC § 163(h)(2)(A).

[24] IRS Pub 463, *Travel, Entertainment, Gift, and Car Expenses,* p. 16.

[25] Rev. Proc. 2001-54.

[26] Ibid.

[27] IRC § 162(f).

[28] IRC § 164(a).

[29] IRC § 280F(a).

[30] IRC § 280F(d)(5)(A).

[31] IRC § 280F(d)(5)(B).

[32] IRC § 168(k)(2)(E)(i), as amended by 2002 Act § 110(a).

[33] Ibid.

[34] IRS Pub 463, *Travel, Entertainment, Gift, and Car Expenses,* p. 20.

[35] IRC § 280F(d)(1).

[36] IRC § 280F(a)(1)(B).

[37] IRC § 280F(d)(3).

[38] IRC § 280F(c).

[39] From Rev. Proc. 2002-14, 2002-5 IRB 450. The complete table covers cars valued at up to $250,000.

[40] Treas. Reg. § 1.280F-7 and IRS Publication 463.

[41] IRC § 62(c).

CHAPTER 8

Other Common Business Deductions

> Next to being shot at
> and missed, nothing
> is quite as satisfying
> as an income tax
> refund.
>
> —F.J. Raymond

The common non-travel deductions available to home-based businesses are discussed in this chapter. (See Chapter 7 for travel and transportation expenses.) These are the deductions that are not limited by the Section 280A home-office rules. That means they can be deducted even if your home office does not meet one of the business-use tests described in Chapter 5.

Who Deducts What, Where?

The business expenses incurred by self-employed individuals are deductible on either Schedule C or C-EZ (Form 1040), Schedule E (Form 1040) for rental real estate, or Schedule F (Form 1040) for farmers.

Business expenses incurred by employees that are unreimbursed by their employer are also deductible, but they must go on Schedule A (line 20) as "Miscellaneous Itemized Deductions."[1] If you are an employee, and your employer reimbursed you for some of your employee business expenses, fill out Form 2106 by following the instructions to that form. If your employer reimbursed you for all of your employee business expenses, you might be able to skip Form 2106 and not report either the reimbursement or the expenses.

Investment related expenses, other than those relating to rental or royalty income, are also Miscellaneous Itemized Deductions.[2] Only the aggregate amount of your Miscellaneous Itemized Deductions in excess of two percent of your Adjusted Gross Income (the amount on line 31 of Form 1040) is deductible.

How About When?

Some costs are deductible in the year they are paid (for a cash method taxpayer) or incurred (for an accrual method taxpayer) if they qualify as ordinary and necessary business expenses under IRC Section 162. Other costs represent the purchase of business or investment assets rather than current expenses. The cost of most of these assets is depreciable or amortizable over the life of the asset. For certain depreciable business property, an election is available to expense its cost in the year it is purchased. This is called a Section 179 election, and is discussed later in this chapter.

Depreciation of Personal Property

Chapter 6 shows how to depreciate the home-office portion of your residence if it qualifies for one of the Section 280A business-use tests. Your home office is real property (or realty), and its depreciation is limited by the Section 280A home-office rules. Even if your home office does not qualify for depreciation, you can claim depreciation for personal property used in connection with your home-based business. Personal property is anything that is not permanently attached to land or buildings. The rules for depreciating personal property vary depending on the type of property, the percentage of time it is used for business, and how and when it was acquired.

The Categories

There are two categories of depreciable personal property that account for just about any kind of depreciable asset used in connection with a home office. They are five-year property and seven-year property.[3]

FIVE-YEAR PROPERTY

This category includes computers and peripheral equipment (such as printers, monitors, data storage systems, and scanners), typewriters, copiers, and other duplicating equipment.[4] Your business car, truck, or van is also in this category. (See Chapter 7, "Planes, Trains, and (Especially) Automobiles," for rules on depreciating business vehicles). The reason it is called five-year property is because the property is presumed to have a depreciable life (or recovery period) of five years, regardless of how long you think the property will be useful to you. Cars, computers, and peripheral equipment are a special type of property called listed property that will be discussed separately later in this chapter.

SEVEN-YEAR PROPERTY

This category includes desks, chairs, lamps, files, safes, fax machines, appliances, carpets, telephones, books, and any other property that is not otherwise classified.[5] It's called seven-year property because—you guessed it—it is presumed to have a depreciable life of seven years.

Many other types of depreciable assets might be used in connection with your home-based business, depending on what business you are in. Their classification can be found in IRS Publication 946, *How to Depreciate Property.* For example, if you are in the business of building ships or boats, Table B-2 of Publication 946 says your tools are five-year property. If you are in the business of manufacturing jewelry, Table B-2 of Publication 946 says your tools are seven-year property.

How Much Is Deductible Each Year?

With the exception of certain listed property, five-year property and seven-year property can be depreciated using the 200 percent declining balance (or double declining balance) method.[6] This is a method that permits larger deductions in the early years than in the later years. You can elect the 150 percent declining balance method or the straight-line method, but the 200 percent method is generally better because the sooner you can claim a deduction the better. However, if you are subject to the Alternative Minimum Tax (AMT), you may want to elect the 150 percent method to avoid an AMT adjustment (see the instructions to Form 6251, "Alternative Minimum Tax—Individuals"). In the later years of an asset's recovery period, when the double declining rate or the 150 percent declining balance rate provides a lower annual deduction than the straight-line rate, you switch the method to the straight-line rate. Table 8.1 shows the percentages to deduct each year under the 200 percent method. Year one is the year you first begin to use the property for business.

TABLE 8.1 200 Percent Declining Balance Method Half-Year Convention

YEAR	5-YEAR PROPERTY	7-YEAR PROPERTY
1	20.00%	14.29%
2	32.00	24.49
3	19.20	17.49
4	11.52	12.49
5	11.52	8.93
6	5.76	8.92
7		8.93
8		4.46

It generally doesn't matter at what point during the year you purchase depreciable personal property (or convert it to business use), because it is assumed to be purchased (or converted) halfway through the year. This is called the "half-year convention."[7] You may have noticed that there are actually six years of depreciation for five-year property, and eight years of depreciation for seven-year property. That's because only half a year is allowed for the first year, so half a year's depreciation is remaining at the end of the five- or seven-year period. Also, if you sell five-year or seven-year property before it is fully depreciated, you are supposed to claim a half year's depreciation in the year of sale, regardless of when during the year it is sold.

NEW 30 PERCENT ALLOWANCE FOR QUALIFIED PROPERTY

The Job Creation and Worker Assistance Act of 2002 allows you to claim a special depreciation allowance equal to 30 percent of the depreciable basis of qualified property.[8] You can claim the special depreciation deduction only for the year the qualified property is placed in service. Here are the general requirements for qualified property:

1. It must be new depreciable property with a recovery period of 20 years or less (certain leasehold improvements also qualify).

2. You must have bought it at any time after September 10, 2001 and before September 11, 2004.

3. Over 50 percent of the property's use must be qualified business use.

Example 8.1

On November 1, 2002, Dorothy bought, and placed in service in her business, qualified property that cost $100,000. Dorothy did not elect to claim a Section 179 deduction (discussed later in this chapter). Dorothy can deduct 30 percent of the cost (30,000) as a special depreciation allowance for 2002. Dorothy uses the remaining $70,000 of cost to figure her regular depreciation deduction for 2002 and later years.

This allowance is deductible for both regular tax and alternative minimum tax (AMT) purposes. There is no AMT adjustment required for any depreciation figured on the remaining basis of the property. You can elect not to use the additional 30 percent allowance if you want to. Also, since the law was signed after most people filed their 2001 return, you are allowed to file an amended return for 2001 to claim the special deduction.

Several additional depreciation benefits are available for property you place in service in the New York Liberty Zone. They include a special depreciation allowance for the year you place the property in service, an increased Section 179 deduction, and the classification of certain leasehold improvement property as 5-year property. The New York Liberty Zone is the area located on or south of Canal Street, East Broadway (east of its intersection with Canal Street), or Grand Street (east of its intersection with East Broadway) in the Borough of Manhattan in the City of New York. To learn more about Liberty Zone benefits, as well as how to elect out of the special 30 percent allowance and how to file an amended 2001 return to claim the allowance, see IRS Publication 3991, *Highlights of the Job Creation and Worker Assistance Act of 2002.*

BASIS FOR DEPRECIATION

The basis of purchased property is the original cost (whether you paid with cash, other property, debt or services), plus sales tax and delivery charges. An asset's adjusted basis is its original basis, plus the cost of any improvements, and minus deductions you have claimed for depreciation and casualty losses. If you trade in an old asset, like a car, for a new one, the basis of the new asset is generally the adjusted basis of the old asset plus any additional payment you make.

Example 8.2

Brad purchased a copier (five-year property) in 2000 for $5,000 to use in his home office. He used it 80 percent of the time in his business activities in 2000, 70 percent in 2001 and 60 percent in 2002. In 2002 he sold the copier for $2,000. Here's how he computes the yearly depreciation and loss on the sale.

Total depreciation claimed for the three-year period (including half-year for 2002) is $2,208. That means the basis of the copier is $2,792 ($5,000 − $2,208) in the year of sale. The sales price of $2,000 less the basis of $2,792 produces a loss of $792. The business portion of this loss (the portion of the time it is used for business in the year of sale) is 60 percent. So a loss of $475 ($792 × 60%) can be claimed. This loss is reported in Part I of Form 4797 (from there Brad just follows the instructions to that form).

YEAR	200% DB RATE	BUSINESS %	BASIS	DEDUCTION
2000	20%	× 80%	× $5,000	= $ 800
2001	32%	× 70%	× $5,000	= $1,120
2002	½ × 19.2%	× 60%	× $5,000	= $ 288
Total				$2,208

If the item is used only partially for business, the basis for depreciation is only the business-use portion of the cost. If you convert property from personal use, its basis is the lesser of its original cost or its fair market value at the time of conversion. If it is used less than 100 percent for business, the business-use percentage of this amount is its depreciable basis.

Notice in Example 8.2 that the percentages for the 200 percent declining balance method are applied to the unadjusted basis of the asset each year; the depreciable basis is not reduced by depreciation claimed in the previous year. (This is not the way the declining balance method is usually computed, but the tables are set up this way to make it easier. Note that in Table 8.1 the total of the percentages for each property equals 100.) Also, notice that it doesn't matter what year the asset is placed in service, the same percentages apply, as long as it is after 1986.

Have You Appreciated Your Depreciation?

Perhaps you just realized that you have been using things in your home office that you could have been depreciating for several years. Maybe you haven't claimed depreciation deductions for previous years. Can you still claim a deduction for the current year? Yes! But you can't start at the beginning of the depreciation table; you must pick up depreciation in the current year as if you had been claiming it all along. Additionally, basis of your depreciable assets must be reduced by depreciation that was allowable in prior years, even if you did not claim it on your return.[9]

You can also file amended returns for previous years and claim any deductions not claimed on the original returns. An amended return can be filed at any time within three years of the date the original return was filed or two

---

Example 8.3

Assume that Brad in Example 8.2 did not claim depreciation for his copier on his 2000 or 2001 tax return. His home office did not qualify for home-office deductions, and Brad mistakenly thought depreciation on his copier was not deductible. Brad can still claim depreciation for the copier on his 2002 return in the amount of $288. He can also file amended returns for 2000 and 2001 to claim allowable depreciation for those years. Even if Brad does not file amended returns, however, the adjusted basis of his copier at the time of sale is still $2,792.

years from the time the tax was paid, whichever is later.[10] Returns that are filed early are deemed to have been filed on the date the return was due.[11]

The Mid-Quarter Convention

There is one situation in which you cannot use the half-year convention for depreciable personal property. This is when over 40 percent of all the depreciable personal property you buy during the year is bought and placed in service during the last three months of the year. (In determining this percentage, don't include any real property purchases or property expensed under Section 179.) In that case you have to use what they call the "mid-quarter convention." This method presumes each item placed in service during any quarter of the calendar year is placed in service during the midpoint of the quarter. For example, any item placed in service in October, November, or December is presumed to be placed in service in the middle of November, so you get one and one-half month's depreciation. Any items placed in service during January, February, or March is presumed to be placed in service in mid-February, so you get eleven and one-half month's depreciation. This is to prevent people from going out in December and purchasing the bulk of their depreciable personal property, then claiming a half year of depreciation. If you must use the mid-quarter convention for a particular year, each item of depreciable personal property placed in service during that year must be depreciated using the mid-quarter convention for its entire recovery period. Tables 8.2 and 8.3 show the percentages to deduct each year under the 200 percent declining balance method, depending on which quarter you begin to use the property for business.

TABLE 8.2 200 Percent Declining Balance Method—Five-Year Property Mid-Quarter Convention

YEAR	FIRST QUARTER	SECOND QUARTER	THIRD QUARTER	FOURTH QUARTER
1	35.00%	25.00%	15.00%	5.00%
2	26.00	30.00	34.00	38.00
3	15.60	18.00	20.40	22.80
4	11.01	11.37	12.24	13.68
5	11.01	11.37	11.30	10.94
6	1.38	4.26	7.06	9.58

TABLE 8.3 200 Percent Declining Balance Method—Seven-year Property Mid-Quarter Convention

YEAR	FIRST QUARTER	SECOND QUARTER	THIRD QUARTER	FOURTH QUARTER
1	25.00%	17.85%	10.71%	3.57%
2	21.43	23.47	25.51	27.55
3	15.31	16.76	18.22	19.68
4	10.93	11.97	13.02	14.06
5	8.75	8.87	9.30	10.04
6	8.74	8.87	8.85	8.73
7	8.75	8.87	8.86	8.73
8	1.09	3.33	5.53	7.64

Example 8.4

Assume Brad in Example 8.2 purchased his copier in November of 2000 for $5,000 and began using it in his home office. He also purchased a fax machine (seven-year property) for $300 in June of 2000 for business use. Over 40 percent of the total depreciable personal property placed in service by Brad in 2000 was placed in service during the last three months. That means Brad must use the mid-quarter convention for the fax machine and the copier during their entire recovery periods. For the fax machine, Brad uses the percentages for the Second Quarter (April through June) from Table 8.3 (the mid-quarter convention table for seven-year property). For the copier, Brad uses the percentages for the Fourth Quarter (October through December) from Table 8.2 (the mid-quarter convention table for five-year property).

Deduct It All in One Year!—The Section 179 Election

Wouldn't it be neat if you could just deduct the cost of your depreciable assets and not have to worry about computing depreciation on them every year? Well, you can; it's called a Section 179 election. There are restrictions, however. Here are the conditions:

1. The property must be purchased for use in a trade or business (not an investment activity). "Purchased" means it was not acquired by gift,

inheritance, or converted from personal use. Also, it cannot be purchased from your spouse, kids, grandkids, parents, or grandparents.[12]

2. The property must be tangible personal property, such as computers, furniture, books, and so on; not land, buildings, or things that are permanently attached to land or buildings.[13]

3. If you acquire property by trading in old property, the cost of the new property that qualifies for the election includes only the amount paid; it does not include the adjusted basis of the property traded in.[14]

4. If you purchase property for both business and nonbusiness use, you can make the election only for the business-use portion, and only if more than 50 percent of the property's use during its entire depreciable life is for business.[15] If you make the election when business use is greater than 50 percent, and in a later year the business-use percentage dips below 50 percent, you might have to report income as a result. It's the difference between what you claimed under Section 179, and the total of what you could have claimed in depreciation. This goes in Part IV of Form 4797 (see instructions to Form 4797).

5. The election is available only for the first year property is "placed in service." That is the year it is first made ready and available for a specific use, whether the use is in a business, investment, or a personal activity. Property placed in service in a use that does not qualify it for the Section 179 deduction (a nonbusiness use) cannot later qualify in another year, even if its use changes to business.

Example 8.5

In 2002 you bought a new computer and placed it in service for personal use. In 2003 you began to use it for business. The fact that you changed its use from personal to business use disqualifies the cost of your computer for a Section 179 deduction. You can claim depreciation for the business use of the computer for 2003.

6. The total cost of Section 179 property that you can elect to deduct in 2002 cannot be more than $24,000.[16] You do not have to claim the full amount, and you can allocate the deduction among different properties any way you want. If you make the election for only part of the cost of property, the amount that you elect to deduct reduces the amount that you can depreciate, but you can claim depreciation on what's left.

Example 8.6

On November 1, 2002, you bought and placed in service in your business property costing $100,000 that qualifies for both the special 30 percent depreciation allowance and the Section 179 allowance. You elect to deduct $24,000 of the property's cost under Section 179. You use the remaining $76,000 of cost to figure your special depreciation allowance of $22,800 ($76,000× 30%). You use the remaining $53,200 of cost to figure your regular depreciation deduction for 2002 and later years.

PLANNING TIP

Generally when you make the Section 179 election, you should choose to expense the property with the longest depreciable life first. That way if you exceed the limit, you can depreciate what's left over a shorter period. You can also use the Section 179 election to avoid the mid-quarter convention. If you have acquired more than 40 percent of your depreciable personal business property during the last quarter, apply the Section 179 election to last quarter purchases to reduce the percentage to below 40 percent.

7. For every dollar of Section 179 property (depreciable tangible personal property) in excess of $200,000 you place in service in one year, the maximum deduction is reduced by one dollar.[17] For example, if you purchase and place in service $211,000 of Section 179 property during 2003, your maximum Section 179 deduction is $14,000 [$25,000 − ($211,000 − $200,000)].

8. The total cost of Section 179 property that you can elect to deduct for any year is limited to your taxable business income during the year.[18] Any excess amount can be carried over to the next year. Taxable business income for this purpose includes the net income (or loss) from all businesses you and your spouse (if filing a joint return) actively conduct during the year. This includes any wages, tips or, other compensation earned as an employee. It is computed without regard to (1) the Section 179 expense deduction; (2) the self-employment tax deduction; and (3) any net operating loss carryback or carryforward.[19]

9. You make the Section 179 election in Part I of Form 4562, "Depreciation and Amortization." If you are an employee and you want to make the election for a business vehicle, use Form 2106, "Employee Business

Example 8.7

Hong and Yan are married and file a joint return. Hong had wages from his position as a clothing store salesman of $5,000 in 2003. Yan is a sole proprietor and had $7,000 of taxable income from her desktop publishing business in 2003, and a $1,500 net operating loss carryforward from 2002. Yan purchased $3,000 of office furniture and $8,000 of computer equipment for her business in 2003. Taxable business income on Hong and Yan's joint return for 2003 is $12,000, because Hong's wages are included, and the net operating loss is ignored. So Yan is able to deduct the entire $11,000 of Section 179 property purchased in 2003.

Expenses." The election must be made no later than the due date (including extensions) for your return for the tax year the property was placed in service.[20]

Treatment of Listed Property

There are limitations and restrictions on the deductions relating to this type of property. Listed property includes:[21]

1. Any passenger automobile. This is defined as any four-wheeled vehicle made primarily for use on public streets, roads, and highways, and rated at 6,000 pounds or less of unloaded gross vehicle weight (6,000 pounds or less of gross vehicle weight for trucks and vans).[22] Vehicles that are not considered passenger automobiles for this purpose are ambulances, hearses, and any vehicle used in the business of transporting people or property for compensation.[23]

2. Certain other property used for transportation, such as trucks, buses, boats, airplanes, and motorcycles.

3. Any computer and related peripheral equipment, unless it is used only at a regular business establishment and is owned or leased by the person operating the establishment. A regular business establishment includes a home office if, and only if, it qualifies under one of the first three business-use tests described in Chapter 5.[24]

4. Any property used for entertainment or recreational purposes (such as photographic, phonographic, communication, and video recording equipment), unless it is used only at a regular business establishment and is owned or leased by the person operating the establishment. A regular

business establishment has the same meaning as for computers and peripheral equipment.[25]

5. Any cellular telephone (or similar telecommunication equipment) placed in service or leased in a tax year beginning after 1989.

"Peripheral equipment" relating to a computer is "any auxiliary machine which is designed to be controlled by the central processing unit of a computer."[26] They are talking about external drives, printers, monitors, modems, scanners, and other such equipment.

HERE IS THE BAD NEWS

For any listed property that is not used more than 50 percent in a "qualified business use" for its entire depreciable life:

- The Section 179 deduction is not available, and
- You must depreciate the property using the straight line method rather than the 200 percent declining balance method.[27]

STRAIGHT LINE FOR LISTED PROPERTY

If your property is considered listed property, and you use it 50 percent or less of the time for "qualified business use" during any year of its recovery period, you must use straight-line depreciation. For seven-year property, the depreciation must be stretched out over a ten-year period rather than seven years.

Qualified business use means any use in your trade or business, but does not include use in an investment activity. However, whether or not you satisfy the greater than 50 percent business-use requirement, you can still claim depreciation for any investment use of the property. (See Example 8.8.)

If you claimed the Section 179 allowance or started to depreciate the property using the 200 percent declining balance method, and then your qualified business use drops to 50 percent or below, you must recompute what you claimed in prior years in excess of straight line depreciation, and report the difference as income. (This goes in Part IV of Form 4797.) So if you have listed property and you think your business use might drop to 50 percent or below, it's a good idea to just use the straight-line method, and the longer recovery period for seven-year property.

Table 8.4 shows the percentages of the business-use portion you can claim each year for computers, cellular phones, and entertainment equipment, using the straight-line method and the half-year convention. Computers and peripheral equipment are five-year property, and cellular phones and equipment that could be used for entertainment are seven-year property (depreciated over 10 years in this case).

Example 8.8

Marge uses a home computer (five-year property) 50 percent of the time to manage investments. Marge also uses the computer 40 percent of the time in her part-time consumer research business. Marge's home computer is listed property because it is not used at a regular business establishment. Because her business use of the computer does not exceed 50 percent, the computer is not predominantly used in a qualified business use. Since she does not meet the 50 percent use test, Marge cannot elect a Section 179 deduction for the computer and she must use straight-line depreciation. However, Marge can combine the time spent on the computer for both business and investment use (90 percent) for determining her depreciation deduction.[28] She will have to allocate the investment and business depreciation to different schedules in her return. (See "Where and How to Report Depreciation and the Section 179 Deduction" on page 181.)

TABLE 8.4   Depreciation Percentages for Listed Property Used Less Than 50 Percent for Business in Any Year

YEAR	5-YEAR PROPERTY	7-YEAR PROPERTY
1	10%	5%
2	20	10
3	20	10
4	20	10
5	20	10
6	10	10
7		10
8		10
9		10
10		10
11		5

THROW IN YOUR INVESTMENT USE

Even though you have listed property that is used less than 50 percent in a qualified business use, you can also claim depreciation for the portion of use that applies to investment activities.

Keep in mind that computers and entertainment equipment are only regarded as "listed property" if your home office does not meet one of the first three business-use requirements discussed in Chapter 5. If you have a deductible home office, there are no restrictions on depreciating the business-use portion of these items, even if it is less than 50 percent. You do not get a Section 179 deduction, however, for any property that is used less than 50 percent for business.[29]

USE BY AN EMPLOYEE

If you are using the listed property as an employee, your use is not considered business use unless:

1. The use is for your employer's convenience, and
2. The use is required as a condition of your employment.[30]

The IRS has taken a pretty strict position on the "condition of employment" requirement with respect to a home computer. In the case of a university professor who purchased a home computer and used it 100 percent for doing scholarly research and applying for research grants, the IRS held that this was not "required," even though the university provided no word-processing facilities.[31] The IRS said:

> Although the benefits of [the taxpayer's] use of the computer may inure to the employer, the purchase of a computer was clearly not required as a condition of employment. The facts suggest that the computer use, although work-related, is not inextricably related to proper performance of the employee's job. Further, there appears no evidence in the facts that those employees who did not purchase a computer were professionally disadvantaged.[32]

The Tax Court, on the other hand, has taken a more liberal approach to this requirement. It decided a case involving a different university professor and his wife, who was a transportation planner. The professor stored much of his research material at his home because of lack of space at the university, and did much of his research at home. He did not have access to a computer at the university, so he bought a home computer for storing information and for word processing in his academic research. The professor's wife used the computer in her work as the chief transportation planner for a local governmental agency. Her job required extensive number crunching which had previously been done on a mainframe computer owned by the state, but the state eliminated access to this computer. Although the couple did not meet the tests relating to deductions for their home office, the Tax Court held that the computer met the "condition of employment" requirement in this case, and the "convenience of the employer" requirement. The court said the computer purchase spared the employers from providing them with suitable computer equipment.[33]

RECORDS YOU SHOULD KEEP

Listed property that is continually used more than 50 percent in a qualified business use is treated the same as any other five-year or seven-year property; except that for all listed property, you must keep adequate records to indicate your business (and investment) use.[34] Your records do not have to conform to any specific format, but you must be able to document the following:

1. The amount of each separate expenditure with respect to an item of listed property.
2. The length of time the item was used for business or investment purposes compared to total use.[35]

If your business-use percentage of listed property is relatively constant throughout the year, you can use a sampling, by maintaining records for a portion of the year or a portion of each month, instead of keeping records for the entire year.[36] For more details on record-keeping for business vehicles, see Chapter 11.

Example 8.9

Ed is self-employed and has a computer that he uses in a home office that does not meet the business-use requirements of Section 280A. Ed documents the business use of his computer for the first three months of the year as 55 percent of total use. As long as Ed can establish that his business usage continues at approximately the same rate for the rest of the year, his records support a deduction based on 55 percent of the cost of the computer (that is, he can use the 200 percent method or the Section 179 election if he wants to).

Where and How to Report Depreciation and the Section 179 Deduction

You are required to fill out and send in Form 4562, "Depreciation and Amortization," only under one or more of the following circumstances:

1. You are claiming depreciation for property placed in service during the year.

2. You are making a Section 179 election, or have a Section 179 deduction carryover.

3. You are claiming depreciation on listed property, regardless of when it was placed in service.

4. You are claiming amortization costs that began during the current year (see below regarding computer software).

5. You are claiming a deduction for any vehicle on any form other than Schedule C (Form 1040) or Schedule C-EZ (Form 1040).

6. You are claiming any depreciation on a corporate income tax return (other than Form 1120S).

If you are claiming depreciation or the Section 179 deduction in more than one business activity, or a business activity and an investment activity, you are supposed to fill out a separate Form 4562 for each activity.[37] You could be using the same asset for different activities; you still have to divide up the depreciation relating to each activity.

If you are making the Section 179 election for property in more than one business activity, fill out Part I of Form 4562 using the aggregate amounts from all your business activities, and write "Summary" at the top. The dollar limitation (Part I, line 5) and the business income limitation (Part I, line 11) apply overall, rather than to each activity. Then allocate a portion of the total Section 179 deduction from this form to each Form 4562 that you prepare for the separate activities.

Follow the instructions to the form, and come up with a total on line 20 for each activity. If you are filing Schedule C (Form 1040), put this amount on line 13. For Schedule F (Form 1040), the amount goes on line 16. If you are claiming deductions as an employee, or if the depreciation relates to an investment activity, the amount on line 20 of Form 4562 goes on line 20 of Schedule A (Form 1040).

If you are only claiming depreciation on property that is not listed property and that was placed in service in a previous year, you do not have to fill out Form 4562. Simply compute the depreciation and put the amount on the appropriate line (or lines) of Schedule C, F, or A. You should write on the appropriate line "See schedule attached," and attach your own depreciation schedule. You have to maintain a depreciation schedule for your records anyway, and I've never seen anyone get into trouble for sending in too many schedules.

Computer Software

If the charge for software is included in the price of a computer without being separately identified, the charge for the software must be consistently treated as

Example 8.10

Laura purchased a business software program and loaded it onto her computer on October 1, 2003. The cost of the program was $300, and Laura uses it entirely for a business purpose. The amount of the purchase price that is deductible each year is:

YEAR	DEDUCTION
2003	$25 ($300 × $\frac{3}{36}$)
2004	$100 ($300 × $\frac{12}{36}$)
2005	$100 ($300 × $\frac{12}{36}$)
2006	$75 ($300 × $\frac{9}{36}$)
Total	$300

The $25 deduction for 2003 is shown in Part VI of Form 4562. After the first year, Laura can simply report the deduction on the appropriate schedule. It is reported exactly the same way as depreciation.

part of the cost of the computer.[38] That means it must be depreciated, or deducted under Section 179, the same as the computer. If the price of the software is separately stated, or the software is purchased separately, it is supposed to be amortized ratably over 36 months, beginning in the month the software is placed in service.[39]

You cannot deduct computer software by making a Section 179 election, because software is intangible property, and the Section 179 election only applies to tangible personal property. However, software often does not remain usable for three years; it becomes obsolete. If this happens to your software, you can deduct the balance of its cost in the year it is no longer usable. To illustrate, if the software Laura bought in the above example becomes obsolete in 2004, she can deduct the balance of the cost of $275 ($300 − $25) in 2004.

Books, Subscriptions, and Supplies

If you purchase books for business or investment purposes having only short-term value (a tax guide like this one, for example), you can deduct their entire cost in the year of purchase.[40] Books of a more lasting value are seven-year property for depreciation purposes. They can be depreciated using the 200 percent declining balance method and the half-year convention.

How to Deduct the Whole Cost

It might be tempting to simply deduct all of the books you purchase that relate to your business or investment activities, and bury them in the "supplies" or "office expense" category. That might work, but if discovered, there's always the threat of the IRS making you depreciate this expense over seven years. Here's a better idea. Because books are tangible personal property, they qualify for the Section 179 election if they are purchased for a business purpose. Instead of burying them in supplies, make the Section 179 election by putting them in Part I of Form 4562, and deduct them as part of your depreciation expense. (Remember that you must make the Section 179 election by the due date of your return, including extensions.)

Take a Chance with Periodicals

Subscriptions to business and investment periodicals are deductible as business or investment expenses.[41] However, the IRS says you cannot deduct the cost of subscriptions for more than one year in advance.[42] In other words, if you subscribe to a periodical in January of 2003 and pay for 3 years, you can only deduct two-thirds of the cost—the amount that applies to 2003 and 2004. The portion of the payment that pertains to 2005 can be deducted in 2004. The problem is that you might forget about it when it comes time to fill out your return for 2004.

The IRS announced this rule at the end of 1986, when the tax rates were to decline dramatically in the following year. The concern was that taxpayers would try to deduct prepaid expenses against the higher 1986 tax rates, and avoid the new Miscellaneous Itemized Deduction limitation that the Tax Reform Act of 1986 imposed for years after 1986. Since tax rates are not currently going down dramatically, agents probably aren't real concerned about enforcing this rule, as long as the amount is not too out of line. Enough said.

Newspapers and magazines can be deducted if they are sufficiently connected to your business, job, or investment activity. That means the primary purpose for subscribing must be for your business or investment activity, not for personal knowledge, enjoyment or entertainment. You might satisfy this requirement even if the newspapers or magazines are aimed at the general public rather than your specific profession. But keep in mind that the burden of proof for your deductions is on you; so have adequate support ready.

Plan Your Supply Purchases

You can deduct the cost of all the materials and supplies you bought during the year for business or investment purposes, even if you have not used them all, provided the unused amount is not excessive.[43] Keep in mind that if you are an employee or in an investment activity, your deductions are Miscellaneous Itemized Deductions and must be reduced by two percent of Adjusted Gross Income on Schedule A (Form 1040). So toward the end of the year, it's a good idea to compare your employee and investment expenses to your expected AGI. If the expenses exceed two percent of AGI, go out and buy some stuff. If you know your employee and investment expenses will not be more than two percent of AGI, put off your purchases until next year.

Telephone Services

Telephones themselves are seven-year depreciable personal property, the treatment of which is discussed above. With respect to the monthly phone bill, IRC Section 262(b) denies a deduction under any IRC section for any charge (including taxes) required to be paid to obtain local telephone service for your first residential phone line. Beyond the basic cost of your first line, any amount spent for business or investment related phone service is deductible,[44] and is not limited by Section 280A.[45] This includes business or investment related long-distance calls on your first line, call waiting, call forwarding, and all costs relating to an additional line used only for business.

Meals and Entertainment

These are deductions that taxpayers have always tried to stretch to the limit— and the IRS has always been there tugging back the other way. Congress has imposed substantial limitations over the years to quell the bickering. The problem is, business expenses cannot be primarily personal,[46] and it is sometimes difficult to know whether a taxpayer is entertaining clients who happen to be friends or entertaining friends who happen to be clients. Because of the inherently personal aspects of these expenses, much tighter rules apply to them than apply to business expenses in general.

Meal and entertainment expenses must be ordinary and necessary, and meet the criteria of all other business expenses under IRC Section 162 (see Chapter 1). In addition, entertainment expenses (including entertainment-related meals) must meet one of the following two tests:

1. They must be directly related to the active conduct of your business, or
2. They must precede or follow a substantial and bona fide business discussion and be associated with the active conduct of your business.[47]

The Directly-Related Test

Generally this test is met if you can show the following:

1. The primary purpose of the combined business and entertainment was the conduct of business,

2. You had the expectation of getting some specific business benefit, al-though a business benefit need not actually result, and

3. During the entertainment period you engaged in some kind of business meeting or discussion with the client in order to pursue the expected business benefit.[48]

Because directly related expenses are incurred for the purpose of conducting business, the entertainment should take place in a clear business setting. Entertainment is generally not considered directly related when it takes place in an area of substantial distractions, like a nightclub, theater, sporting event, cocktail party, or country club.

The Associated Test

Expenses that do not meet the directly related test might meet this test. Generally, entertainment that directly precedes or follows a substantial business discussion is associated with your business if there is a clear business purpose for the expense. The purpose may be to obtain new business or to encourage the continuation of an existing business relationship.[49] If you are entertaining people who are not closely connected with a person who engaged in the substantial business discussion, the expenses allocable to them are not deductible. It is generally okay to deduct the expenses allocable to the spouse of the person who engaged in the discussion, however.

SUBSTANTIAL BUSINESS DISCUSSION

Whether a meeting, negotiation, or discussion constitutes a "substantial and bona fide business discussion" depends on the facts of each case.[50] The meeting does not have to be for any specific length of time, and there need not be more time devoted to the business discussion than to the entertainment. But the primary purpose of the combined business and entertainment activity should be the business discussion.

DIRECTLY BEFORE OR AFTER A BUSINESS DISCUSSION

Entertainment that occurs on the same day as a substantial business discussion will be considered to directly precede or follow the discussion.[51] If the entertainment and the business discussion are not on the same day, the facts of each case must be considered to see if the associated test is met. Factors that can be taken into account are whether you or your business associates are from out of town, and if so, the date of arrival and departure. For example, if a group of business associates comes from out of town to hold a substantial business discussion, and you entertain them and their spouses on the evening before the discussion, the expenses meet the associated test. They would also meet the test if the entertainment took place on the evening of the day following the business discussion.[52]

Which Costs Are Deductible?

MEALS AS A FORM OF ENTERTAINMENT

You can deduct the cost of meals you provide customers or clients, (and their spouses) as long as they satisfy one of the above deductibility tests. You (or an employee) must be present at the meal,[53] so your meal is also deductible. The law provides that such meals must not be "lavish or extravagant," but expenses will not be disallowed just because the meals take place at deluxe restaurants, hotels, nightclubs, or resorts. Something you cannot do is join a group of business acquaintances for lunch on a regular basis, and take turns picking up the check to deduct as entertainment.[54]

CLUB DUES

The Code says "no deduction shall be allowed . . . for amounts paid or incurred for membership in any club organized for business, pleasure, recreation, or other social purpose."[55] That seems to pretty much cover the gamut of clubs, although the IRS will probably not disallow dues to clubs that are primarily for public service or volunteerism, such as Kiwanis, Lions, Rotary, and so on, if there is a business purpose for being a member. Also, even though the dues are not deductible, actual entertainment at a club is deductible if it meets one of the deductibility tests.

TICKETS AND SKYBOXES

If you buy tickets to an entertainment event, like a basketball game or play, you can only deduct the face value of the tickets, regardless of how much you have to pay to get them.[56] That means you cannot deduct service fees to ticket agencies or any excess payments to scalpers. This limitation applies before the 50 percent limit discussed next.

Different rules apply when the cost of a ticket to a sports event benefits a charitable organization. You can deduct the full price of the ticket, even if it is more than the face value, if the event is mainly to benefit a qualified charity, the entire proceeds of the event go to the charity, and the event uses volunteers to perform substantially all the event's work.[57] As an extra bonus, you do not have to reduce the cost of the tickets by 50 percent like other entertainment expenses.[58]

If you rent a skybox at a sports arena for more than one event, your deduction is limited to the price of regular nonluxury box seat tickets.[59] This limitation applies before the 50 percent limit. If the bill for food and beverages in the skybox is separately stated, these costs can be deducted in addition, as long as they meet one of the deductibility tests.

BUSINESS GIFTS

Business gifts are deductible to the extent of $25 per donee per year.[60] If you give out items that cost $4 or less that have your name printed on them, like pens, magnets, or desk sets, they are not included in the $25 limit for business gifts. Business gifts are not treated the same as entertainment expenses because they are not subject to the 50 percent limitation. Therefore, if an item could be considered either a gift or entertainment, you have to determine what to call it. Generally you can choose whatever classification is most advantageous.[61]

The 50 Percent Limitation

In 1993 the party poopers in Washington decided you should only be allowed to deduct 50 percent of your meal and entertainment expenses.[62] Before that you could deduct 80 percent. This reduction applies to employees or their employers, and to self-employed persons or their clients, depending on whether the expenses are reimbursed. If the expenses are reimbursed, then the limitation applies to the one who is doing the reimbursing rather than the one who incurred the expense. In other words, for a single expense, the reduction applies only once, and is assigned to the one who ultimately pays for the meals or entertainment. (See Example 8.11.)

Example 8.11

Judy is a self-employed literary agent for Bob, who wrote a book. Judy adequately accounts for meals and entertainment expenses to clients who reimburse her for those expenses. Judy entertained some publishing executives to discuss Bob's book, and spent $500. Bob's reimbursement to Judy is included in her income, and she can deduct the full $500. Bob's deduction for his reimbursement to Judy is reduced by 50 percent.

The 50 percent reduction applies to all meals, whether incurred as travel costs or entertainment. The limitation does not apply to other travel expenses, such as lodging and transportation.

Free Meals and Lodging for You and the Whole Family?!

There is a rumor circulating among some home-office workers that the Internal Revenue Code allows a deduction for meals consumed by the worker and the worker's family at the home owned by the worker. Rumor also has it that there is an additional deduction for the cost of lodging for the whole family if one is clever enough to take advantage of it. Forget it—these deductions do not exist.

Section 119 of the Code is the source of the rumors. Section 119 is actually an exclusion section rather than a deduction section. It allows an employee to exclude from gross income the value of meals and lodging provided by an employer. The requirements are that the meals and lodging be provided for the convenience of the employer, and be furnished on the employer's business premises. In the case of lodging, the employee is required to accept such lodging on the business premises of the employer as a condition of employment.[63]

For anyone who is self-employed, this is nothing special—they don't include the value of their meals and lodging in their income anyway. This provision is only an advantage if a home-based worker, as his or her own employer, can also deduct the cost of the meals and lodging as a business expense. Meals and lodging are generally considered an ordinary and necessary business expense only if they are incurred in traveling away from home on business, or in entertaining clients or customers. The costs of meals at home and maintaining the family residence are not considered ordinary and necessary business expenses, and are not deductible.

What if you were doing business as a partnership or S corporation, the business entity owned the residence in which you lived and required you to reside there as a condition of employment? In this case, could the partnership or S corporation take advantage of Section 119 by deducting your meals and the costs of maintaining the home, while allowing you to avoid income? In one court case, the owner of an S corporation was a rancher who lived in a house on the ranch owned by the S corporation. The S corporation tried to deduct the rancher's home heating costs, costs of groceries, telephone and electricity costs, and depreciation on the house, and the rancher tried to exclude the same costs from income under Section 119. Had this rancher been successful in this, ranchers everywhere would organize as S corporations and deduct their living expenses. The court noted this, and said:

> This would hardly be a fair result unless all business owners who must live in the city to be near their business for a variety of reasons were allowed to deduct their food and lodging expenses as well. Such a result is unthinkable and this Court will not construe the [Internal Revenue Code] to reach this outcome.[64]

Business Liability Insurance

If you have business insurance separate from the amount that covers your dwelling unit, such as coverage for professional liability or damage to business property and inventory, the premiums are not limited by Section 280A because they do not relate to the dwelling unit. If you are self-employed, the premiums are deductible on Schedule C (line 15) or Schedule F (line 22). If you have paid the premiums for one or two years in advance, the IRS says you can only deduct the amount of the premium that is applicable to the current year.[65] The First Circuit Court of Appeals[66] and the Tax Court[67] both say the same thing. However, the Eighth Circuit Court of Appeals says that a cash method taxpayer can deduct the amount paid during the year, even if it relates to one or two future years, as long as it is done consistently from year to year.[68] The Eighth Circuit Court said:

> The taxpayer has uniformly . . . charged all insurance premiums paid as a business expense in the year paid. This appears to be an entirely proper procedure under the cash method of accounting.[69]

If you are on the cash method and have prepaid business insurance premiums, deduct them when paid if the amount is not substantial and you do not live within the jurisdiction of the First Circuit Court of Appeals.[70] You have adequate authority to do this. Even if the amount is substantial, if you happen to live within the jurisdiction of the Eighth Circuit Court of Appeals, you can probably thumb your nose at the IRS on this one; they are not going to go to court. (The Eighth Circuit takes in Minnesota, North Dakota, South Dakota, Nebraska, Arkansas, Missouri, and Iowa.) Be aware, however, that if you live anywhere else in the country, or you are using an accrual method of accounting, the IRS has adequate authority to make you amortize the premiums.

Health Insurance and Medical Savings Accounts

Because employees can exclude the cost of health insurance paid for by their employers, it only seems fair to permit self-employed individuals to deduct their health insurance premiums as a business expense above the line (that is, in arriving at adjusted gross income). Prior to 2003, however, such was not the case. Self-employed people could claim only part of the health insurance premiums for themselves, their spouses, and their dependents as a business expense, subject to additional limitations. The balance of the premiums could be claimed as an itemized deduction on Schedule A, where the deduction was subject to the 7.5 percent of AGI reduction for medical expenses.

For 1995 and 1996 the maximum business deduction allowed was 30 percent of the premiums. The deduction increased to 40 percent of premiums in 1997, and to 45 percent in 1998. Under the Tax and Trade Relief Extension Act of 1998, the above-the-line percentage for 1999 through 2001 was 60 percent. The percentage deductible above the line increased to 70 percent in 2002 and is 100 percent in 2003 and later. Health insurance premiums for both medical and dental may be included, as well as eligible long-term care insurance premiums. These percentages are also available to partners of partnerships and shareholders of S corporations who own more than two percent of the stock.[71]

Additional Limitations

The deduction is only permitted to the extent it does not exceed your net earned income from your business. Also, it is not available for any calendar month you were eligible to participate in any subsidized health plan maintained by an employer of you or your spouse.[72] The deduction is claimed on page one of Form 1040, because it is not allowed to reduce your net income on Schedule C for the purpose of self-employment tax. Any amount you do not deduct on page one is deductible on Schedule A (Form 1040). But be sure not to claim a deduction for the same amount on page one and on Schedule A.

Eligible Long-Term Care Premiums

The self-employed health insurance deduction also applies to "eligible long-term care" insurance premiums. The deductibility of long-term care services and long-term care insurance premiums were new medical expense deductions beginning in 1997.[73] The annual deductible long-term care insurance premiums are limited according to the taxpayer's age and are adjusted each year for inflation. For those not over 40 by the end of the year, the annual limit for 2002 is $240; for ages 41 through 50 the amount is $450; for ages 51 through 60 it is $900; for ages 61 through 70, $2,390; and for taxpayers 71 or older the limit is $2,990.[74] These are per individual limitations rather than per return. So if spouses over 70 have both paid long-term care insurance premiums in 2002, up to $5,980 can qualify as a deductible amount on their joint return. If you are planning to buy long-term care insurance, make sure the policy qualifies under the tax law. Your agent should provide you with this information.

An Advantage of Employing Your Spouse

If you are self-employed, any amount of your medical insurance premiums you cannot deduct under the above rules must be deducted as a medical expense on Schedule A. There it is reduced by 7.5 percent of your AGI, which usually doesn't leave much left to deduct.

An employee who is a participant in an employer-provided health care plan gets a better deal. The employee does not include in income amounts paid by the employer to reimburse the employee (directly or indirectly) for medical care of the employee, his or her spouse, and any of the employee's dependents.[75] Also, any health insurance premiums paid by the employer for the employee's coverage under a health plan are not considered income to the employee.[76] Payments by the employer for health coverage of an employee and his or her family are deductible by the employer as ordinary and necessary business expenses under IRC Section 162. This means they escape the 7.5 percent reduction.

With all this in mind, think about how you could maximize your deduction for your family's medical care by hiring your spouse. Let's say you are self-employed and do not have health care coverage. You hire your spouse as your only employee. Let's assume that there is no question about the bona fide employer-employee relationship between you and your spouse. Your spouse receives from you compensation for services he or she performs (which is deductible on your Schedule C), and includes the compensation as gross income on your jointly filed tax return. (This is a wash—it does not change your Adjusted Gross Income.) You also adopt a written employer-provided accident and health plan that, by its terms, covers all employees of your business. During the year, you reimburse your spouse under the plan for medical expenses incurred on behalf of the spouse, his or her spouse (which is you), and their dependents (which are your kids). You deduct the medical reimbursements to your spouse on Schedule C as a business expense under Section 162. By doing this you completely avoid the 7.5 percent of AGI reduction on Schedule A.

Do you think the IRS would go along with this? No problem. In a recent technical advice memorandum[77] sharing the same facts, the IRS ruled that the amounts paid to the husband-employee under the plan as reimbursement for medical expenses are deductible as a business expense under Section 162. The Service further ruled that the husband-employee may exclude the reimbursements from gross income.[78] The ruling was premised on the fact that there was a legitimate employer-employee relationship between the couple—it was not just a scheme cooked up to maximize their medical expense deduction. See a knowledgeable health insurance agent if you want to set this up.

Medical Savings Accounts

The Health Insurance Portability and Accountability Act of 1996 added a new section to the Code[79] to allow eligible individuals to establish medical savings accounts (MSAs) under a pilot program beginning in 1997. The purpose of the provision is to encourage taxpayers to purchase high-deductible medical insurance and provide for the co-payments through tax deductible savings accounts. This will provide taxpayers with lower health insurance premiums and permit them to deduct the co-payment costs in full. It is hoped this will make Americans more cost conscious in purchasing medical services, thereby slowing the growth in the overall costs of health care.

Generally, to be eligible for an MSA, you must either be self-employed (or the spouse of someone who is) or be employed by a small employer (50 or fewer employees). You also must be covered by a high-deductible health plan. If you are eligible, you can arrange for the establishment of an MSA without waiting for IRS approval, and any insurance company or bank can be a qualified MSA custodian.

Contributions to the MSA can be made by either you or your employer, and are deductible (if made by you) or excludable (if made by your employer) from your gross income. Earnings from the MSA are exempt from tax as long as the account remains an MSA,[80] and distributions from an MSA are excluded from income if used for qualified medical expenses.[81] Distributions not used for qualified medical expenses are subject to regular tax and an additional 15 percent penalty. The penalty does not apply to distributions after you have turned 65, died, or become disabled.[82]

A HIGH DEDUCTIBLE HEALTH PLAN

A "high deductible health plan" is defined as a plan with an annual deductible between \$1,650 and \$2,500 for individuals and between \$3,300 and \$4,950 for families in 2002.[83] The annual out-of-pocket expenses required to be paid (other than for premiums) for covered benefits must not exceed \$3,300 for self-coverage and \$6,050 for family coverage in 2002.[84] All of these dollar amounts are indexed annually for a cost-of-living adjustment.

DEDUCTION LIMITATIONS

The amount allowable as a deduction to an individual for contributions to an MSA is generally 65 percent of the annual deductible under the coverage if the individual has self-only coverage. The amount is 75 percent of the deductible if an individual has the whole family covered.[85] An employee covered by an employer plan is not taxed on employer MSA contributions of up to the MSA deduction limit applicable to the individual.[86]

Wages for Home-Office Workers

Wages paid for cleaning and repair work in your home office are subject to the Section 280A limitations. However, wages for regular office work are business expenses that are not related to the dwelling unit, so they go directly on Schedule C (Form 1040) or Schedule F (Form 1040) and are not reported on Form 8829.[87]

Pay Your Kid to Clean Up Your Room

In addition to employing your spouse, discussed above, there are advantages to putting your child to work in your home office. If your child does cleaning and repair work in the home office, his or her wages would be a direct home-office expense. You could also pay your kid a reasonable amount for answering the phone, doing filing, keeping the books, or other business-related chores. These wages are business expenses, but would not be related to your home office, and would not be reported on Form 8829.[88] As long as they are reasonable (about what you would pay an unrelated individual) they are deductible, even if you do not qualify for home-office deductions. Report these wages on line 26 of Schedule C (Form 1040), or line 24 of Schedule F (Form 1040). You do not have to withhold Social Security tax if your child is under 18,[89] and wages of up to $4,700 (in 2002) received by a dependent child will be offset by the child's standard deduction.

Retirement Plans for the Self-Employed

Through a retirement plan you get tax advantages for setting aside money for your retirement, and for the retirement of your employees, if you have any. The Economic Growth and Tax Relief Reconciliation Act of 2001 (EGTRRA) significantly expanded the deferral benefits available under retirement plans for 2002 and beyond. This section provides a brief explanation of the benefits for the self-employed. For a more detailed discussion of the rules, see IRS Publication 560, *Retirement Plans for Small Business* and IRS Publication 590, *Individual Retirement Arrangements.*

As a sole proprietor, you can set up a simplified employee pension (SEP), a Keogh plan, or a Savings Incentive Match Plan for Employees (SIMPLE). A Keogh plan can also be set up by a partnership, but not by the individual partners. SEP and SIMPLE plans can be set up by a sole proprietor, a partnership, an S corporation, or a C corporation.

Contributions to these plans are deductible, and the earnings on them remain tax free, until you receive distributions from the plan in later years. Generally, a 10 percent early withdrawal penalty applies if you take the money out before you are 59½ years old, but there are exceptions.

Each of these plans requires you to make contributions for eligible employees. You can avoid making retirement contributions for your employees if you simply set up an individual retirement account (IRA) for yourself (and your spouse), but the maximum amount that you can put away each year is much lower for an IRA.

Simplified Employee Pensions

A SEP is a written plan that allows you to make contributions directly to an individual retirement arrangement (SEP-IRA) that is owned by you, and separate accounts owned by each of your employees. You can deduct as much as 25 percent of your net earnings from self-employment beginning in 2002 (up from 15 percent in 2001) up to a maximum of $200,000 of self-employment income in 2002. The compensation limit is increased for inflation after 2002. Your net earnings from self-employment for this purpose are computed with the deduction you get for one-half of your self-employment tax, and the deduction for the contribution to the SEP. That means the real percentage for your contributions on net income after the self-employment tax deduction is 20 percent.

You must involve your employees if you set up a SEP. The contributions for employees must generally be the same percentage of their wages as you make for yourself.[90] Prior to 1997, a SEP could have been designed for certain small businesses so that employees could fund all or part of their own contributions through a salary reduction arrangement (SARSEP).[91] An employer is no longer allowed to establish a SARSEP after 1996. However, participants (including new ones) in a SARSEP established before 1997 can continue to elect to have their employer contribute part of their pay to the plan. Employees who participate may elect to have contributions made to the SEP as a reduction of their salary (called an elective deferral), or take the amount in cash. Elective deferrals cannot exceed $11,000 in 2002. The limitation on elective deferrals increases $1,000 per year to $15,000 in 2006, and is then increased each year for inflation.

Whether you have employees or not, this is something you will need professional help with. There are a lot of financial institutions that will help you set up and administer a SEP.

Keogh Plans

Although setting up a Keogh plan is more involved, it has the advantage of providing greater benefits than a SEP. The two basic kinds of Keogh plans are defined contribution plans and defined benefit plans.

DEFINED CONTRIBUTION PLANS

A defined contribution plan does not fix a specific retirement benefit, but rather, sets the amount of annual contributions so that the amount of retirement benefits depends on contributions and income earned on those contributions. If contributions are geared to company profits, the plan is a profit-sharing plan. A plan that requires fixed contributions regardless of profits is a money-purchase plan. You can be more flexible in making contributions to a profit-sharing plan than to a money purchase plan or a defined benefit plan, but the maximum contributions may be less under a profit-sharing plan, which has the same limits as a SEP.

For a money-purchase plan you can generally contribute and deduct for yourself 20 percent of net earnings from self-employment up to $200,000 for 2002.[92] The 20 percent is after considering the contribution (it is 25 percent before considering the contribution). The deduction limit for employees is the lesser of $40,000 or 100 percent of their taxable compensation. You must comply with a complicated set of nondiscrimination rules for employee contributions. Also, employee contributions must be fixed and not based on the employer's net profit. For 2002 and beyond, a plan can permit participants who are age 50 or over at the end of the year to also make catch-up contributions. The catch-up contribution limit for 2002 is $1,000, and it goes up $1,000 per year thereafter until it reaches $5,000 in 2006. After that it is adjusted for inflation.

DEFINED BENEFIT PLANS

Defined benefit plans fix a specific retirement benefit that is payable regardless of the amount of contribution or income earned on the contribution. Contributions to defined benefit plans are based on actuarial assumptions on what is needed to provide specific future benefits to the plan participants.

You can get help setting up and administering a Keogh from banks, mutual funds, insurance companies, and trade or professional organizations. They act as plan providers, and can provide IRS-approved master or prototype plans.

The Savings Incentive Match Plan for Employees (SIMPLE)

The SIMPLE plan was authorized by the Small Business Job Protection Act of 1996. Congress wanted to encourage small business owners to adopt retirement plans by making the rules much simpler than the rules that apply to qualified plans in general. Beginning in 1997, this plan allows you to contribute to a retirement account on behalf of each employee, including yourself, under the following rules. The SIMPLE plan

1. Can be used only by an employer with 100 or fewer employees who received at least $5,000 of compensation from the employer for the preceding year. As a self-employed individual, you are considered an employee;

2. Can be established as an IRA or as part of a Section 401(k) plan;

3. Allows each employee to elect to contribute a percentage of his or her compensation to the SIMPLE plan under a salary reduction arrangement. The contribution is indexed for inflation and cannot exceed $7,000 in 2002. The limit increases by $1,000 each year after 2002 until it reaches $10,000 in 2005. After that it is increased for inflation. Catch-up contributions are also allowed for participants over 50 at the end of the year. For 2002 the catch-up contribution limit is $500. The limit increases by $500 each year after that until it reaches $2,500 in 2006. It is then increased each year for inflation.

4. Requires the employer to match employee's contributions on a dollar-for-dollar basis, up to 3 percent of compensation, or the employer may elect to make a 2 percent non-elective contribution on behalf of all eligible employees; and,

5. Must be the only retirement plan of the employer.

Whether it is established in IRA form or as part of a Section 401(k) plan, a SIMPLE plan is not subject to the complex reporting and nondiscrimination rules that are generally applicable to qualified plans. Distributions from a simple plan are generally taxed under the rules for IRAs, except that an increased early withdrawal penalty (25 percent rather than 10 percent) applies to distributions within the first two years you participate in the plan.

New Options for Individual Retirement Arrangements (IRAs)

THE TRADITIONAL IRA

Whether you are an employee or self-employed, you can set up and make contributions to a deductible IRA if you received taxable compensation during the year and were under 70½ years of age at the end of the year.[93] Compensation generally includes any kind of personal service income, including self-employment income, as well as taxable alimony and separate maintenance payments received.[94] Your allowable contributions to an IRA are deductible (subject to the limitations described below), and the earnings on the contributions are not taxable until withdrawn. There is generally a 10 percent penalty for withdrawing any of the funds before you are 59½ years old.[95]

The 2001 tax act, EGTRRA, increases the amount that you can contribute to an IRA. In 2002, the amount is the lesser of $3,000 or your taxable compensation. The limit increases to $4,000 to 2005 through 2007, and $5,000 for 2008 and beyond. If you file a joint return, you can make a contribution of up to the same dollar limit to the IRA of each spouse, as long as you don't contribute more than the total compensation of both of you.[96] Catch-up contributions to an IRA are also available for individuals 50 and older. The additional amount that can be contributed and deducted is $500 for 2002 through 2005, and $1,000 for 2006 and later.[97]

The amount of your contributions you can deduct depends on your adjusted gross income (AGI) if you or your spouse were actively participating in an employer's retirement plan. If neither you nor your spouse participated in an employer's retirement plan, during the year, your IRA contributions are deductible in full regardless of your AGI. The Taxpayer Relief Act of 1997 increases the floor for phasing out IRA deductions for individuals who are active participants in an employer-sponsored retirement plan. For 2002, IRA contributions are deductible in full if your AGI on a joint return is $54,000 or less ($34,000 or less if you are single), and the limit is increased annually to $80,000 for years after 2006 ($50,000 for years after 2004 if you are single).[98] In 2002 there is a phase-out of the deduction between $54,000 and $64,000 of AGI ($34,000 and $44,000 if single). Also under the '97 Act, the above limits on deductible IRA contributions no longer apply to an individual who is not an active participant in a pension plan but whose spouse is. For these people, the maximum deductible IRA contribution is not phased out until their AGI (combined with that of their spouse) is greater than $150,000.[99] The law also provides for waiver of the 10 percent early withdrawal penalty on up to $10,000 of IRA funds used by first-time home buyers, and on funds used to pay for higher education expenses.[100]

THE ROTH IRA

Probably the most significant IRA development from the Taxpayer Relief Act of 1997 was the introduction of the Roth IRA (named for Senator William Roth, chair of the Senate Finance Committee).[101] Joint filers can now make annual nondeductible contributions of up to the same contribution limits for traditional IRAs (minus their other IRA contributions) if their AGI is $150,000 or less. The allowable contribution is phased out for AGI up to $160,000. The contribution that can be made by single individuals is phased out for AGI between $95,000 and $110,000. Active participation in a qualified plan does not matter. The benefit of the Roth IRA is that earnings accumulate tax-free, and qualified distributions are completely non-taxable. Distributions are qualified if they are made after the account holder is 59½ years old, deceased, disabled, or is paying expenses (up to $10,000) in connection with a first-time home purchase. However, the Roth IRA must exist for at least five years before any distribution is qualified. If distributions are not qualified, they are only taxable after any contributions are recovered tax-free. Contributions to Roth IRAs for any year, as well as regular IRAs, can be made until April 15 of the following year.

Additional Resources

IRS publications that address topics discussed in this chapter include Publication 334, *Tax Guide for Small Business;* Publication 535, *Business Expenses;* Publication 946, *How to Depreciate Property;* Publication 463, *Travel, Entertainment, Gift, and Car Expenses;* Publication 527, *Residential Rental Property;* Publication 560, *Retirement Plans for the Self-Employed;* and Publication 590, *Individual Retirement Arrangements (IRAs).* IRS Publication 1339, *Highlights of the Job Creation and Worker Assistance Act of 2002,* provides information on depreciation and retirement benefits for 2002 and beyond.

You can get IRS publications free by calling the IRS at (800) TAX-FORM [(800) 829-3676]. If you have access to TTY/TDD equipment, you can call (800) 829-4059. To download them from the Internet, go to *www.irs.gov* (World Wide Web), or *ftp.irs.gov* (FTP). If you would like to get forms and instructions (not publications) by FAX, dial (703) 368-9694 to reach IRS Tax Fax.

As an alternative to downloading files from the Internet, you can order *IRS Federal Tax Products* on CD-ROM. This CD includes over 2,000 tax products, including all of the above publications and forms. It can be ordered by calling

(800) 233-6767. Also, Publication 3207, *Small Business Resource Guide,* is an interactive CD-ROM that contains information important to small businesses. It is available in mid-February. You can get one free copy by calling (800) 829-3676.

Notes

[1] IRC § 62(a)(1); IRC § 67(b).

[2] IRC § 62(a)(4); IRC § 67(b).

[3] Under the Modified Accelerated Cost Recovery System (MACRS) of IRC Section 168.

[4] IRS Publication 946, Table B-1.

[5] IRS Publication 946, Tables B-1 and B-2.

[6] IRC § 168(b)(1).

[7] IRC § 168(d)(4).

[8] IRC § 168(k), added by § 101(a), P.L. 107-147, 3/9/2002.

[9] IRC § 1016(a)(2).

[10] IRC § 6511(a).

[11] IRC § 6513(a).

[12] IRC § 179(d)(2).

[13] IRC § 179(d)(1).

[14] IRC § 179(d)(3).

[15] Reg. § 1.179-1(d).

[16] IRC § 179(b)(1).

[17] IRC § 179(b)(2).

[18] IRC § 179(b)(3).

[19] IRS Publication 534, p. 9.

[20] IRS Publication 534.

[21] IRC § 280F(d)(4).

[22] IRC § 280F(d)(5)(A).

[23] IRC § 280F(d)(5)(B).

[24] Reg. § 1.280F-6T(b)(5).

[25] Reg. § 1.280F-6T(b)(3).

[26] IRS Publication 534, p. 25.

[27] IRC § 280F(b).

[28] From IRS Publication 534, p. 26.

[29] Reg. § 1.179-1(C)(1).

[30] IRC § 280F(d)(3)(A).

[31] LTR 8615024.

[32] Ibid.

[33] *Cadwallader v. Commissioner,* T.C. Memo 1989-356.

[34] IRC § 274(d); Reg. § 1.274-5T(c)(2)(C).

[35] Reg. § 1.274-5T(b)(6).

[36] Reg. § 1.274-5T(c)(3)(ii).

[37] See Instructions to Form 4562.

[38] H Rep No. 93-111 (PL 103-66) p. 767.

[39] IRC § 167(f)(1); H Rep No. 103-111 (PL 103-66) p. 767.

[40] Reg. § 1.162-6; IRC § 212.

[41] Ibid.

[42] IR 86-169.

[43] Reg. § 1.162-3.

[44] *Shepherd v. Commissioner,* T.C. Memo 1976-48; *Barry v. Commissioner,* T.C. Memo 1978-250.

[45] Prop. Reg. § 1.280A-2(i)(7).

[46] IRC § 262.

[47] IRC § 274(a)(1)(A).

[48] Treas. Reg. § 1.274-2(c)(3).

[49] Treas. Reg. § 1.274-2(d)(2).

[50] Treas. Reg. § 1.274-2(d)(3).

[51] Treas. Reg. § 1.274-2(d)(3).

[52] IRS Publication 463, *Travel, Entertainment, Gift, and Car Expenses,* p. 12.

[53] IRC § 274(k)(1)(B).

[54] IRS Publication 463.

[55] IRC § 274(a)(3).

[56] IRC § 274(I).

[57] IRC § 274(I)(1)(B).

[58] IRC § 274(n).

[59] IRC § 274(I)(2).

[60] IRC § 274(b)(1).

[61] IRS Publication 463, p. 14.

[62] IRC § 274(n).

[63] IRC § 119(a).

[64] Dilts v. U.S., 73 AFTR 2d 94-1633, 03/11/1994.

[65] Rev. Rul. 70-413, 1970-2 C.B. 103.

[66] *Commissioner v. Boylston Market Assn.,* 131 F2d 966, 30 AFTR 512 (1st Cir., 1942).

[67] Waldheim Realty & Investment Co., 25 T.C. 1216 (1956), rev'd, 245 F2d 823, 51 AFTR 801 (8th Cir. 1957).

[68] *Waldheim Realty & Investment Co. v. Commissioner,* 245 F2d 823, 51 AFTR 801, (8th Cir. 1957), rev'g 25 T.C. 1216 (1956).

[69] 245 F.2d 823 at 827.

[70] The First Circuit takes in Maine, New Hampshire, Massachusetts, and Rhode Island.

[71] IRC § 162(l)(5).

[72] IRC § 162(l)(2).

[73] IRC § 213(d)(1)(D) and (d)(10).

[74] Rev. Proc. 2001-59, 2001-52 IRB 1.

[75] IRC § 105(b).

[76] IRC § 106.

[77] LTR 9409006, citing Rev. Rul. 71-588, 1971-2 C.B. 91.

[78] Under IRC § 105(b).

[79] IRC § 220.

[80] IRC § 220(e).

[81] IRC § 220(f)(1).

[82] IRC § 220(f)(4).

[83] Rev. Proc. 99-42, 1999-46 IRB.

[84] Rev. Proc. 98-61.

[85] IRC § 220(b)(2).

[86] IRC § 106(b)(1).

[87] *Dollard v. Commissioner,* T.C. Memo 1987-346.

[88] Ibid.

[89] IRC § 3121(b)(3)(A).

[90] IRC § 408(k)(3).

[91] IRC § 408(k)(6).

[92] The limitation under IRC § 401(a)(17) is indexed annually for inflation. Notice 99-55, 1999-49 IRB 638, provides the adjusted amounts for 2000.

[93] IRC § 219.

[94] IRC § 219(f)(1).

[95] IRC § 72(q).

[96] IRC § 219(c), as amended by the Small Business Job Protection Act of 1996.

[97] IRC § 219(b)(5)(B).

[98] IRC § 219(g)(3)(B) as amended by the Taxpayer Relief Act of 1997, Act § 301(a)(1).

[99] IRC § 219(g)(7).

[100] IRC § 72(t).

[101] IRC § 408A, added by the Taxpayer Relief Act of 1997, Act § 302(a).

CHAPTER 9

Other Taxes

> If you get up early,
> work late, and pay
> your taxes, you will
> get ahead—if you
> strike oil.
>
> —J. Paul Getty

When you start a home-based business, it would be nice if you could simply concentrate on making as much profit as possible. Unfortunately, you must also concern yourself with trying to stay out of trouble with city, state, and federal taxing authorities. This chapter discusses the major tax considerations you have as a home-based business owner, apart from your federal income tax return.

State and Local Taxes

One of the first things you should do as a new business owner is to call your state's Department of Revenue and ask them to send you information on all the tax requirements for a small business operating in your state. Your business might be subject to state and local income taxes, franchise taxes, sales taxes, and occupational taxes. If you organize as a C corporation, S corporation, limited liability company, or limited liability partnership (see Chapter 3), you might be subject to entity level taxes by your state government that do not apply at the federal level. If you hire one or more employees, you should contact your state unemployment insurance office to get details about your state unemployment tax obligations (see *Employment Taxes*, later in this chapter). You should also check with City Hall. As more people establish home businesses, cities are increasingly seeing revenue opportunities. Some cities charge business licensing fees, and/or a gross receipts tax.

Self-Employment Tax

Self-employment (SE) tax is what you pay as a self-employed individual to finance your coverage under the Social Security system. SE tax is computed on

Schedule SE, *Self-Employment Tax* (Form 1040). The tax is based on your net earnings from self-employment, and the combined rate is 15.3 percent. The combined rate is the sum of 12.4 percent for Social Security (old-age, survivors, and disability insurance) and 2.9 percent for Medicare (hospital insurance). The maximum amount of earnings from self-employment subject to the Social Security part (12.4 percent) for 2002 is $89,400. All of your net earnings from self-employment are subject to the Medicare part (2.9 percent). If your net earnings from self-employment are less than $400 (less than $108.28 as a church employee) you do not have to pay SE tax.[1]

This tax might be a real eye-popper for some people the first year they have income from their small business. As an employee, your employer generally pays half of your Social Security tax and withholds the other half from your paycheck. As a self-employed person, you are on your own for the whole bill. Because net earnings from self-employment are determined differently than your taxable income, you could have a substantial SE tax liability even when you owe little or no income tax. Your combined obligation for SE tax and income tax on self-employment income should be paid in quarterly estimated payments, explained later in this chapter.

Example 9.1

Ed Nord had self-employment income in 2002 of $30,000. Ed and his wife filed a joint return, and neither one received wages subject to Social Security and Medicare taxes. The Nords have five dependent children and claimed itemized deductions of $9,000 on their 2002 return. The Nords' taxable income is zero, so no income tax is due [$30,000 − $9,000 (itemized deductions) − $21,000 (7 exemptions × $3,000) = $0]. However, they owe Self-Employment tax of $4,239 ($30,000 × 92.35% × 15.3%). The tax is computed on only 92.35 percent of $30,000 because half of the SE tax is deductible. See Example 9.2.

Who Must Pay Self-Employment Tax?

Income received from carrying on a business as a sole proprietor (or independent contractor) or a member of a partnership is generally self-employment income.[2] Your business need not be full time; you could have a small part-time business in addition to your regular job. Any wages you earn reduce the self-employment tax base for retirement and disability benefits, so that you do not pay this amount on more than $89,400 in SE and wage income. See "Computing the SE Tax" on page 207.

You are only subject to the tax on active business income—not on investment income. To determine whether you have business income, the same rules generally apply as for income tax purposes (see Chapter 2). Even if you are retired from your regular job and receiving Social Security benefits, you will still owe SE tax on your self-employment income.

NOT EMPLOYEES, USUALLY

Employees share their Social Security tax obligation (FICA) with their employers so they do not pay SE tax. Sometimes employers try to classify employees as independent contractors to avoid their share of the Social Security tax. On the other side, IRS agents have been known to be overly zealous in trying to reclassify workers as employees.[3] Nevertheless, whether someone is an independent contractor or an employee depends on the facts in each case, not on how their employer classifies them. If an employer misclassifies an employee as an independent contractor, the employer can be held liable for unpaid employment taxes for that worker plus a penalty.

Generally, you are an independent contractor if you are receiving payments from someone who has the right to control or direct only the result of your work, not specifically what you will do or how you will do it. You are generally not an independent contractor if the person paying you controls what you will do and how and when you will do it. This applies even if you are performing the work in your home office. What matters is that the employer has the legal right to control the details of how your services are performed.

The determination of whether you are an employee or are self-employed generally follows the same tests for both income tax and Social Security tax purposes, but there are some differences. Some people are classified as employees for Social Security tax purposes but are self-employed for income tax purposes. Others are treated just the opposite.

STATUTORY EMPLOYEES

For example, if you earned wages as a "statutory employee," you are considered an employee for FICA purposes and do not pay SE tax. A statutory employee is anyone who performs services as an agent-driver or commission-driver, as a full-time life insurance sales representative, as a home worker, or as a traveling or city salesperson, under the conditions stated in the Code.[4] If you are a statutory employee, the box titled "Statutory employee" in box 15 of your Form W-2 (Wage and Tax Statement) that you get from your employer at the end of the year will be checked.

Although your employer withholds Social Security tax from your paycheck, you are not an employee for income tax purpose. You can report your wages on Schedule C (or Schedule C-EZ) and deduct any allowable related expenses.

This avoids having to claim these deductions on Schedule A as employee expenses where they are reduced by 2 percent of your Adjusted Gross Income (AGI).

ORDAINED MINISTERS

Conversely, if you are a duly ordained, commissioned, or licensed minister of a church, you are treated as self-employed for SE tax purposes,[5] but are probably an employee for income tax purposes. That means you must pay SE tax on your net earnings, but cannot use Schedule C or C-EZ to claim related deductions. Your employee expenses must be claimed on Schedule A as itemized deductions, subject to the two percent of AGI reduction.

FORM SS-8

If you are now confused about this and wondering whether you are an employee or self-employed, or are treating workers you hire correctly, get IRS Publication 15-A, *Employer's Supplemental Tax Guide*. This publication has information that helps to determine whether an individual is an employee or independent contractor. If you believe you might be wrongly classified, or might be wrongly classifying your workers, you can get a written determination from the IRS by completing and filing Form SS-8, "Determination of Employee Work Status for Purposes of Federal Employment Taxes and Income Tax Withholding." Either the employer or the worker, or both can complete this form. See "Additional Resources" at the end of this chapter.

PARTNERS

If you are a general partner in a partnership that carries on a trade or business, your distributive share of income or loss from the trade or business is included in your income from self-employment. If you are a limited partner, only guaranteed payments for services performed during the year are included in your self-employment income.[6]

If your partnership is not engaged in a business, then your distributive share of income or loss is not included in your income from self-employment. For example, if you are a member of an investment club partnership that limits its activities to investing in securities and collecting interest and dividends for its members' accounts, the income is not self-employment income.

What Is Not Self-Employment Income

Even if you are self-employed, all the income or loss from your business might not be included in self-employment income. Here are a few things that are not included:

- *Gains and losses.* Gains and losses from property that you are not in the business of selling are not included in self-employment income. Examples are gains and losses from investment property, and depreciable property or other fixed assets used for business.[7]

- *Real estate rent.* Rent from real estate and from personal property leased with the real estate is not self-employment income, unless you receive the income as part of your business as a real estate dealer. If you are a dealer, include the rental income and deductions with your other real estate income on Schedule C or C-EZ (Form 1040). If you are not a real estate dealer, include the income and deductions from rental property on Schedule E (Form 1040).

- *Corporate shareholders.* The only self-employment income you might receive from a corporation is director fees. This is generally income you receive for going to directors' meetings or serving on committees, not compensation for your active involvement in the operation of the corporation.

  Even if you own all the stock of a C corporation, your work performed for the corporation is in the capacity of an employee, and compensation you receive is not self-employment income. It is subject to withholding by the corporation for Social Security and Medicare taxes. If you are a shareholder in an S corporation, your share of the corporation's income is not self-employment income, even though you must report it for income tax purposes. Payments from your S corporation for services are employee wages, subject to withholding by the corporation.

Computing the SE Tax

If you owe SE tax, you must file Form 1040 to report the tax, even if you owe no income tax. SE tax is shown on line 56 of Form 1040, and is computed on Schedule SE (Form 1040). If you file a joint return, you must compute the self-employment income of you and your spouse separately; so if you both have self-employment income you have to file two schedules.

WHAT IS DEDUCTIBLE?

The tax is computed on net earnings from self-employment, which is generally self-employment income reduced by the business deductions that are allowable for income tax. If you have more than one business, combine the net income or loss from each to determine your net earnings from self-employment. Some of the deductions that reduce taxable income for income tax purposes but do not count in determining net income from self-employment are the following:

1. Deductions for personal and dependency exemptions.

2. The standard deduction or itemized deductions.

3. The net operating loss deduction (meaning business losses from other years that are carried to the current year).

4. Contributions on your behalf to a retirement plan, including an IRA.

5. The self-employed health insurance deduction.

For income tax purposes, you can deduct half of your SE tax computed on Schedule SE.[8] This deduction goes on line 29 of Form 1040 rather than on Schedule SE. Instead of allowing this deduction for SE tax purposes (which would create a simultaneous equation), the Code allows you to compute the tax on only 92.35 percent of net earnings from self-employment (100% − 7.65%)

HOW MUCH IS TAXABLE?

The maximum amount that is subject to the 12.4 percent rate is $89,400 in 2002, reduced by any wages you earned that were subject to Social Security tax. All of your net earnings from self-employment are subject to the additional 2.9 percent rate (Medicare). So if your combined wages and net earnings from self-employment were less than $89,400, all of your net self-employment earnings are taxed at 15.3 percent. If net earnings from self-employment are greater than the excess of $89,400 over wages, only the amount equal to the excess is taxed at 15.3 percent; the rest is taxed at 2.9 percent.

The instructions to Schedule SE tell you how to use either the nonfarm or farm optional method to figure the tax if you have a loss or a small amount of income from self-employment and you want to receive credit for Social Security benefit coverage.

Example 9.2

Jeff Ferd had net income from self-employment of $70,000 in 2002, and received $33,200 in wages subject to Social Security and Medicare taxes. Jeff's net earnings from self-employment are $64,645 ($70,000 × 0.9235). The maximum income subject to the 15.3% SE tax rate is $56,200 ($89,400 − $33,200). The tax at 15.3% is $8,598.60. The balance of Jeff's net self-employment earnings is taxed at 2.9%. That amount is $244.91 ($8,445 × 2.9%). That makes Jeff's total SE tax $8,843.51 ($8,598.60 + $244.91). One half of this amount, or $4,421.76, is deductible on line 29 of Form 1040. See the computation on page 2 of Schedule SE in Figure 9.1.

Schedule SE (Form 1040) 2002 — Attachment Sequence No. **17** — Page **2**

Name of person with **self-employment** income (as shown on Form 1040)
Jeff Ferd

Social security number of person with **self-employment** income ▶ 999 : 88 : 7777

Section B—Long Schedule SE

Part I Self-Employment Tax

Note. If your only income subject to self-employment tax is **church employee income,** skip lines 1 through 4b. Enter -0- on line 4c and go to line 5a. Income from services you performed as a minister or a member of a religious order **is not** church employee income. See page SE-1.

A If you are a minister, member of a religious order, or Christian Science practitioner **and** you filed Form 4361, but you had $400 or more of **other** net earnings from self-employment, check here and continue with Part I. . . . ▶ ☐

1	Net farm profit or (loss) from Schedule F, line 36, and farm partnerships, Schedule K-1 (Form 1065), line 15a. **Note.** Skip this line if you use the farm optional method. See page SE-3 .	1		
2	Net profit or (loss) from Schedule C, line 31; Schedule C-EZ, line 3; Schedule K-1 (Form 1065), line 15a (other than farming); and Schedule K-1 (Form 1065-B), box 9. Ministers and members of religious orders, see page SE-1 for amounts to report on this line. See page SE-2 for other income to report. **Note.** Skip this line if you use the nonfarm optional method. See page SE-3.	2	70,000	
3	Combine lines 1 and 2	3	70,000	
4a	If line 3 is more than zero, multiply line 3 by 92.35% (.9235). Otherwise, enter amount from line 3	4a	64,645	
b	If you elect one or both of the optional methods, enter the total of lines 15 and 17 here .	4b		
c	Combine lines 4a and 4b. If less than $400, **do not** file this schedule; you do not owe self-employment tax. **Exception.** If less than $400 and you had **church employee income,** enter -0- and continue ▶	4c	64,645	
5a	Enter your **church employee income** from Form W-2. **Caution.** See page SE-1 for definition of church employee income . . .	5a		
b	Multiply line 5a by 92.35% (.9235). If less than $100, enter -0- . .	5b		
6	**Net earnings from self-employment.** Add lines 4c and 5b	6	64,645	
7	Maximum amount of combined wages and self-employment earnings subject to social security tax or the 6.2% portion of the 7.65% railroad retirement (tier 1) tax for 2002	7	84,900	00
8a	Total social security wages and tips (total of boxes 3 and 7 on Form(s) W-2) and railroad retirement (tier 1) compensation	8a	20,000	
b	Unreported tips subject to social security tax (from Form 4137, line 9)	8b		
c	Add lines 8a and 8b	8c	20,000	
9	Subtract line 8c from line 7. If zero or less, enter -0- here and on line 10 and go to line 11 . ▶	9	56,200	
10	Multiply the **smaller** of line 6 or line 9 by 12.4% (.124)	10	6,968	80
11	Multiply line 6 by 2.9% (.029)	11	1,874	71
12	**Self-employment tax.** Add lines 10 and 11. Enter here and on **Form 1040, line 56** . .	12	8,843	51
13	**Deduction for one-half of self-employment tax.** Multiply line 12 by 50% (.5). Enter the result here and on **Form 1040, line 29** .	13		

Part II Optional Methods To Figure Net Earnings (See page SE-3.)

Farm Optional Method. You may use this method **only** if:
Your gross farm income[1] was not more than $2,400 **or**
Your net farm profits[2] were less than $1,733.

14	Maximum income for optional methods	14	1,600	00
15	Enter the **smaller** of: two-thirds (²⁄₃) of gross farm income[1] (not less than zero) **or** $1,600. Also include this amount on line 4b above	15		

Nonfarm Optional Method. You may use this method **only** if:
Your net nonfarm profits[3] were less than $1,733 and also less than 72.189% of your gross nonfarm income[4] **and**
You had net earnings from self-employment of at least $400 in 2 of the prior 3 years.
Caution. You may use this method no more than five times.

16	Subtract line 15 from line 14	16		
17	Enter the **smaller** of: two-thirds (²⁄₃) of gross nonfarm income[4] (not less than zero) **or** the amount on line 16. Also include this amount on line 4b above	17		

[1]From Sch. F, line 11, and Sch. K-1 (Form 1065), line 15b. [3]From Sch. C, line 31; Sch. C-EZ, line 3; Sch. K-1 (Form 1065), line 15a; and Sch. K-1 (Form 1065-B), box 9.
[2]From Sch. F, line 36, and Sch. K-1 (Form 1065), line 15a. [4]From Sch. C, line 7; Sch. C-EZ, line 1; Sch. K-1 (Form 1065), line 15c; and Sch. K-1 (Form 1065-B), box 9.

Schedule SE (Form 1040) 2002

FIGURE 9.1

Federal Estimated Tax Payments

Even though your final tax liability cannot be determined until you file your income tax return at the end of the year, the government wants you to pay your taxes in installments throughout the year. This requires you to estimate the amount of tax (including alternative minimum tax and self-employment tax) you expect to owe for the year, after subtracting tax credits and tax withheld by employers. If you are required to make estimated tax payments, and do not send in enough each quarter by the due date, you might be charged a penalty, even though you are due a refund when you file your tax return. Corporations, as well as individuals, are required to make estimated tax payments.

General Rules for Individuals

You might owe an underpayment penalty if you did not pay, in the form of withholding and/or equal quarterly estimated payments, at least the smaller of:

- 90 percent of the tax shown on your tax return for the current year; or
- 100 percent of the tax shown on your tax return for the preceding year.

The tax shown on your return means all taxes you were required to pay, reduced only by the earned income credit and the credit for federal tax paid on fuels; not your withholding and estimated tax payments.

Higher income individuals are required to pay a higher percentage based on the preceding year to avoid an estimated tax underpayment penalty. If your adjusted gross income (AGI) on your 2001 return exceeded $150,000 ($75,000 for married taxpayers filing separately) your required annual payment in figuring 2002 estimated tax is the lesser of 90 percent of the tax for 2002 or 112 percent of the tax for 2001. The preceding year tax percentage goes down to 110 percent for years after 2001.[9]

You will not owe a penalty if you had no tax liability for the preceding year, and you were a U.S. citizen or resident for the entire year. Also, you will not be penalized for any year in which the tax liability shown on your return, minus withholding, is less than $1,000 for years after 1997 ($500 for prior years).[10]

General Rule for Corporations

A corporation is generally subject to an underpayment penalty if it has a tax liability of $500 or more for the current year and did not timely pay, in quarterly installments, at least the smaller of:

- 100 percent of the tax liability on its current year return; or
- 100 percent of the tax liability on its preceding year return.[11]

The preceding year is only taken into account if the corporation filed a return for the preceding year showing at least some tax liability.

Making the Payments

For estimated tax purposes, the year is divided into four payment periods, and each period has a due date. If you do not pay enough tax by each of these due dates, you might owe a penalty. The due dates for a calendar year individual are: April 15 (for the first quarter); June 15 (for the second quarter); September 15 (for the third quarter); and January 15 of the following year (for the fourth quarter).[12] You can skip the fourth quarter payment if you file your return and pay the tax due by January 31.[13]

The first three dates are the same for a calendar year corporation, but the last payment is due on December 15 of the same year.[14] A fiscal year taxpayer uses corresponding dates for his or her taxable year. Due dates are always postponed to the next working day if they fall on a weekend or holiday.

You can use the Estimated Tax Worksheet in the instructions to Form 1040-ES (the payment vouchers) to compute your estimated tax payments for your individual return. To compute corporate estimated tax payments, use Form 1120-W, "Estimated Tax for Corporations."

The simplest and safest way to figure the payments for your individual return is to take the tax liability from your previous year's return, subtract the tax you

---

Example 9.3

Jim and Julie showed a cobined tax liability on their 2002 jointly filed Form 1040 of $13,000 (line 61) before any credit for withholding or estimated taxes. The tax was attributable to income tax on Julie's wages, and income and self-employment tax on Jim's home-based business income. In 2003, Julie expects to pay $9,500 in federal income tax withholding through her employer.

Jim and Julie will avoid underpayment penalties for 2003 if they pay, in equal quarterly installments, enough additional tax to equal 90 percent of their 2003 combined tax liability, or 100 percent of their 2002 tax liability. To be safe, they make four quarterly payments of $875 beginning April 15, 2003. That is $3,500 ($13,000 − $9,500) divided by four.

expect to be withheld during the current year on wages for you and/or your spouse (if filing jointly), and use the difference for your total estimated tax payments. One-fourth of the total should be sent in by the due date for each quarter.

If you discover late in the year that your estimated payments and withholding will not equal at least 90 percent of your tax liability, and you or your spouse are earning wages subject to withholding, the best way to make up the deficit is to request that your (or your spouse's) employer increase the withholding. The penalty for each quarter is computed by assuming your employer withholds income tax proportionately throughout the year, even if it is all taken out of your last paycheck.[15] Your estimated payments, however, are not applied until they are actually paid.

The Penalty

The underpayment penalty charged to individuals and corporations is redetermined by the Treasury each quarter and is tied to the current yield on U.S. government short-term bonds.[16] As of this writing (summer of 2002), the rate is 6 percent for all taxpayers except for large corporations, which are charged 8 percent.[17]

If you failed to make adequate estimated payments, you can compute the underpayment penalty for Form 1040 on Form 2210, "Underpayment of Estimated Tax by Individuals, Estates, and Trusts." The underpayment for corporations is computed on Form 2220, "Underpayment of Estimated Tax by Corporations." You do not have to compute the underpayment penalty if you don't want to (it's complicated). In fact, the IRS encourages you to send your return in and let them calculate the penalty. They will send you a bill, and it will not cost you any more for them to do it as long as your return is filed by the due date, and you pay the penalty by the date specified on the bill. If you want to do this, just leave the penalty line on your return blank (line 69 on Form 1040) and do not file Form 2210 .[18]

If you operate a seasonal business where your income varies quite a bit during the year, you might be able to lower or eliminate some or all of the quarterly penalties by using the annualized income installment method to compute the penalties. See the instructions to Form 2210 or Form 2220. You must complete and file the form to do this.

All or part of an underpayment will be waived if the IRS determines that the underpayment was due to a casualty, disaster, or other unusual circumstance, and it would be inequitable to impose the penalty.[19] If you wish to request a waiver, you must complete and file Form 2210 (or Form 2220) and follow the instructions for requesting a waiver. Don't count on much sympathy from the IRS unless your excuse is a pretty good one.

Employment Taxes

Most home-based business owners work solo; but if you have the need and desire for an employee, and a place to put one, you should first learn about your employment tax obligations. You might also go out and buy an extra filing cabinet to handle all the paperwork.

Employer Identification Number (EIN)

Your EIN is like your business's Social Security number. You generally don't need an EIN if you are a sole proprietor without employees or a deferred compensation plan. But if you are considering hiring an employee you should get one. You are required to have an EIN if you:

1. Have employees;
2. Have a Keogh plan;
3. Operate your business as a corporation or partnership; or
4. File any of these tax returns:
   a) Employment,
   b) Excise, or
   c) Alcohol, tobacco, and firearms.

You can get an EIN by filling out Form SS-4, "Application for Employer Identification Number," and sending it in. It will take at least four or five weeks to get the number. A quicker way is to apply over the phone. To find the local phone number to call, either look in the instructions to Form SS-4, or call the IRS at (800) 829-1040, and ask for the entity control phone number for your area. If you apply by phone you will get your number immediately.

Tax Withholding

Your employees should fill out Form W-4, "Employee's Withholding Allowance Certificate," when starting work. You will use the filing status and withholding allowances shown on this form to figure the amount of income tax to withhold. Then you need to get IRS Publication 15, *Circular E, Employer's Tax Guide*, to calculate the proper withholding.

Social Security and Medicare taxes are generally levied on both you and your employees. You must withhold and deposit the employees' part, and pay a matching amount. The deposits for withheld income and Social Security tax are reported on Form 941, and are generally made quarterly. See Publication 15 for the details on when and where to send the deposits.

If you operate your home-based business as a sole proprietor, and you employ your child who is under 18, the child's wages will not be subject to Social

Security and Medicare taxes.[20] Also, wages of your child who is under the age of 21 are not subject to federal unemployment taxes (FUTA). These exemptions apply only to your child—just any kid will not do. In addition, the employment must be directly by you, the parent. If the child is employed by a partnership or corporation, even if controlled by you, the exemptions will not apply.

Federal Unemployment (FUTA) Tax

The federal unemployment tax pays unemployment compensation to workers who lose their jobs. The FUTA tax rate is 6.2 percent through 2007,[21] and the federal wage base is $7,000.[22] Most employers pay both a federal and a state unemployment tax. Your state wage base may be different. You should contact your state unemployment insurance offices to receive your state reporting number, state experience rate, and details about your state unemployment tax obligations. The federal government allows a credit for FUTA paid, or allowed under a merit rating system, to your state. The credit cannot exceed 5.4 percent of the covered wages, so the amount you pay to the IRS could be as low as 0.8 percent (6.2% – 5.4%). You report and pay FUTA tax separately from withheld taxes, and it is all paid out of your funds. You use Form 940 or 940-EZ, "Employer's Annual Federal Unemployment (FUTA) Tax Return" to report this tax.

Additional Resources

The IRS publication that addresses self-employment tax is Publication 533, *Self-Employment Tax.* For further guidance in determining whether you are an employee or self-employed, get IRS Publication 15A, *Employer's Supplemental Tax Guide.* IRS Publication 505, *Tax Withholding and Estimated Tax,* shows detailed examples of how to compute estimated tax payments and figure the underpayment penalty. IRS Publication 15, *Circular E, Employer's Tax Guide,* gives information on the computation and reporting of employment taxes. IRS Publication 1066, *Small Business Tax Workshop Workbook,* gives detailed lessons on how to comply with all the requirements related to having employees.

You can get IRS publications free by calling the IRS at (800) TAX-FORM [(800) 829-3676]. If you have access to TTY/TDD equipment, you can call (800) 829-4059. To download them from the Internet, go to *www.irs.gov* (World Wide Web), or *ftp.irs.gov* (FTP). If you would like to get forms and instructions (not publications) by FAX, dial (703) 368-9694 to reach IRS Tax Fax.

As an alternative to downloading files from the Internet, you can order *IRS Federal Tax Products* on CD-ROM. This CD includes over 2,000 tax products, including all of the above publications and forms. It can be ordered by calling (800) 233-6767. Also, Publication 3207, *Small Business Resource Guide,* is an interactive CD-ROM that contains information important to small businesses. It is available in mid-February. You can get one free copy by calling (800) 829-3676.

Notes

[1] IRC § 1402(b)(2).

[2] IRC § 1402(a).

[3] See *W&S Distributing Inc. v. US,* 78 AFTR2d Par. 96-5254 (D.C.E. Mich., 1996).

[4] IRC § 3121(d)(3).

[5] IRC § 1402(c); IRC § 3121(b)(8)(A).

[6] IRC § 1402(a)(13).

[7] IRC § 1402(a)(3).

[8] IRC § 164(f).

[9] IRC § 6654(d).

[10] IRC § 6654(e)(1).

[11] IRC § 6655(d).

[12] IRC § 6654(c).

[13] IRC § 6654(h).

[14] IRC § 6655(c).

[15] IRC § 6654(g).

[16] IRC § 6621.

[17] Rev. Rul. 2000-16, 2000-12 IRB 780.

[18] Instructions for Form 2210.

[19] IRC § 6654(e)(3).

[20] IRC § 3121(b)(3).

[21] IRC § 3301.

[22] IRC § 3306(b).

CHAPTER 10

Sale of Your Residence

The personal
residence is the last
true tax shelter in
the U.S. income tax
system.

—Someone down at
the office

The tax rules pertaining to the sale of your principal residence were substantially changed by the Taxpayer Relief Act of 1997 (TRA '97). The changes also affect the tax treatment of your home office. Under the new rules, you can generally avoid paying tax on gain from the sale of your residence (up to $500,000 if filing jointly, $250,000 if single). However, gain attributable to your home office might be taxable, at least in part. In this chapter, you learn how to report the sale of your residence when you have a home office. Because the rules in effect prior to TRA '97 are sometimes relevant in computing gain under the new rules the old provisions are briefly discussed first.

The Sale of a Principal Residence Before and After the Taxpayer Relief Act of 1997

The Old Rules

Prior to TRA '97, Section 1034 of the Code generally allowed you to defer the recognition of gain on the sale of your principal residence, as long as a new principal residence was purchased for as much as or more than what your old home sold for. The replacement residence was required to be purchased within two years before or two years after the sale of the old residence. This was a gain deferral, or "rollover" provision, because the basis of your replacement residence was reduced by the unrecognized gain. If you sold your home and did not purchase a replacement for an equal or greater amount, gain was recognized to the extent that the cost of the new residence was less than the "adjusted sales price" of the old residence. There was no provision for deducting a loss on the sale of the personal use portion of your home—a feature that has not changed.

If, in your later years, you wanted to sell your home and acquire smaller and less expensive living quarters, the gain that was previously deferred under Section 1034 became taxable. Therefore, former Code Section 121 allowed a once in a lifetime exclusion of gain from the sale of a principal residence that was not reinvested in another residence. The exclusion was limited to $125,000, and applied only if you or your spouse had turned 55 before the date of sale. The form used to report the sale of your residence prior to 1998 was Form 2119, which is now obsolete.

The New Rules

Congress felt that the Section 1034 rules promoted an inefficient use of taxpayers' financial resources by encouraging them to buy more expensive houses than they otherwise would, just to avoid a tax liability. In addition, prior law discouraged some older taxpayers from selling their homes, either because they would recognize gain in excess of the $125,000 exclusion, or because they had already used the exclusion. In response, the 1997 Act replaces the old provisions with a much more generous Section 121 exclusion that can be used every two years.

The new law exempts from federal income tax the first $250,000 of gain ($500,000 on a joint return) from the sale of a principal residence. To qualify for the full exclusion, you must own and use the property as your principal residence for at least two out of five years prior to the sale. No age requirements exist, and the exclusion applies as long as you do not sell more than one principal residence within a two-year period. Additionally, you get a partial exclusion if you are forced to sell early because of a change in employment, health reasons, or other unforeseen circumstances specified in yet-to-be published regulations.[1]

The new exclusion applies to any sale or exchange of a principal residence occurring after May 6, 1997. However, the repeal of the Section 1034 rollover provision was not effective until August 5, 1997, the date the president signed the new law. Therefore, if you sold your home after May 6, 1997, but before August 5, 1997, or had a binding commitment to sell during that period, or had a binding commitment to purchase a replacement residence during that period, you had a choice to make. You could have elected to apply either the old rules under Section 1034, or the new rules permitting the exclusion, whichever provided the greater advantage. If you had a gain in excess of $250,000 ($500,000 on a joint return), and wanted to purchase a bigger house, the old rules were your preferred option. Any gain in excess of the exclusion limit would be taxed under the new rules, regardless of how much you pay for your replacement residence. However, anyone with gain of less than $250,000 ($500,000 on a joint return) is probably better off under the new rules.

Tax Treatment of Your Home Office

THE OLD RULES

Under the rollover provision of Section 1034, the IRS considered your home office a business asset separate from your personal residence, and any gain allocated to it was taxed in the year of sale.[2] On the other hand, if you sold your residence for a loss, the portion allocable to your home office was deductible. If you sold your house under the old rules, you could avoid gain recognition on your home office by simply not claiming home-office deductions in the year of sale.[3]

THE NEW RULES

Under the new rules, your home office is considered a separate business asset only if it does not qualify as your principal residence under the two out of five year test. In such case, gain allocable to it is taxable. On the other hand, If you did not deduct home-office expenses for at least two of the five years preceding the sale, your home office qualifies as part of your principal residence and is not treated as a separate business asset. Your home office also qualifies for the partial exclusion if you are forced to sell early because of a change in employment or health reasons.

Whether or not your home office qualifies for gain exclusion, the new law says that gain must be recognized to the extent of any depreciation allowable with respect to the business use of your residence for periods after May 6, 1997.[4] If your home office qualifies as your principal residence, you can exclude any gain attributable to depreciation taken before May 7, 1997. Gain attributable to depreciation for periods after May 6, 1997 is taxed at the maximum rate of 25 percent under TRA '97. This gain recognition cannot be avoided by not claiming the depreciation on your tax return. If this sounds confusing, the examples in the next section should help to clear things up.

Reporting Post-Taxpayer Relief Act of 1997 Sales

As indicated earlier, after 1997 you are no longer required to file Form 2119, *Sale of Your Home,* to report a sale. That's because most taxpayers can now fully exclude gain on home sales. The new rules greatly simplify the record keeping and reporting requirements for selling your principal residence.

However, even though you might not be required to report the sale for tax purposes, it is still important to maintain records detailing the original cost of your home and capital improvements. If your home office qualifies, you will need to be able to allocate a portion of the property's basis for depreciation purposes.

If you need to figure a reduced exclusion, or your gain is more than $500,000, use the worksheet in Publication 523, *Selling Your Home.* Any taxable gain not attributable to your home office should be reported on Schedule D (Form 1040).

Any reportable gain or loss attributable to your home office is reported first on Form 4797, "Sales of Business Property." If it's a gain, and there are no losses reported on Form 4797, it is transferred to Schedule D as capital gain. If you report a loss from your home office, and there are no gains reported on Form 4797, the loss will end up on the front page of Form 1040 (line 14) as an ordinary loss.

If you purchase a replacement residence, the year you begin depreciating your new home office you are supposed to file Form 4562, "Depreciation and Amortization." Simply copy the information from Part III of Form 8829 (for your new home office) to line 15(i) of Form 4562. Remember to only claim depreciation for the portion of the year that you occupy your new home office. Include the amount on line 15(i), column (g) of Form 4562 in the total on line 21 of that form, and show the same amount on lines 40 and 28 of Form 8829.

Example 10.1 demonstrates the reporting requirements for the sale of your home when your home office qualifies for the Section 121 exclusion. In that case, you need not divide the transaction into two sales, but you must report gain attributable to depreciation claimed after May 6, 1997. Example 10.2 demonstrates the reporting requirements when your home office does not qualify for the Section 121 exclusion, in which case you must report the entire gain or loss attributable to your home office.

Example 10.1

Lloyd Brown sold his principal residence at 314 Elm Street on July 10, 2002. Lloyd owned and occupied the residence for six years. Lloyd used an area in his house as his principal place of business since January 2001, but the office had been used as living space prior to that. Relevant numbers are:

314 Elm Street:

Selling price	$240,000
Expenses of sale	$19,200

Example 10.1

(Continued)

Original cost of home	$165,000
Original value of lot included in cost of new house	$15,000
Area used regularly and exclusively for business	200 sq. ft.
Total living space	2,000 sq. ft.
Indirect operating costs for 2002 to date of sale:	
Home mortgage interest	$8,500
Real estate taxes	$1,800
Homeowner's insurance	$400
Repairs and maintenance	$50
Utilities	$1,250
Tentative profit for 2002 from Schedule C, line 29 (before home-business expenses)	$30,500

Since Lloyd has owned and occupied his residence for more than two of the five years preceding the sale, gain on the sale of the residence is excluded under Section 121. The selling price ($240,000) is less than the exclusion limit ($250,000), so there is no reporting requirement beyond the home office portion. Because Lloyd has owned and occupied the residence for six years, but has only used his home office for about a year and a half, his home office space qualifies as his principal residence and is eligible for the Section 121 exclusion. He still must report gain attributable to the depreciation claimed, however.

Lloyd's allowable home-business deductions are calculated on Form 8829, shown in Figure 10.1. Note that only $16,455 is included on line 8 rather than the total amount from Schedule C, line 29. This is because Lloyd only occupied his home office for 190 days during 2002, so only a corresponding share of Schedule C income is allocable to it. Also, depreciation gain from the sale of his home must be added. Lloyd will attach the following schedule (Figure 10.2) to his return showing the computation.

Form **8829**	**Expenses for Business Use of Your Home**	OMB No. 1545-1266
Department of the Treasury Internal Revenue Service (99)	File only with Schedule C (Form 1040). Use a separate Form 8829 for each home you used for business during the year. See separate instructions.	**2002** Attachment Sequence No. **66**

Name(s) of proprietor(s)	Your social security number
Lloyd Brown	999 : 33 : 4444

Part I Part of Your Home Used for Business

1	Area used regularly and exclusively for business, regularly for day care, or for storage of inventory or product samples (see instructions)	1	200
2	Total area of home	2	2,000
3	Divide line 1 by line 2. Enter the result as a percentage	3	10 %
	For day-care facilities not used exclusively for business, also complete lines 4–6. **All others, skip lines 4–6 and enter the amount from line 3 on line 7.**		
4	Multiply days used for day care during year by hours used per day .	4	hr.		
5	Total hours available for use during the year (365 days 24 hours) (see instructions)	5	8,760 hr.		
6	Divide line 4 by line 5. Enter the result as a decimal amount . .	6	.		
7	Business percentage. For day-care facilities not used exclusively for business, multiply line 6 by line 3 (enter the result as a percentage). All others, enter the amount from line 3 . . . ▶	7	10 %

Part II Figure Your Allowable Deduction

8	Enter the amount from Schedule C, line 29, **plus** any net gain or (loss) derived from the business use of your home and shown on Schedule D or Form 4797. If more than one place of business, see instructions	8	16,455

			(a) Direct expenses	(b) Indirect expenses		
	See instructions for columns (a) and (b) before completing lines 9–20.					
9	Casualty losses (see instructions)	9				
10	Deductible mortgage interest (see instructions) .	10		8,500		
11	Real estate taxes (see instructions) . . .	11		1,800		
12	Add lines 9, 10, and 11	12		10,300		
13	Multiply line 12, column (b) by line 7 . .	13		1,030		
14	Add line 12, column (a) and line 13				14	1,030
15	Subtract line 14 from line 8. If zero or less, enter -0- .				15	15,425
16	Excess mortgage interest (see instructions) .	16				
17	Insurance	17		400		
18	Repairs and maintenance	18		50		
19	Utilities	19		1,250		
20	Other expenses (see instructions) . . .	20				
21	Add lines 16 through 20	21		1,700		
22	Multiply line 21, column (b) by line 7	22		170		
23	Carryover of operating expenses from 2001 Form 8829, line 41 .	23				
24	Add line 21 in column (a), line 22, and line 23				24	170
25	Allowable operating expenses. Enter the **smaller** of line 15 or line 24				25	170
26	Limit on excess casualty losses and depreciation. Subtract line 25 from line 15				26	15,255
27	Excess casualty losses (see instructions)	27				
28	Depreciation of your home from Part III below	28		209		
29	Carryover of excess casualty losses and depreciation from 2001 Form 8829, line 42	29				
30	Add lines 27 through 29				30	209
31	Allowable excess casualty losses and depreciation. Enter the **smaller** of line 26 or line 30 .				31	209
32	Add lines 14, 25, and 31				32	1,409
33	Casualty loss portion, if any, from lines 14 and 31. Carry amount to **Form 4684**, Section B .				33	
34	Allowable expenses for business use of your home. Subtract line 33 from line 32. Enter here and on Schedule C, line 30. If your home was used for more than one business, see instructions ▶				34	1,409

Part III Depreciation of Your Home

35	Enter the **smaller** of your home's adjusted basis or its fair market value (see instructions) .	35	165,000
36	Value of land included on line 35	36	15,000
37	Basis of building. Subtract line 36 from line 35	37	150,000
38	Business basis of building. Multiply line 37 by line 7	38	15,000
39	Depreciation percentage (see instructions)	39	1.391 %
40	Depreciation allowable (see instructions). Multiply line 38 by line 39. Enter here and on line 28 above	40	209

Part IV Carryover of Unallowed Expenses to 2003

41	Operating expenses. Subtract line 25 from line 24. If less than zero, enter -0-	41	
42	Excess casualty losses and depreciation. Subtract line 31 from line 30. If less than zero, enter -0- .	42	

For Paperwork Reduction Act Notice, see page 4 of separate instructions.   Cat. No. 13232M   Form **8829** (2002)

FIGURE 10.1

Portion of Schedule C tentative income attributable to business use of home based on days occupied:	
190/365 × $30,500	$ 15,877
Depreciation gain:	
Depreciation claimed on home office for 2001	
(see Table 6.1): 15,000 × 2.461%	$ 369
Depreciation claimed	
on home office for 2002 (see Form 8829):	$ 209
Total depreciation gain: Form 4797, Line 7	$ 578
Total net business income: Form 8829, Line 8	$ 16,455
Form 4797 Allocation of Business-Use Portion of Residence	
1. Selling price of home	$240,000
2. Business-use percentage (Form 8829, Line 7)	10%
3. Line 1 × Line 2: put on Form 4797, Line 2(d)	$ 24,000
4. Expenses of sale	$ 19,200
5. Line 2 × Line 4	$ 1,920
6. Business basis of residence (Form 8829, Line 38)	$ 15,000
7. Line 5 + Line 6: put on Form 4797, Line 2(f)	$ 16,920
8. Total depreciation claimed on business basis: put on Form 4797, Line 2(e)	$ 578

FIGURE 10.2 Schedule for Form 8829, Line 8 and Form 4797, Line 7

If Lloyd acquires a new residence with a home office, he must file an additional Form 8829 to claim home-office deductions for the new home office. Both Forms 8829 should be filed with his return, with the total allowable home office deductions accounted for on line 30 of Schedule C.

Because Lloyd's home office qualifies for the Section 121 exclusion (owned and occupied as a residence for two of five years preceding the sale), the excluded portion is recorded as a loss on line 2 of Form 4797, column (g) (Figure 10.3). The loss shown as "Section 121 Exclusion" on line 2 of Form 4797 is simply the total gain attributable to the home office minus the depreciation gain

Form **4797**

Department of the Treasury
Internal Revenue Service (99)

Sales of Business Property

(Also Involuntary Conversions and Recapture Amounts
Under Sections 179 and 280F(b)(2))

▶ **Attach to your tax return.** ▶ **See separate instructions.**

OMB No. 1545-0184

20**02**

Attachment
Sequence No. **27**

Name(s) shown on return

Lloyd Brown

Identifying number

999-33-4444

1 Enter the gross proceeds from sales or exchanges reported to you for 2002 on Form(s) 1099-B or 1099-S (or substitute statement) that you are including on line 2, 10, or 20 (see instructions) . . . . | **1** |

Part I **Sales or Exchanges of Property Used in a Trade or Business and Involuntary Conversions From Other Than Casualty or Theft—Most Property Held More Than 1 Year** (See instructions.)

(a) Description of property	(b) Date acquired (mo., day, yr.)	(c) Date sold (mo., day, yr.)	(d) Gross sales price	(e) Depreciation allowed or allowable since acquisition	(f) Cost or other basis, plus improvements and expense of sale	(g) Gain or (loss) Subtract (f) from the sum of (d) and (e)
2 314 Elm						
Home office	1996	2002	24,000	578	16,920	7,658
Section 121 exclusion						(7,080)

3	Gain, if any, from Form 4684, line 39	**3**	
4	Section 1231 gain from installment sales from Form 6252, line 26 or 37	**4**	
5	Section 1231 gain or (loss) from like-kind exchanges from Form 8824	**5**	
6	Gain, if any, from line 32, from other than casualty or theft	**6**	
7	Combine lines 2 through 6. Enter the gain or (loss) here and on the appropriate line as follows: . .	**7**	578

Partnerships (except electing large partnerships) and S corporations. Report the gain or (loss) following the instructions for Form 1065, Schedule K, line 6, or Form 1120S, Schedule K, line 5. Skip lines 8, 9, 11, and 12 below . . .

All others. If line 7 is zero or a loss, enter the amount from line 7 on line 11 below and skip lines 8 and 9. If line 7 is a gain and you did not have any prior year section 1231 losses, or they were recaptured in an earlier year, enter the gain from line 7 as a long-term capital gain on Schedule D and skip lines 8, 9, 11, and 12 below.

8	Nonrecaptured net section 1231 losses from prior years (see instructions)	**8**	
9	Subtract line 8 from line 7. If zero or less, enter -0-. If line 9 is zero, enter the gain from line 7 on line 12 below. If line 9 is more than zero, enter the amount from line 8 on line 12 below and enter the gain from line 9 as a long-term capital gain on Schedule D (see instructions)	**9**	

Part II **Ordinary Gains and Losses**

10 Ordinary gains and losses not included on lines 11 through 17 (include property held 1 year or less):

11	Loss, if any, from line 7	**11**	(	)
12	Gain, if any, from line 7 or amount from line 8, if applicable	**12**		
13	Gain, if any, from line 31	**13**		
14	Net gain or (loss) from Form 4684, lines 31 and 38a	**14**		
15	Ordinary gain from installment sales from Form 6252, line 25 or 36	**15**		
16	Ordinary gain or (loss) from like-kind exchanges from Form 8824	**16**		
17	Recapture of section 179 expense deduction for partners and S corporation shareholders from property dispositions by partnerships and S corporations (see instructions)	**17**		
18	Combine lines 10 through 17. Enter the gain or (loss) here and on the appropriate line as follows: . . .	**18**		

a **For all except individual returns.** Enter the gain or (loss) from line 18 on the return being filed.

b **For individual returns:**

(1) If the loss on line 11 includes a loss from Form 4684, line 35, column (b)(ii), enter that part of the loss here. Enter the part of the loss from income-producing property on Schedule A (Form 1040), line 27, and the part of the loss from property used as an employee on Schedule A (Form 1040), line 22. Identify as from "Form 4797, line 18b(1)." See instructions . . . . | **18b(1)** |

(2) Redetermine the gain or (loss) on line 18 excluding the loss, if any, on line 18b(1). Enter here and on Form 1040, line 14 . . . . | **18b(2)** |

For Paperwork Reduction Act Notice, see page 7 of the instructions.   Cat. No. 13086I   Form **4797** (2002)

FIGURE 10.3

Example 10.2

Tess Milbourn sold her home at 225 Oak Street on March 1, 2002. Tess has used a room in her Oak Street home regularly and exclusively as her principal place of business since 1993, and continued to do so until she sold her house. Tess must report capital gain from the sale attributable to her home office. She has accumulated home-business deductions that were disallowed in previous years that will offset part of the gain. Here are relevant amounts that relate to the residence:

225 Oak Street:

Selling price	$185,000
Expenses of sale	$16,000
Adjusted basis when acquired, plus improvements	$140,000
Value of land when acquired	$10,000
Accumulated depreciation on business use portion for prior years	$2,883
Depreciation for 2002 (see Form 8829, Line 40)	$70
Area used regularly and exclusively for business	180 sq. ft.
Total living space	1,800 sq. ft.
Home mortgage interest (two months)	$600
Real estate taxes (two months)	$200
Homeowner's insurance (two months)	$50
Utilities (two months)	$175
Carryover of operating expenses	
from 2001 Form 8829, Line 41	$4,200
Carryover of excess depreciation	
from 2001 Form 8829, Line 42	$1,450
Tentative profit for 2002 from Schedule C, line 29 (before home-business expenses)	$4,500

($7,658 – $578 = $7,080). The depreciation gain shown on Form 4797, line 7, is combined with other business gains and losses Lloyd might have. If there are no offsetting losses on Form 4797, it is transferred to Schedule D, line 11 as long-term capital gain. In computing Lloyd's tax in Part IV of Schedule D, this gain is referred to as "unrecaptured section 1250 gain," and is taxed at a maximum rate of 25 percent.

Turning to Example 10.2, since Tess has owned and occupied her residence for more than two of the five years preceding the sale, gain on the sale of the residence is excluded under Section 121. The selling price ($185,000) is less than the exclusion limit ($250,000), so there is no reporting requirement beyond the home-office portion.

Figure 10.4 shows the portion of the selling price, expenses of sale, and the adjusted basis of 225 Oak Street allocable to home office use, and provides the numbers for figuring gain on Form 4797. Figure 10.5 shows the calculation of "unrecaptured section 1250 gain," which is the portion of the capital gain that is reported on line 25 of Schedule D and taxed at the maximum rate of 25 percent. Figure 10.7 shows the gain attributable to the business portion computed on Form 4797. Assuming no other sales are reported on her Form 4797, Tess will report the gain of $6,853 on Schedule D as long-term capital gain.

Tess's allowable home-business deductions are calculated on Form 8829, shown in Figure 10.6. Note that $7,580 is included on line 8 rather than the total amount from Schedule C, line 29. This is because Tess only occupied her home office for 59 days during 2002, so only a corresponding share of Schedule

1. Selling price of home	$185,000
2. Business-use percentage (Form 8829, Line 7)	10%
3. Line 1 × line 2: put on Form 4797, Line 2(d)	$ 18,500
4. Expenses of sale	$ 16,000
5. Line 2 × line 4	$ 1,600
6. Business basis of residence before depreciation (Form 8829, Line 38)	$ 13,000
7. Line 5 + line 6: put on Form 4797, Line 2(f)	$ 14,600
8. Total depreciation (current and prior year) claimed on business basis: put on Form 4797, line 2(e)	$ 2,953

FIGURE 10.4   Sale of Residence Allocation of Business-Use Portion

Portion of Schedule C tentative income attributable to business use of home based on days occupied:	
59/365 × $4,500	$ 727
Gain from Form 4797, line 2(g)	$6,853
Total net business income: Form 8829, line 8	$7,580
Computation of unrecaptured section 1250 gain, Schedule D, line 25:	
Depreciation claimed on home office for 1997:	
$13,000 × 2.564% = $333	
Percentage of days after May 6, 1997: 239/365	
Post May 6, 1997, depreciation: 239/365 × 333	$ 218
Depreciation claimed on home office for 1998–2001:	
$13,000 × 2.564% × 4 years	$1,333
Depreciation from 2002 (see Form 8829):	$ 70
Unrecaptured section 1250 gain	$1,621

FIGURE 10.5 Schedule for Form 8829, Line 8 and Schedule D

C income is allocable to it. Also, gain from the sale of her home office must be added. Tess will attach the following schedule (Figure 10.5) to her return showing the computation.

If Tess acquires a new residence with a home office, she must file an additional Form 8829 to claim home-office deductions for the new home office. Both Forms 8829 should be filed with her return, with the total allowable home-office deductions accounted for on line 30 of Schedule C. Incidentally, if your home-office deductions are limited on Form 8829 and must be carried over, you will not lose them as long as you continue your business somewhere else.

Should You Always Claim Home-Office Deductions?

Notice in Example 10.2 that Tess was required to report a gain of $6,853 attributable to her home office. Of the entire gain, only $1,621 was attributable to depreciation recapture. Any gain in excess of depreciation recapture would not have been recognized had Tess used her home office as personal space for at least two years during the five years preceding the sale. In some situations it is

Form **8829**	**Expenses for Business Use of Your Home**	OMB No. 1545-1266
Department of the Treasury Internal Revenue Service (99)	File only with Schedule C (Form 1040). Use a separate Form 8829 for each home you used for business during the year. **See separate instructions.**	**2002** Attachment Sequence No. **66**

Name(s) of proprietor(s) Tess Milbourn	Your social security number 999 ⦙ 66 ⦙ 9999

Part I **Part of Your Home Used for Business**

1	Area used regularly and exclusively for business, regularly for day care, or for storage of inventory or product samples (see instructions)	**1**	180
2	Total area of home	**2**	1,800
3	Divide line 1 by line 2. Enter the result as a percentage	**3**	10 %

For day-care facilities not used exclusively for business, also complete lines 4–6.
All others, skip lines 4–6 and enter the amount from line 3 on line 7.

4	Multiply days used for day care during year by hours used per day .	**4**	hr.
5	Total hours available for use during the year (365 days 24 hours) (see instructions)	**5**	8,760 hr.
6	Divide line 4 by line 5. Enter the result as a decimal amount . .	**6**	.
7	Business percentage. For day-care facilities not used exclusively for business, multiply line 6 by line 3 (enter the result as a percentage). All others, enter the amount from line 3 . . . ▶	**7**	10 %

Part II **Figure Your Allowable Deduction**

8	Enter the amount from Schedule C, line 29, **plus** any net gain or (loss) derived from the business use of your home and shown on Schedule D or Form 4797. If more than one place of business, see instructions		**8**	7,580

See instructions for columns (a) and (b) before completing lines 9–20.

		(a) Direct expenses	(b) Indirect expenses		
9	Casualty losses (see instructions) . . .	**9**			
10	Deductible mortgage interest (see instructions) .	**10**		600	
11	Real estate taxes (see instructions) . . .	**11**		200	
12	Add lines 9, 10, and 11	**12**		800	
13	Multiply line 12, column (b) by line 7 . .	**13**		80	
14	Add line 12, column (a) and line 13			**14**	80
15	Subtract line 14 from line 8. If zero or less, enter -0- .			**15**	7,500
16	Excess mortgage interest (see instructions) .	**16**			
17	Insurance	**17**		50	
18	Repairs and maintenance	**18**			
19	Utilities	**19**		175	
20	Other expenses (see instructions) . . .	**20**			
21	Add lines 16 through 20	**21**		225	
22	Multiply line 21, column (b) by line 7	**22**	23		
23	Carryover of operating expenses from 2001 Form 8829, line 41 .	**23**	4,200		
24	Add line 21 in column (a), line 22, and line 23			**24**	4,223
25	Allowable operating expenses. Enter the **smaller** of line 15 or line 24			**25**	4,223
26	Limit on excess casualty losses and depreciation. Subtract line 25 from line 15 . . .			**26**	3,277
27	Excess casualty losses (see instructions)	**27**			
28	Depreciation of your home from Part III below	**28**	70		
29	Carryover of excess casualty losses and depreciation from 2001 Form 8829, line 42	**29**	1,450		
30	Add lines 27 through 29			**30**	1,520
31	Allowable excess casualty losses and depreciation. Enter the **smaller** of line 26 or line 30 .			**31**	1,520
32	Add lines 14, 25, and 31			**32**	5,823
33	Casualty loss portion, if any, from lines 14 and 31. Carry amount to **Form 4684**, Section B .			**33**	
34	Allowable expenses for business use of your home. Subtract line 33 from line 32. Enter here and on Schedule C, line 30. If your home was used for more than one business, see instructions ▶			**34**	5,823

Part III **Depreciation of Your Home**

35	Enter the **smaller** of your home's adjusted basis or its fair market value (see instructions) .	**35**	140,000
36	Value of land included on line 35	**36**	10,000
37	Basis of building. Subtract line 36 from line 35	**37**	130,000
38	Business basis of building. Multiply line 37 by line 7	**38**	13,000
39	Depreciation percentage (see instructions)	**39**	.535 %
40	Depreciation allowable (see instructions). Multiply line 38 by line 39. Enter here and on line 28 above	**40**	70

Part IV **Carryover of Unallowed Expenses to 2003**

41	Operating expenses. Subtract line 25 from line 24. If less than zero, enter -0-	**41**	
42	Excess casualty losses and depreciation. Subtract line 31 from line 30. If less than zero, enter -0- .	**42**	

For Paperwork Reduction Act Notice, see page 4 of separate instructions.   Cat. No. 13232M   Form **8829** (2002)

FIGURE 10.6

Form **4797**	**Sales of Business Property**	OMB No. 1545-0184
Department of the Treasury Internal Revenue Service (99)	(Also Involuntary Conversions and Recapture Amounts Under Sections 179 and 280F(b)(2)) ▶ **Attach to your tax return.** ▶ **See separate instructions.**	20**02** Attachment Sequence No. **27**

Name(s) shown on return	Identifying number
Tess Milbourn	999-666-9999

1 Enter the gross proceeds from sales or exchanges reported to you for 2002 on Form(s) 1099-B or 1099-S (or substitute statement) that you are including on line 2, 10, or 20 (see instructions) . . . . | **1** |

Part I **Sales or Exchanges of Property Used in a Trade or Business and Involuntary Conversions From Other Than Casualty or Theft—Most Property Held More Than 1 Year** (See instructions.)

(a) Description of property	(b) Date acquired (mo., day, yr.)	(c) Date sold (mo., day, yr.)	(d) Gross sales price	(e) Depreciation allowed or allowable since acquisition	(f) Cost or other basis, plus improvements and expense of sale	(g) Gain or (loss) Subtract (f) from the sum of (d) and (e)
2 225 Oak Street						
Home office	1993	2002	18,500	2,953	14,600	6,853

3 Gain, if any, from Form 4684, line 39 . . . . **3**

4 Section 1231 gain from installment sales from Form 6252, line 26 or 37 . . . . **4**

5 Section 1231 gain or (loss) from like-kind exchanges from Form 8824 . . . . **5**

6 Gain, if any, from line 32, from other than casualty or theft **6**

7 Combine lines 2 through 6. Enter the gain or (loss) here and on the appropriate line as follows: **7**   6,853

Partnerships (except electing large partnerships) and S corporations. Report the gain or (loss) following the instructions for Form 1065, Schedule K, line 6, or Form 1120S, Schedule K, line 5. Skip lines 8, 9, 11, and 12 below . .

All others. If line 7 is zero or a loss, enter the amount from line 7 on line 11 below and skip lines 8 and 9. If line 7 is a gain and you did not have any prior year section 1231 losses, or they were recaptured in an earlier year, enter the gain from line 7 as a long-term capital gain on Schedule D and skip lines 8, 9, 11, and 12 below.

8 Nonrecaptured net section 1231 losses from prior years (see instructions) **8**

9 Subtract line 8 from line 7. If zero or less, enter -0-. If line 9 is zero, enter the gain from line 7 on line 12 below. If line 9 is more than zero, enter the amount from line 8 on line 12 below and enter the gain from line 9 as a long-term capital gain on Schedule D (see instructions) **9**

Part II **Ordinary Gains and Losses**

10 Ordinary gains and losses not included on lines 11 through 17 (include property held 1 year or less):

11 Loss, if any, from line 7 . . . .   **11** ( )

12 Gain, if any, from line 7 or amount from line 8, if applicable **12**

13 Gain, if any, from line 31 . . . .   **13**

14 Net gain or (loss) from Form 4684, lines 31 and 38a **14**

15 Ordinary gain from installment sales from Form 6252, line 25 or 36 . . . .   **15**

16 Ordinary gain or (loss) from like-kind exchanges from Form 8824 . . . .   **16**

17 Recapture of section 179 expense deduction for partners and S corporation shareholders from property dispositions by partnerships and S corporations (see instructions) **17**

18 Combine lines 10 through 17. Enter the gain or (loss) here and on the appropriate line as follows: . . .   **18**

a **For all except individual returns.** Enter the gain or (loss) from line 18 on the return being filed.

b **For individual returns:**

(1) If the loss on line 11 includes a loss from Form 4684, line 35, column (b)(ii), enter that part of the loss here. Enter the part of the loss from income-producing property on Schedule A (Form 1040), line 27, and the part of the loss from property used as an employee on Schedule A (Form 1040), line 22. Identify as from "Form 4797, line 18b(1)." See instructions . . . .   **18b(1)**

(2) Redetermine the gain or (loss) on line 18 excluding the loss, if any, on line 18b(1). Enter here and on Form 1040, line 14 . . . .   **18b(2)**

For Paperwork Reduction Act Notice, see page 7 of the instructions.   Cat. No. 13086I   Form **4797** (2002)

FIGURE 10.7

wise not to claim home office deductions for at least two years during the five years preceding a sale of your residence in order to avoid paying tax on this gain. In Tess's case, $5,650 of carryover deductions from previous years was deductible on her 2002 return as a result of including the gain on the home office. Tess must weigh the benefit of these deductions against the cost of reporting the additional gain. For example, if Tess was in the 27 percent bracket in 2002, the extra deductions would have been worth $1,526 ($5,650 × 27%). The capital gain on the sale of the residence (exclusive of depreciation recapture) is taxed at a maximum rate of 20 percent, so its cost was $1,046 ($6,853 − $1,621 × 20%). Tess therefore receives a slight benefit by reporting the gain ($1,526 − $1,046).

In most cases, it is difficult to judge whether claiming deductions for a particular year is beneficial, if it is not certain when the residence will be sold. Remember that you can file an amended return at any time up to three years after the due date of the original return. This allows you to use hindsight to cancel your home-office deductions for previous years if it is more beneficial not to claim them. It is unlikely that the IRS will question an amended return on which you choose to reclaim deductions and pay additional tax. Probably the best reason to give for any amended return canceling home-office deductions is, "The office space was not used exclusively for business." Since at least minimal nonbusiness activities take place in most home offices, this will usually be an accurate statement.

Additional Resources

IRS Publication 523, *Selling Your Home,* discusses additional issues, such as computation of basis when the home is received through inheritance, and the rules for when a home is sold in connection with a divorce. IRS Publication 537, *Installment Sales,* will be useful if you provide financing for the buyer of your home. IRS Publication 936, *Home Mortgage Interest Deduction,* tells about how to treat seller paid points.

You can get IRS publications free by calling the IRS at (800) TAX-FORM [(800) 829-3676]. If you have access to TTY/TDD equipment, you can call (800) 829-4059. To download them from the Internet, go to *www.irs.gov* (World Wide Web), or *ftp.irs.gov* (FTP). If you would like to get forms and instructions (not publications) by FAX, dial (703) 368-9694 to reach IRS Tax Fax.

As an alternative to downloading files from the Internet, you can order *IRS Federal Tax Products* on CD-ROM. This CD includes over 2,000 tax products, including all of the above publications and forms. It can be ordered by calling (800) 233-6767. Also, Publication 3207, *Small Business Resource Guide,* is an interactive CD-ROM that contains information important to small businesses. It is available in mid-February. You can get one free copy by calling (800) 829-3676.

Notes

[1] IRC § 121 as amended by TRA '97 § 312(a).
[2] Reg. § 1.1034-1(c)(3)(ii).
[3] Rev. Rul. 82-26, 1982-1 CB 114.
[4] IRC § 121(d)(6), as amended by TRA '97.

CHAPTER 11

Records You Better Keep

Though tax records
are generally looked
upon as a nuisance,
the day may come
when historians will
realize that tax
records tell the real
story behind civilized
life.

—Charles Adams

A n old and often-cited Supreme Court decision says that deductions are allowed only by "legislative grace."[1] In other words, to deduct is not a constitutional right, but a privilege granted by Congress, and the burden is on you to prove your entitlement. The lawmakers require you to maintain records sufficient to substantiate your claims, and the IRS tries to make sure that you do.

This chapter tells you what records are necessary to ensure that your deductions will be allowed if you happen to get audited. It also offers a few suggestions about the easiest ways to comply with the substantiation requirements.

General Bookkeeping and Substantiation Requirements

Adequate and accurate record keeping is fundamental to running any business. Records tell you what you own and what you owe, whether you are making a profit or are incurring a loss, and whether you are building equity in your enterprise. In addition, maintaining accurate records is the only way to ensure that you are paying the proper tax liability. It might also affect whether a loss will be allowed, because it is one factor the IRS uses to determine whether your activity is a legitimate business or simply a hobby (see Chapter 2). Keep in mind that the IRS is not obliged to prove that an item is *not* deductible—it is up to you to show that it *is*.[2]

You do not have to be a certified public accountant to keep adequate records (although it wouldn't hurt). Even if you have no accounting background, you can maintain a very simple record-keeping system sufficient to show your profit or loss. Following are a few suggestions for general record keeping if you are operating a business. Whether you are an employee or self-employed, there are specific requirements for accounting for travel, transportation, entertainment and gift expenses, and for the use of listed property. These will be described later in the chapter.

Your Business Checking Account and Credit Card

One of the first things you should do when you start a business is to open a separate checking account for it. Banks like to charge a lot of money for business checking accounts, so shop around. If you are a sole proprietor just starting out, and you do not have an assumed name for your business, you might try to operate your business through a personal checking account. The IRS will have no problem with this, but the bank might.

Use this separate account only for business items, and don't run business items through your personal account. If you run out of money in your business account, transfer funds to it rather than writing checks from your personal account. Pay for all of your business expenditures with checks (or your business credit card) rather than cash, and avoid writing checks payable to cash; write checks to yourself only when you want to withdraw money from the business. Be sure to reconcile your checkbook with your bank statements on a regular basis, and at the end of the year.

You should also get a credit card that is designated for business purchases. It does not have to be a "business" credit card. When you pay the credit-card bill, use your business checking account. Your credit-card charges are considered paid when you charge them,[3] making them deductible at that time rather than when you pay the bill. So be sure that all unpaid credit-card charges are recorded in your business books at the end of the year.

Simply keeping your business income and expenditures separate from your personal items will greatly simplify your record keeping. It will also demonstrate to the IRS that you are serious about your business. Your checking account and credit-card receipts are your primary sources of information for recording transactions in your business books.

Keeping the Books

The purpose of keeping books is to record and identify each transaction, and to summarize all transactions at the end of the year to establish an accurate income statement and balance sheet. How you accomplish this is up to you, as long as you record sufficient information to accurately present your income or loss.

COMPUTER PROGRAMS

If you use a computer, the easiest way to keep your business books may be to buy a computer bookkeeping program. Before you buy, though, get some advice on which one is best for you. The easiest ones are based on a simple single-entry system, allowing you to record receipts and expenditures just like in your checkbook. These programs can also replace your checkbook. They print out checks and even make electronic funds transfers. They reconcile your bank account, and produce instant profit and loss statements, balance sheets, and other reports. If you get the program that is right for you, it will be a painless way to satisfy your record-keeping requirements.

MANUAL SYSTEMS

If you are not a computer person, you should find complete single-entry bookkeeping ledger systems at you favorite office supply store for less than $35. There is one brand that even gives you a lesson in bookkeeping with filled-in ledger sheets. You can get systems for either cash or accrual accounting. These systems make bookkeeping pretty easy, even for the completely uninitiated.

BAILING OUT

You might be thinking you want no part of this. Perhaps you are an ideas person and don't care to be a bean counter. Okay, if you can afford the luxury, hire someone. But if you simply want someone to do the bookkeeping, and are not looking for a full-fledged business or tax consultant, you do not need a CPA. There are probably plenty of bookkeeping services in your area that employ qualified people at much lower hourly rates.

DO NOT TRUST THE BOOKKEEPER!

Whatever you do, do not turn over the entire financial affairs of your business to any one person. If you hire a bookkeeper, continue to write the checks and deposit the funds yourself; let the bookkeeper record the transactions. This is called internal control, and is essential to safeguard the monetary assets of your business. If you grow to the point where you can no longer pay the bills and do the banking yourself, you had better hire an accountant to keep an eye on the bookkeeper. If the bookkeeper and the accountant get really friendly, fire one of them and hire someone else. The world abounds with those who tread the straight and narrow path simply for want of opportunity. Do not allow your business to become their fortuitous circumstance.

Substantiating Your Expenses

For each business purchase, you should have evidence of the date, the amount, the payee, and the business purpose of the expenditure. Your canceled checks and credit-card statements will provide evidence of the first three, but you also need the invoice or receipt from the vendor to indicate business purpose.

For example, let's say you bought some office furniture for your home office during the year from Bob's Furniture, and it cost $1,000. You claim the furniture as a Section 179 deduction on your tax return, and your friendly neighborhood IRS agent pays you a visit. The agent simply wants proof that you bought the furniture during the year, and that you paid $1,000 for it. You can show the agent your record of the transaction in your books, and the agent can visibly inspect the furniture in your home office. But from viewing the books and inspecting the furniture, the agent still does not know for sure that you spent all or any of the $1,000 paid to Bob's Furniture on that particular furniture. You could have bought a dining room table from Bob's and received the office furniture as a gift from Aunt Harriet. What the agent needs to see is the invoice or receipt from Bob's Furniture showing that you did in fact pay $1,000 for office furniture.

Regarding documents from any business transaction, instead of trying to figure out what to keep and what to throw away, just keep everything. Later in this chapter you will be given some guidelines on when it is safe to throw stuff away.

Special Substantiation Requirements

The Cohan Rule

The first few decades following the enactment of our income tax in 1913 were the days of development for our tax laws. A lot of landmark cases were decided in the courts back then that still have relevance today. In the years 1921 through 1923, the great song-and-dance man George M. Cohan claimed to have spent over $50,000 in traveling expenses, and in entertaining actors, employees, and "drama critics."[4] The problem was he had no receipts to show for it. The Tax Court (Board of Tax Appeals back then) simply threw out his deductions for lack of substantiation. But Mr. Cohan found a fan in Judge Learned Hand on the Second Circuit Court of Appeals. In instructing the lower court to reconsider the evidence, Judge Hand wrote:

The question is how far this refusal is justified, in view of the finding that he had spent much and that the sums were allowable expenses. Absolute certainty in such matters is usually impossible and is not necessary; the Board should make as close an approximation as it can, bearing heavily if it chooses upon the taxpayer whose inexactitude is of his own making. But to allow nothing at all appears to us inconsistent with saying that something was spent.[5]

Cohan was therefore allowed to deduct part of his expenses, based purely on the notion that some money must have been spent under the circumstances.

Although this case is still relevant for some business deductions, the Cohan case created concern in Congress about the inflated expense accounts of taxpayers who were not maintaining adequate records. So now Section 274(d) of the Code mandates specific substantiation requirements for deductions relating to (1) travel (including meals and lodging while away from home), (2) entertainment, (3) gifts, and (4) any listed property.

The regulations under Section 274 specifically state that the Cohan rule will not apply to these expenses.[6] That means that unless you comply with the rules under Section 274(d), your deductions could be completely disallowed. Following are the elements you must prove for each type of expense and the rules for how you are expected to do so.

The Elements of Travel Expenses

The elements you must be able to prove for travel away from home expenses are the following:

1. *Amount.* The amount of each separate expenditure, such as the cost of transportation or lodging, except that the daily cost of your own breakfast, lunch, and dinner and of expenditures incidental to such travel may be aggregated, if put in reasonable categories. For example, you could have these expenses categorized as meals, car expenses, and taxi fares. If you are using a per diem allowance for meals (or, if reimbursed by an employer, for meals and lodging) you may not need proof of these expenses (see page 160, "How to Report Travel and Transportation Deductions on Your Return" in Chapter 7).

2. *Time.* The dates you left and returned home for each trip, and the number of days spent on business while away.

3. *Place.* Where you went.

4. *Business purpose.* The business reason for your travel, or the nature of the business benefit derived or expected to be derived as a result of the travel.

The Elements of Entertainment Expenses

IN GENERAL

The elements you must be able to prove for an entertainment expense are the following:

1. *Amount.* The amount of each separate entertainment expense, except incidental items such as taxi fares and telephone calls can be totaled on a daily basis.
2. *Time.* When the entertainment took place.
3. *Place.* The name, if any, location, and type of entertainment, such as dinner or theater, if that is not apparent from the name.
4. *Business purpose.* The business reason for the entertainment, or the business benefit gained or expected to be gained, and the nature of any business discussion or activity that took place.
5. *Business relationship.* Occupation or other information about the person(s) being entertained. If you entertain a large number of people, you do not have to describe everyone if they are members of a particular identifiable group. Just describe the group.

BEFORE OR AFTER A BUSINESS DISCUSSION

If you claim a deduction for entertainment directly preceding or following a business discussion, you must be able to prove Items (1), (2), (3), and (5) for general entertainment, plus the following:

1. *Time.* The date and length of the business discussion.
2. *Place.* The place of the business discussion.
3. *Business purpose.* The nature of the business discussion and the business benefit gained or expected to be gained.
4. *Business relationship.* Identification of the people who were entertained who also took part in the business discussion.

The Elements of a Gift

The elements you must be able to prove with respect to a gift are the following:

1. *Amount.* What you spent for the gift.
2. *Time.* When the gift was made.
3. *Description.* What the gift was.
4. *Business purpose.* The business reason for the gift, or the business benefit derived or expected to be derived from the gift.

5. *Business relationship.* Occupation or other information about the person receiving the gift.

If you have receipts for the gifts, you can write down items (4) and (5) on the receipts. Also, if you buy a number of small gifts for a large group, like customers, you can simply describe the group of recipients, as long as you are not trying to avoid the annual $25 limit on gifts to one person.

The Elements for Local Business Use of Your Car

To deduct local business use of your car you must be able to prove the following:

1. *Amount.* The purchase price and capital improvements. If you deduct actual car expenses, you must also be able to prove each separate expense for operating the car, such as lease payments, insurance, interest, taxes, licenses, maintenance, repairs, gas and oil.

2. *Use.* The mileage for each business or investment use of the car, and the total miles you drove the car during the year.

3. *Time.* The date of the expense or use.

4. *Business purpose.* The reason for the expense or use, unless the business purpose, such as a sales route, is clear from the surrounding circumstances.

Whether you are using the actual expense method or the standard mileage rate for local transportation, you still need to determine your allowable business mileage and total mileage for the year. Review the rules for deductibility of local transportation in Chapter 7, and go buy a mileage log book at the office supply store. Keep the book on the dashboard of your car with a pen or pencil attached. Start logging your mileage now, even if it is well into the year. Record the date you start and the odometer reading. Write down just your business mileage, but record the odometer reading at regular intervals to indicate your total mileage during that period. If there are places you make regular visits to (and the mileage is deductible) you only need to write down the miles to and from once, then just record the name of the place. You do not necessarily need to do this all year. See *Sampling* under *How to Prove the Required Elements.*

The Elements Regarding Other Listed Property

Listed property is generally your business car, your home computer (but only if your home office is not deductible), and your cellular phone. See Chapter 8 under "Depreciation of Personal Property" on page 168 for a more detailed description. The elements you must prove are the following:

1. *Amount.* The expenditures for each item of listed property, including costs of acquisition, capital improvements, lease payments, and repairs and maintenance.

2. *Uses.* The amount of each business/investment use, and the total use of the listed property for the year.

3. *Time.* The date of each expenditure or use.

4. *Business purpose.* The business purpose for the expenditure or use.

How to Prove the Required Elements

The Code says you can substantiate the required elements of each of the above expenses either by "adequate records" or by sufficient evidence supporting your own written or oral statement.[7]

ADEQUATE RECORDS

Adequate records generally consist of your accounting for each expense in a diary or log, and documentary evidence, such as receipts or paid bills to support the expenditure. The regulations say you should make your recordings of each expense or use while you still remember everything; a log maintained on a weekly basis is okay.[8] It is not necessary to write everything down in your log if the information is on a receipt, as long as you keep the information in an orderly manner.[9] If the business purpose of any of the designated expenses can be inferred from the facts and circumstances, it is not necessary to explain it in your log. Examples are traveling expenses for calling on customers on an established sales route, or the entertainment expense of having lunch with a steady client.[10]

There is a variety of little log books and diaries available at your office supply store that try to make the record-keeping task as easy as possible. They all fit into your coat pocket. Get one and start using it. Do not wait until you receive a notice from the IRS that says they would like to examine your expense records from two years ago. You might be able to salvage your deductions from two years ago by reconstructing the information (see page 241), but it will probably generate more frustration and anxiety than it is worth. If you at least buy a log book and make a noble effort to comply with the record-keeping requirements you will sleep sounder at night.

The regulations generally require documents to support your expense records, such as paid bills and receipts, except in the following situations:[11]

1. You incur meals or lodging expenses while traveling away from home for which you account to your employer under an accountable plan, and you use a per diem allowance method that includes meals and/or lodging.

2. Your expense, other than lodging while traveling away from home, is less than $75.

3. You incur a transportation expense for which a receipt is not readily available.

This does not mean that you should throw away all of your receipts for less than $75, because you might forget to record the expenditures in your log book. Be sure to get a receipt for each business expenditure you make, and write on it the required elements that are not contained on the receipt itself, such as business purpose. These receipts will constitute adequate records if you keep them in an orderly manner. You could simply staple them to the appropriate page of your expense log. If your log gets a little fat after awhile, go buy another one; they are very inexpensive. There is no better way to defang an IRS agent on the prowl for expense records than to pull out a stack of big fat log books.

WHEN YOUR RECORDS ARE NOT ADEQUATE

So you did not go out and buy a log book, huh? And now the IRS wants to see your expense records? Well, there is still a ray of hope. The regulations say that if you do not have adequate records, you can prove the required expense elements by the following:[12]

1. Your own statement, whether written or oral, that contains specific information about the element, and

2. Other supporting evidence that is sufficient to establish the element.

Your statement that an expense was incurred will not be accepted without some kind of supporting evidence. A canceled check or credit-card receipt will suffice if other evidence shows the expense was for a business purpose. This evidence could be circumstantial, such as a check to a hotel in Atlanta for a stay during the week of your trade association's national convention there.

However, if the missing element is the description of a gift, or the cost, time, place, or date of an expense, the evidence must be direct. The regulations suggest that a written statement or oral testimony of persons entertained or witnesses, setting forth detailed information about the element, would be acceptable.[13] This is where it might get difficult. It seems that burdening your clients or business associates with this favor might be more costly in quid pro quos than just paying the tax. Perhaps that is what the authors of the regulations had in mind—they wanted to encourage you to keep adequate records.

SAMPLING

With respect to the use of listed property, such as your car, it is permissible to maintain an adequate record for portions of the year, and use that to substantiate the business use of the property for the rest of the year. You must be able to demonstrate by other evidence, though, that the sample periods are representative of use for the rest of the year.[14]

Example 11.1

Jane, a sole proprietor, operates an interior-decorating business out of her home. Jane uses her car for local business transportation to visit the homes or offices of clients, and to meet with suppliers and other subcontractors. There is no other business use of the automobile, but Jane and other members of her family also use the car for personal purposes. Jane maintained adequate records for the first three months of the year indicating that 75 percent of the use of the car was in Jane's business. Invoices from subcontractors and paid bills indicate that Jane's business continued at approximately the same rate for the remainder of the year. If other circumstances do not change (like Jane getting a second car for exclusive use in her business), the determination that the business use of the automobile for the taxable year is 75 percent is based on sufficient supporting evidence.[15]

Example 11.2

The facts are the same as in Example 11.1, except that Jane maintains adequate records during the first week of every month, which indicate that 75 percent of the use of the car is in Jane's business. The invoices from Jane's business indicate that Jane's business continued at the same rate during the remaining weeks of each month, so Jane's weekly records are representative of each month's business use of the automobile. The determination that the business use of the automobile for the taxable year is 75 percent is based on sufficient supporting evidence.[16]

When Is It Safe to Throw Stuff Away?

You should keep records as long as the transaction involved could be questioned by the IRS, or has an effect on an item that could be questioned by the IRS. That generally means you should keep all records that support an item of income or deduction on a return until the period of limitations for that return expires. The period of limitations is the length of time after you file your return in which the return can be amended to claim a credit or refund, or in which the IRS can assess additional tax.

Income and Expense Records

The normal period of limitations for your return generally expires three years after the return is filed.[17] That means you should never throw anything away for at least three years. If you have a net operating loss in a later year, and you carry the loss back to the current year, the period of limitations for the current year can be as long as six years.[18] In that situation, you should keep all your records for at least six years. If the transaction relates to a bad debt deduction or a loss from worthless securities, the period of limitations is extended to seven years,[19] so keep that stuff for seven years. If you have employees, you must keep all employment tax records for at least four years after the tax is due or is paid, whichever comes later.

Asset Records

The cost of an asset, and any capital improvements, could be questioned by the IRS for up to three years after you dispose of the asset in a taxable transaction. Keep all of your records until that time.

The gain or loss on certain asset dispositions is not recognized if the property is replaced, and this affects the basis of the replacement property. For example, if you trade in a business automobile, the basis of the new car is determined, in part, by the basis of the car you traded in. That means you have to keep the records for the old car as well as the new car. All records should be kept until the period of limitations expires for the year the new property is disposed of in a taxable sale.

Although most taxpayers no longer need to report the sale and purchase of a personal residence on their tax return, you must still establish a basis in your personal residence to claim a home-office deduction, and it is still necessary to report gain on a sale attributable to claimed depreciation. It's a good idea, therefore, to keep a permanent file for each personal residence. The closing papers from the purchase of your home should go into this file, as well as receipts for all capital improvements. Keep this file for at least three years after you have sold your house and moved to a retirement home.

Additional Resources

IRS publications that address topics discussed in this chapter include Publication 583, *Starting a Business and Keeping Records;* and Publication 463, *Travel, Entertainment, Gift, and Car Expenses.* Publication 583 contains an example of a simple manual bookkeeping system.

You can get IRS publications free by calling the IRS at (800) TAX-FORM [(800) 829-3676]. If you have access to TTY/TDD equipment, you can call (800) 829-4059. To download them from the Internet, go to *www.irs.gov* (World Wide Web), or *ftp.irs.gov* (FTP). If you would like to get forms and instructions (not publications) by FAX, dial (703) 368-9694 to reach IRS Tax Fax.

As an alternative to downloading files from the Internet, you can order *IRS Federal Tax Products* on CD-ROM. This CD includes over 2,000 tax products, including all of the above publications and forms. It can be ordered by calling (800) 233-6767. Also, Publication 3207, *Small Business Resource Guide,* is an interactive CD-ROM that contains information important to small businesses. It is available in mid-February. You can get one free copy by calling (800) 829-3676.

Notes

[1] *New Colonial Ice Co., Inc. v. Helvering,* 292 U.S. 435 (1934).

[2] *Welch v. Helvering,* 290 U.S. 111 (1933); *New Colonial Ice Co., Inc. v. Helvering,* 292 U.S. 435, 440 (1934).

[3] Rev. Rul. 78-38, 1978-1 CB 67; Rev. Rul. 78-39, 1978-1 CB 73.

[4] *Cohan v. Commissioner,* 39 F.2d 540 (2nd Cir. 1930).

[5] *Cohan v. Commissioner,* F.2d 540, 544 (2nd Cir. 1930).

[6] Treas. Reg. § 1.274-5T(a).

[7] IRC § 274(d).

[8] Treas. Reg. § 1.274-5T(c)(2).

[9] Ibid.

[10] Treas. Reg. § 1.274-5T(c)(2)(ii)(B).

[11] Treas. Reg. § 1.274-5T(c)(2)(iii).

[12] Treas. Reg. § 1.274-5T(c)(3).

[13] Ibid.

[14] Treas. Reg. § 1.274-5T(c)(3)(ii).

[15] Treas. Reg. § 1.274-5T(c)(3)(ii), Example (1).

[16] Treas. Reg. § 1.274-5T(c)(3)(ii), Example (2).

[17] IRC § 6511(a).

[18] IRC § 6511(d)(2).

[19] IRC § 6511(d)(1).

A Comprehensive Example

For most of us, the best way to learn how to do something is to see how some-one else did it. So this chapter shows you how George and Judy Jackson pre-pared their 2002 joint income tax return. The Jacksons' return is typical of many couples: one spouse is employed outside the home and the other spouse runs a home-based service business as a sole proprietor. This example shows the completion of Form 1040, including the following schedules and forms:

Schedule A (Itemized Deductions)

Schedule C (Profit or Loss from Business)

Schedule SE (Self-Employment Tax)

Form 4562 (Depreciation and Amortization)

Forms 8829 (Expenses for Business use of Your Home)

The Jacksons' 2003 estimated tax payments are also computed. These forms appear at the end of this chapter on pages 250 to 257.

Judy's Business

Until December of 2001, Judy was employed by a printing company as a graphic artist. While still employed, she got frequent requests from clients for help in creating a home page on the World Wide Web. Judy recognized the opportunity to start her own business in a growing and lucrative field. So she quit her job and started Judy's Web Page Design in 2002 as a cash method sole proprietorship.

She spent January equipping her home office and organizing her business, and began dealing with clients in February.

Judy maintained a mileage log that showed she drove 2,200 business miles during 2002, out of a total of 8,500 miles driven. She chose to use the standard mileage rate, which was 36.5 cents per mile, giving her a deduction of $803. This amount, combined with her parking fees of $55 (totaling $858) is shown on line 10 of Schedule C (Figure 12.3).

Judy had a personal computer she bought for personal use in 2000 for $2,500. She converted it to 100 percent business use when she began her business. She estimated its value at that time to be $1,800. She also purchased additional equipment and furniture for her office in January of 2002. Table 12.1 shows Judy's business income and expenditures for the year, exclusive of amounts spent for her home office. The income and deductions from Table 12.1 are shown on the appropriate lines on Schedule C (Figure 12.3).

For the depreciable items eligible, Judy elected to deduct the entire purchase price under Section 179. None of the assets qualify for the additional 30

TABLE 12.1 Schedule C Worksheet

ITEM	INCOME	DEDUCT	ASSET	BUSINESS USE	DATE	DEPRECIATION LIFE	SECTION 179
Receipts	35,400						
Advertising		1,000					
Entertainment		800					
Office supplies		1,400					
Parking		45					
Books (on Web page design)			300	100%	2/98	7 yrs	300
Software			750	100%	2/98	3 yrs	
Computer			1,800	100%	2/98	5 yrs	
Printer			500	100%	2/98	5 yrs	500
Fax/copier			900	100%	2/98	5 yrs	900
Bus. telephone			120	100%	2/98	7 yrs	120
Office furniture			1,200	100%	2/98	7 yrs	1,200
Filing cabinet			150	100%	2/98	7 yrs	150
Lamp			75	100%	2/98	7 yrs	75
Bookcase			300	100%	2/98	7 yrs	300
Totals	35,400	3,245	6,095				3,545

percent allowance. Of the depreciable assets placed in service, only those that are tangible and purchased during the year qualify for the Section 179 deduction. The software is not tangible, and the computer was converted from personal use, so they do not qualify. Form 4562 (Figure 12.5) shows the depreciation for the computer on line 19b, and the amortization for the software on line 16.

The total on line 22 of Form 4562 includes $201 for home-office depreciation on line 19i (see *The Home Office,* below). The $201 is reported on Form 8829, line 40 (Figure 12.6), and the balance from Form 4562 ($4,334) is shown on Schedule C, line 13.

The Home Office

Beginning in February, Judy used her home office regularly and exclusively as her place of business. Judy earned her income by designing computerized graphic images at the demand of her clients. Her work was done mostly at the computer in her home office, where she also did her administrative and management work. Her home office therefore constituted her principal place of business (see Chapter 5).

George and Judy bought their home in 1986 for $120,000, and have made no significant improvements. Judy estimates that the lot their house sits on was worth $12,000 at the time of purchase. These amounts are used in Part III of Form 8829 (Figure 12.6) to arrive at the basis of the building ($108,000) on line 37.

The house has a useable area of 2,000 square feet. Judy converted the spare bedroom to an office, which measures about 150 square feet. That means 7.5 percent of the house is used for business, as shown on lines 3 and 7 of Form 8829 in Figure 12.6. This is the percentage that is applied to the basis of the building to arrive at the business basis of the building ($8,100) on line 38 of Form 8829.

The conversion of Judy's home office included the following repairs and improvements:

Paint (not including Judy's labor)	$50
New blinds	$200
New carpet and installation (tacked down)	$850

Painting is a repair expense that is directly related to Judy's home business. It is shown on line 18 of Form 8829 in column (a) (Figure 12.6). The new blinds are personal property; not an improvement to the home itself. They are seven-year recovery property,[1] and are eligible for the Section 179 allowance. The cost of the blinds is therefore combined with the other Section 179 property shown in Table 12.1, and the total of $3,745 is shown on line 6 on Form 4562 (Figure 12.5).

The new carpet is considered an improvement to the home office,[2] and therefore has a recovery period of 39 years. Depreciation for the carpet and Judy's home office (the amount from line 38 of Form 8829) is shown on line 15(i) of Form 4562 (Figure 12.5), and is combined on Form 8829, line 40 (Figure 12.6). The depreciation percentage of 2.247 percent is used to compute depreciation on the carpet and Judy's home office. This is taken from Table 6.1 in Chapter 6 for real property placed in service in February.

The Jacksons incurred the following expenses during the year relating to their residence, none of which benefited Judy's office exclusively:

Home mortgage interest	$9,000
Real estate taxes	$2,900
Homeowner's insurance	$800
Repairs and maintenance	$400
Utilities	$1,550

Recall that Judy began doing business in February, so her home office was only used for 11 months during the year. Therefore, only $\frac{11}{12}$ of these costs are listed as indirect expenses on Form 8829 (Figure 12.6). The business percentage from line 7 is allocated to Judy's home office. The nonbusiness portion of home mortgage interest [$9,000 − ($9,000 × $\frac{11}{12}$ × 7.5%) = $8,381] and real estate taxes [$2,900 − ($2,900 × $\frac{11}{12}$ × 7.5%) = $2,701] is deducted on Schedule A (Figure 12.2).

Other Return Items

George works as an accountant for Acme Accounting Services. His taxable wages were $45,000 in 2002. George participated in Acme's pension plan during the year, and Acme provided George and Judy with health insurance. George was reimbursed by Acme for all business-related expenses, so none are shown on his return. Acme withheld $8,912 of federal income tax from George's wages, and $4,000 for the state of Minnesota.

George and Judy received a refund of $300 from the state of Minnesota in 2002. The only other deductible item George and Judy had in 2002 was $1,345 in cash charitable contributions to their church, which are reported on Schedule A.

Estimated Tax Payments for 2003

Notice on line 73 of Form 1040 (Figure 12.1) that George and Judy have a tax iability to pay in the amount of $1,445. This is due to Judy's failure to make estimated tax payments relating to her business income. The minimum tax payments to avoid the underpayment penalty were not made, so an underpayment penalty is due. But rather than try to compute the amount, George and Judy opted to let the IRS send them a bill by simply not filling in line 74. As long as they pay the bill when due, no additional penalty or interest will be charged.

Judy would like to avoid this situation for 2003. She could have used the worksheet in the instructions to Form 1040-ES (Estimated Tax for Individuals), but it looked pretty confusing. Instead, she read Chapter 9 of this book and computed her 2003 estimated payments using the following schedule:

Required annual payment based on 100 percent of 2002 taxes	$10,357
Estimated amount of federal income tax withholding for 2003 (on George's wages)	($8,912)
Total estimated tax payments needed for 2003	$1,445

As long as George's employer withholds at least as much from George's wages as in 2002, this method will avoid the underpayment penalty. If Judy's business income increases in 2003, she should increase her estimated tax payments accordingly.

Judy pays her estimated taxes by completing the Form 1040-ES payment vouchers, and sending in the vouchers and payments to the IRS according to the following schedule:

Payment 1: Due April 15, 2003	$361
Payment 2: Due June 15, 2003	$361
Payment 3: Due September 15, 2003	$361
Payment 4: Due January 15, 2004	$362

Notes

[1] LTR 8848039.

[2] *Walgreen Co. & Subsidiaries v. Commissioner,* 103 T.C. 582 (1994).

| Form **1040** | Department of the Treasury—Internal Revenue Service
U.S. Individual Income Tax Return **2002** | (99) | IRS Use Only—Do not write or staple in this space. |

For the year Jan. 1–Dec. 31, 2002, or other tax year beginning , 2002, ending , 20   OMB No. 1545-0074

Label
(See instructions on page 19.)
Use the IRS label. Otherwise, please print or type.

Your first name and initial	Last name	Your social security number
George	Jackson	999 : 22 : 1111
If a joint return, spouse's first name and initial	Last name	Spouse's social security number
Judy	Jackson	999 : 11 : 2222

Home address (number and street). If you have a P.O. box, see page 19.   Apt. no.
654 Pierce Avenue

▲ **Important!** ▲ You **must** enter your SSN(s) above.

City, town or post office, state, and ZIP code. If you have a foreign address, see page 19.
Bassville, MN 55222

Presidential Election Campaign (See page 19.)
Note. Checking "Yes" will not change your tax or reduce your refund.
Do you, or your spouse if filing a joint return, want $3 to go to this fund? ▶ ☐ Yes ☐ No   ☐ Yes ☐ No

Filing Status
Check only one box.
1. ☐ Single
2. ☑ Married filing jointly (even if only one had income)
3. ☐ Married filing separately. Enter spouse's SSN above and full name here. ▶
4. ☐ Head of household (with qualifying person). (See page 19.) If the qualifying person is a child but not your dependent, enter this child's name here. ▶
5. ☐ Qualifying widow(er) with dependent child (year spouse died ▶). (See page 19.)

Exemptions
6a ☑ Yourself. If your parent (or someone else) can claim you as a dependent on his or her tax return, **do not** check box 6a
b ☑ Spouse
c Dependents:

(1) First name Last name	(2) Dependent's social security number	(3) Dependent's relationship to you	(4)✓ if qualifying child for child tax credit (see page 20)
	:		☐
	:		☐
	:		☐
	:		☐
	:		☐

If more than five dependents, see page 20.

No. of boxes checked on 6a and 6b **2**
No. of children on 6c who:
• lived with you
• did not live with you due to divorce or separation (see page 20)
Dependents on 6c not entered above
Add numbers on lines above ▶ **2**

d Total number of exemptions claimed

Income

Attach Forms W-2 and W-2G here. Also attach Form(s) 1099-R if tax was withheld.

If you did not get a W-2, see page 21.

Enclose, but do not attach, any payment. Also, please use Form 1040-V.

7	Wages, salaries, tips, etc. Attach Form(s) W-2	7	45,000
8a	Taxable interest. Attach Schedule B if required	8a	
b	Tax-exempt interest. **Do not** include on line 8a	8b	
9	Ordinary dividends. Attach Schedule B if required	9	
10	Taxable refunds, credits, or offsets of state and local income taxes (see page 22)	10	300
11	Alimony received	11	
12	Business income or (loss). Attach Schedule C or C-EZ	12	26,150
13	Capital gain or (loss). Attach Schedule D if required. If not required, check here ▶ ☐	13	
14	Other gains or (losses). Attach Form 4797	14	
15a	IRA distributions 15a b Taxable amount (see page 23)	15b	
16a	Pensions and annuities 16a b Taxable amount (see page 23)	16b	
17	Rental real estate, royalties, partnerships, S corporations, trusts, etc. Attach Schedule E	17	
18	Farm income or (loss). Attach Schedule F	18	
19	Unemployment compensation	19	
20a	Social security benefits 20a b Taxable amount (see page 25)	20b	
21	Other income. List type and amount (see page 27)	21	
22	Add the amounts in the far right column for lines 7 through 21. This is your **total income** ▶	22	71,450

Adjusted Gross Income

23	Educator expenses (see page xx)	23	
24	IRA deduction (see page 27)	24	
25	Student loan interest deduction (see page 28)	25	
26	Tuition and fees deduction (see page XX)	26	
27	Archer MSA deduction. Attach Form 8853	27	
28	Moving expenses. Attach Form 3903	28	
29	One-half of self-employment tax. Attach Schedule SE	29	1,848
30	Self-employed health insurance deduction (see page 30)	30	
31	Self-employed SEP, SIMPLE, and qualified plans	31	
32	Penalty on early withdrawal of savings	32	
33a	Alimony paid b Recipient's SSN ▶	33a	
34	Add lines 23 through 33a	34	1,848
35	Subtract line 34 from line 22. This is your **adjusted gross income** ▶	35	69,602

For Disclosure, Privacy Act, and Paperwork Reduction Act Notice, see page 72.   Cat. No. 11320B   Form **1040** (2002)

FIGURE 12.1

Form 1040 (2002)
Page **2**

Tax and Credits	**36**	Amount from line 35 (adjusted gross income)		**36**	69,602
	37a	Check if: ☐ **You** were 65 or older, ☐ Blind; ☐ **Spouse** was 65 or older, ☐ Blind.			
Standard Deduction for—		Add the number of boxes checked above and enter the total here ▶ **37a**			
	b	If you are married filing separately and your spouse itemizes deductions, or you were a dual-status alien, see page 31 and check here ▶ **37b** ☐			
People who checked any box on line 37a or 37b **or** who can be claimed as a dependent, see page 31.	**38**	**Itemized deductions** (from Schedule A) **or** your **standard deduction** (see left margin).		**38**	16,427
	39	Subtract line 38 from line 36		**39**	53,175
	40	If line 36 is $103,000 or less, multiply $3,000 by the total number of exemptions claimed on line 6d. If line 36 is over $103,000, see the worksheet on page 32		**40**	6,000
All others:	**41**	**Taxable income.** Subtract line 40 from line 39. If line 40 is more than line 39, enter -0-		**41**	47,175
Single, $4,700	**42**	**Tax** (see page 33). Check if any tax is from: **a** ☐ Form(s) 8814 **b** ☐ Form 4972		**42**	6,662
Head of household, $6,900	**43**	**Alternative minimum tax** (see page 34). Attach Form 6251		**43**	
Married filing jointly or Qualifying widow(er), $7,850	**44**	Add lines 42 and 43 ▶		**44**	
	45	Foreign tax credit. Attach Form 1116 if required	**45**		
	46	Credit for child and dependent care expenses. Attach Form 2441	**46**		
	47	Credit for the elderly or the disabled. Attach Schedule R	**47**		
Married filing separately, $3,925	**48**	Education credits. Attach Form 8863	**48**		
	49	Retirement savings contributions credit. Attach Form 8880	**49**		
	50	Child tax credit (see page XX)	**50**		
	51	Adoption credit. Attach Form 8839	**51**		
	52	Credits from: **a** ☐ Form 8396 **b** ☐ Form 8859	**52**		
	53	Other credits. Check applicable box(es): **a** ☐ Form 3800 **b** ☐ Form 8801 **c** ☐ Specify	**53**		
	54	Add lines 45 through 53. These are your **total credits**		**54**	
	55	Subtract line 54 from line 44. If line 54 is more than line 44, enter -0- ▶		**55**	6,662
Other Taxes	**56**	Self-employment tax. Attach Schedule SE		**56**	3,695
	57	Social security and Medicare tax on tip income not reported to employer. Attach Form 4137		**57**	
	58	Tax on qualified plans, including IRAs, and other tax-favored accounts. Attach Form 5329 if required		**58**	
	59	Advance earned income credit payments from Form(s) W-2		**59**	
	60	Household employment taxes. Attach Schedule H		**60**	
	61	Add lines 55 through 60. This is your **total tax** ▶		**61**	10,357
Payments	**62**	Federal income tax withheld from Forms W-2 and 1099	**62**	8,912	
	63	2002 estimated tax payments and amount applied from 2001 return	**63**		
If you have a qualifying child, attach Schedule EIC.	**64**	**Earned income credit (EIC)**	**64**		
	65	Excess social security and tier 1 RRTA tax withheld (see page 51)	**65**		
	66	Additional child tax credit. Attach Form 8812	**66**		
	67	Amount paid with request for extension to file (see page 51)	**67**		
	68	Other payments from: **a** ☐ Form 2439 **b** ☐ Form 4136 **c** ☐ Form 8885	**68**		
	69	Add lines 62 through 68. These are your **total payments** ▶		**69**	8,912
Refund	**70**	If line 69 is more than line 61, subtract line 61 from line 69. This is the amount you **overpaid** ▶		**70**	
Direct deposit? See page 51 and fill in 71b, 71c, and 71d.	**71a**	Amount of line 70 you want **refunded to you** ▶		**71a**	
	b	Routing number	▶ **c** Type: ☐ Checking ☐ Savings		
	d	Account number			
	72	Amount of line 70 you want **applied to your 2003 estimated tax** ▶	**72**		
Amount You Owe	**73**	**Amount you owe.** Subtract line 69 from line 61. For details on how to pay, see page 52 ▶		**73**	1,445
	74	Estimated tax penalty (see page 52)	**74**		

Third Party Designee	Do you want to allow another person to discuss this return with the IRS (see page 53)? ☐ **Yes.** Complete the following. ☐ **No**
	Designee's name ▶ Phone no. ▶ ( ) Personal identification number (PIN) ▶

Sign Here	Under penalties of perjury, I declare that I have examined this return and accompanying schedules and statements, and to the best of my knowledge and belief, they are true, correct, and complete. Declaration of preparer (other than taxpayer) is based on all information of which preparer has any knowledge.		
Joint return? See page 19.	Your signature	Date Your occupation	Daytime phone number ( )
Keep a copy for your records.	Spouse's signature. If a joint return, **both** must sign.	Date Spouse's occupation	

Paid Preparer's Use Only	Preparer's signature ▶	Date	Check if self-employed ☐	Preparer's SSN or PTIN
	Firm's name (or yours if self-employed), address, and ZIP code ▶		EIN	
			Phone no.	( )

Form **1040** (2002)

FIGURE 12.1 (Continued)

SCHEDULES A&B	Schedule A—Itemized Deductions	OMB No. 1545-0074

(Form 1040)	(Schedule B is on back)	2002
Department of the Treasury Internal Revenue Service (99)	▶ Attach to Form 1040. ▶ See Instructions for Schedules A and B (Form 1040).	Attachment Sequence No. 07

Name(s) shown on Form 1040	Your social security number
George and Judy Jackson	999 ¦ 22 ¦ 1111

Medical and Dental Expenses		Caution. Do not include expenses reimbursed or paid by others.			
	1	Medical and dental expenses (see page A-2) . .	1		
	2	Enter amount from Form 1040, line 36 ⌊ 2 ⌋			
	3	Multiply line 2 above by 7.5% (.075)	3		
	4	Subtract line 3 from line 1. If line 3 is more than line 1, enter -0-		4	
Taxes You Paid (See page A-2.)	5	State and local income taxes	5	4,000	
	6	Real estate taxes (see page A-2)	6	2,701	
	7	Personal property taxes	7		
	8	Other taxes. List type and amount ▶ _ _ _ _ _ _ _ _ _ _ _	8		
	9	Add lines 5 through 8		9	6,701
Interest You Paid (See page A-3.)	10	Home mortgage interest and points reported to you on Form 1098	10	8,381	
	11	Home mortgage interest not reported to you on Form 1098. If paid to the person from whom you bought the home, see page A-3 and show that person's name, identifying no., and address ▶			
Note. Personal interest is not deductible.		_ _	11		
	12	Points not reported to you on Form 1098. See page A-3 for special rules	12		
	13	Investment interest. Attach Form 4952 if required. (See page A-3.)	13		
	14	Add lines 10 through 13		14	8,381
Gifts to Charity If you made a gift and got a benefit for it, see page A-4.	15	Gifts by cash or check. If you made any gift of $250 or more, see page A-4	15	1,345	
	16	Other than by cash or check. If any gift of $250 or more, see page A-4. You **must** attach Form 8283 if over $500	16		
	17	Carryover from prior year	17		
	18	Add lines 15 through 17		18	1,345
Casualty and Theft Losses	19	Casualty or theft loss(es). Attach Form 4684. (See page A-5.)		19	
Job Expenses and Most Other Miscellaneous Deductions (See page A-5 for expenses to deduct here.)	20	Unreimbursed employee expenses—job travel, union dues, job education, etc. You **must** attach Form 2106 or 2106-EZ if required. (See page A-5.) ▶ _ _ _ _ _ _ _ _ _			
		_ _	20		
	21	Tax preparation fees	21		
	22	Other expenses—investment, safe deposit box, etc. List type and amount ▶ _ _ _ _ _ _ _ _ _ _ _ _ _ _ _ _ _			
		_ _	22		
	23	Add lines 20 through 22	23		
	24	Enter amount from Form 1040, line 36 ⌊ 24 ⌋			
	25	Multiply line 24 above by 2% (.02)	25		
	26	Subtract line 25 from line 23. If line 25 is more than line 23, enter -0- . . .		26	
Other Miscellaneous Deductions	27	Other—from list on page A-6. List type and amount ▶ _ _ _ _ _ _ _ _ _ _ _ _ _ _ _ _ _ _			
		_ _		27	
Total Itemized Deductions	28	Is Form 1040, line 36, over $137,300 (over $68,650 if married filing separately)?			
		☐ **No.** Your deduction is not limited. Add the amounts in the far right column for lines 4 through 27. Also, enter this amount on Form 1040, line 38. ▶		28	16,427
		☐ **Yes.** Your deduction may be limited. See page A-6 for the amount to enter.			

For Paperwork Reduction Act Notice, see Form 1040 instructions.   Cat. No. 11330X   Schedule A (Form 1040) 2002

FIGURE 12.2

SCHEDULE C (Form 1040)	**Profit or Loss From Business** (Sole Proprietorship)	OMB No. 1545-0074 **2002**

Department of the Treasury Internal Revenue Service (99)

▶ Partnerships, joint ventures, etc., must file Form 1065 or 1065-B.
▶ Attach to Form 1040 or 1041. ▶ See Instructions for Schedule C (Form 1040).

Attachment Sequence No. **09**

Name of proprietor **Judy Jackson**	Social security number (SSN) **999 : 11 : 2222**

A Principal business or profession, including product or service (see page C-1 of the instructions)
Web Page Design

B Enter code from pages C-7 & 8 ▶

C Business name. If no separate business name, leave blank.
Judy's Web Page Design

D Employer ID number (EIN), if any

E Business address (including suite or room no.) ▶ -
City, town or post office, state, and ZIP code

F Accounting method: (1) ☑ Cash (2) ☐ Accrual (3) ☐ Other (specify) ▶ - - - - - - -

G Did you "materially participate" in the operation of this business during 2002? If "No," see page C-2 for limit on losses ☐ Yes ☐ No

H If you started or acquired this business during 2002, check here . . . . ▶ ☐

Part I Income

1	Gross receipts or sales. **Caution.** If this income was reported to you on Form W-2 and the "Statutory employee" box on that form was checked, see page C-2 and check here . . . . ▶ ☐	1	35,400
2	Returns and allowances	2	
3	Subtract line 2 from line 1	3	35,400
4	Cost of goods sold (from line 42 on page 2)	4	
5	**Gross profit.** Subtract line 4 from line 3	5	35,400
6	Other income, including Federal and state gasoline or fuel tax credit or refund (see page C-3) . .	6	
7	**Gross income.** Add lines 5 and 6 . . . . ▶	7	35,400

Part II Expenses. Enter expenses for business use of your home **only** on line 30.

8	Advertising	8	1,000	19 Pension and profit-sharing plans	19	
9	Bad debts from sales or services (see page C-3) .	9		20 Rent or lease (see page C-4):		
				a Vehicles, machinery, and equipment .	20a	
10	Car and truck expenses (see page C-3) . . .	10	858	b Other business property .	20b	
11	Commissions and fees .	11		21 Repairs and maintenance .	21	
12	Depletion	12		22 Supplies (not included in Part III)	22	1,400
13	Depreciation and section 179 expense deduction (not included in Part III) (see page C-3) .	13	4,334	23 Taxes and licenses . . 24 Travel, meals, and entertainment: a Travel	23 24a	
14	Employee benefit programs (other than on line 19) .	14		b Meals and entertainment		
15	Insurance (other than health) .	15		c Enter nondeductible amount included on line 24b (see page C-5) .		
16	Interest:			d Subtract line 24c from line 24b .	24d	400
a	Mortgage (paid to banks, etc.) .	16a		25 Utilities	25	
b	Other	16b		26 Wages (less employment credits) .	26	
17	Legal and professional services . . .	17		27 Other expenses (from line 48 on page 2)	27	
18	Office expense . . .	18				

28	**Total expenses** before expenses for business use of home. Add lines 8 through 27 in columns ▶	28	7,992
29	Tentative profit (loss). Subtract line 28 from line 7	29	27,408
30	Expenses for business use of your home. Attach **Form 8829**	30	1,258
31	**Net profit or (loss).** Subtract line 30 from line 29. If a profit, enter on **Form 1040, line 12,** and **also** on **Schedule SE, line 2** (statutory employees, see page C-5). Estates and trusts, enter on Form 1041, line 3. If a loss, you **must** go to line 32.	31	26,150
32	If you have a loss, check the box that describes your investment in this activity (see page C-6). If you checked 32a, enter the loss on **Form 1040, line 12,** and **also** on **Schedule SE, line 2** (statutory employees, see page C-5). Estates and trusts, enter on Form 1041, line 3. If you checked 32b, you **must** attach **Form 6198.**	32a ☐ All investment is at risk. 32b ☐ Some investment is not at risk.	

For Paperwork Reduction Act Notice, see Form 1040 instructions. Cat. No. 11334P Schedule C (Form 1040) 2002

FIGURE 12.3

Schedule C (Form 1040) 2002   **Judy Jackson**   999-11-2222 page 2

Part III   **Cost of Goods Sold** (see page C-6)

33 Method(s) used to value closing inventory: **a** ☐ Cost   **b** ☐ Lower of cost or market   **c** ☐ Other (attach explanation)

34 Was there any change in determining quantities, costs, or valuations between opening and closing inventory? If "Yes," attach explanation . . . .   ☐ Yes   ☐ No

35 Inventory at beginning of year. If different from last year's closing inventory, attach explanation .	**35**	
36 Purchases less cost of items withdrawn for personal use	**36**	
37 Cost of labor. Do not include any amounts paid to yourself	**37**	
38 Materials and supplies	**38**	
39 Other costs	**39**	
40 Add lines 35 through 39	**40**	
41 Inventory at end of year	**41**	
42 **Cost of goods sold.** Subtract line 41 from line 40. Enter the result here and on page 1, line 4 .	**42**	

Part IV   **Information on Your Vehicle.** Complete this part **only** if you are claiming car or truck expenses on line 10 and are not required to file Form 4562 for this business. See the instructions for line 13 on page C-3 to find out if you must file.

43 When did you place your vehicle in service for business purposes? (month, day, year)   02 / 01 / 2002

44 Of the total number of miles you drove your vehicle during 2002, enter the number of miles you used your vehicle for:

a Business   2,200   **b** Commuting   **c** Other   6,300

45 Do you (or your spouse) have another vehicle available for personal use? . . . . ☑ Yes   ☐ No

46 Was your vehicle available for personal use during off-duty hours? . . . . ☑ Yes   ☐ No

47a Do you have evidence to support your deduction? . . . . ☑ Yes   ☐ No

   b If "Yes," is the evidence written? . . . . ☑ Yes   ☐ No

Part V   **Other Expenses.** List below business expenses not included on lines 8–26 or line 30.

48 **Total other expenses.** Enter here and on page 1, line 27	**48**	

                                                         Schedule C (Form 1040) 2002

FIGURE 12.3 (Continued)

SCHEDULE SE		OMB No. 1545-0074
(Form 1040)	**Self-Employment Tax**	2002
Department of the Treasury Internal Revenue Service (99)	Attach to Form 1040. See Instructions for Schedule SE (Form 1040).	Attachment Sequence No. 17

Name of person with **self-employment** income (as shown on Form 1040) Judy Jackson	Social security number of person with **self-employment** income ▶	999 : 11 : 2222

Who Must File Schedule SE

You must file Schedule SE if:

You had net earnings from self-employment from **other than** church employee income (line 4 of Short Schedule SE or line 4c of Long Schedule SE) of $400 or more **or**

You had church employee income of $108.28 or more. Income from services you performed as a minister or a member of a religious order **is not** church employee income. See page SE-1.

Note. Even if you had a loss or a small amount of income from self-employment, it may be to your benefit to file Schedule SE and use either "optional method" in Part II of Long Schedule SE. See page SE-3.

Exception. If your only self-employment income was from earnings as a minister, member of a religious order, or Christian Science practitioner **and** you filed Form 4361 and received IRS approval not to be taxed on those earnings, **do not** file Schedule SE. Instead, write "Exempt–Form 4361" on Form 1040, line 56.

May I Use Short Schedule SE or Must I Use Long Schedule SE?

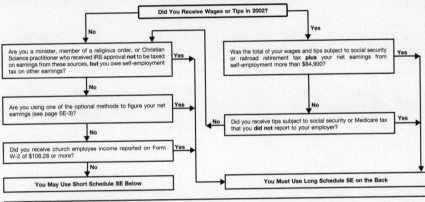

Section A—Short Schedule SE. Caution. Read above to see if you can use Short Schedule SE.

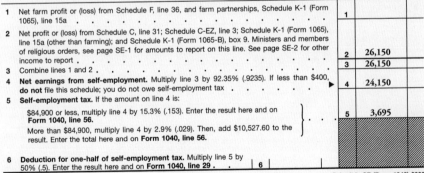

1	Net farm profit or (loss) from Schedule F, line 36, and farm partnerships, Schedule K-1 (Form 1065), line 15a	**1**	
2	Net profit or (loss) from Schedule C, line 31; Schedule C-EZ, line 3; Schedule K-1 (Form 1065), line 15a (other than farming); and Schedule K-1 (Form 1065-B), box 9. Ministers and members of religious orders, see page SE-1 for amounts to report on this line. See page SE-2 for other income to report	**2**	26,150
3	Combine lines 1 and 2	**3**	26,150
4	**Net earnings from self-employment.** Multiply line 3 by 92.35% (.9235). If less than $400, **do not** file this schedule; you do not owe self-employment tax . . . . . . ▶	**4**	24,150
5	**Self-employment tax.** If the amount on line 4 is: $84,900 or less, multiply line 4 by 15.3% (.153). Enter the result here and on **Form 1040, line 56.** More than $84,900, multiply line 4 by 2.9% (.029). Then, add $10,527.60 to the result. Enter the total here and on **Form 1040, line 56.**	**5**	3,695
6	**Deduction for one-half of self-employment tax.** Multiply line 5 by 50% (.5). Enter the result here and on **Form 1040, line 29** . .	**6**	

For Paperwork Reduction Act Notice, see Form 1040 instructions.   Cat. No. 11358Z   Schedule SE (Form 1040) 2002

FIGURE 12.4

Form **4562**	**Depreciation and Amortization**	OMB No. 1545-0172
Department of the Treasury Internal Revenue Service	**(Including Information on Listed Property)** ▶ See separate instructions. ▶ Attach to your tax return.	**20**02 Attachment Sequence No. **67**
Name(s) shown on return **Judy Jackson**	Business or activity to which this form relates **Web Page Design**	Identifying number **999-11-2222**

Part I   **Election To Expense Certain Tangible Property Under Section 179**

Note: *If you have any listed property, complete Part V before you complete Part I.*

1	Maximum amount. See page 2 of the instructions for a higher limit for certain businesses	**1**	$24,000
2	Total cost of section 179 property placed in service (see page 3 of the instructions).	**2**	
3	Threshold cost of section 179 property before reduction in limitation .	**3**	$200,000
4	Reduction in limitation. Subtract line 3 from line 2. If zero or less, enter -0-	**4**	
5	Dollar limitation for tax year. Subtract line 4 from line 1. If zero or less, enter -0-. If married filing separately, see page 2 of the instructions	**5**	24,000

(a) Description of property	(b) Cost (business use only)	(c) Elected cost	
6 **Miscellaneous Business Assets**	3,745	3,745	

7	Listed property. Enter the amount from line 29 **7**		
8	Total elected cost of section 179 property. Add amounts in column (c), lines 6 and 7	**8**	3,745
9	Tentative deduction. Enter the **smaller** of line 5 or line 8	**9**	3,745
10	Carryover of disallowed deduction from line 13 of your 2001 Form 4562.	**10**	
11	Business income limitation. Enter the smaller of business income (not less than zero) or line 5 (see instructions)	**11**	24,000
12	Section 179 expense deduction. Add lines 9 and 10, but do not enter more than line 11	**12**	3,745
13	Carryover of disallowed deduction to 2003. Add lines 9 and 10, less line 12 ▶ **13**		

Note: *Do not use Part II or Part III below for listed property. Instead, use Part V.*

Part II   **Special Depreciation Allowance and Other Depreciation (Do not** include listed property.)

14	Special depreciation allowance for qualified property (other than listed property) placed in service during the tax year (see page 3 of the instructions)	**14**	
15	Property subject to section 168(f)(1) election (see page 4 of the instructions)	**15**	
16	Other depreciation (including ACRS) (see page 4 of the instructions)	**16**	229

Part III   **MACRS Depreciation (Do not** include listed property.) (See page 4 of the instructions.)

Section A

17	MACRS deductions for assets placed in service in tax years beginning before 2002	**17**	
18	If you are electing under section 168(i)(4) to group any assets placed in service during the tax year into one or more general asset accounts, check here ▶ ☐		

Section B—Assets Placed in Service During 2002 Tax Year Using the General Depreciation System

(a) Classification of property	(b) Month and year placed in service	(c) Basis for depreciation (business/investment use only—see instructions)	(d) Recovery period	(e) Convention	(f) Method	(g) Depreciation deduction
19a 3-year property						
b 5-year property		1,800	5 yr	HY	DDB	360
c 7-year property						
d 10-year property						
e 15-year property						
f 20-year property						
g 25-year property			25 yrs.		S/L	
h Residential rental property			27.5 yrs.	MM	S/L	
			27.5 yrs.	MM	S/L	
i Nonresidential real property	2-1-2002	850	39 yrs.	MM	S/L	19
	2-1-2002	8,100	39 yrs	MM	S/L	182

Section C—Assets Placed in Service During 2002 Tax Year Using the Alternative Depreciation System

20a Class life					S/L	
b 12-year			12 yrs.		S/L	
c 40-year			40 yrs.	MM	S/L	

Part IV   **Summary** (see page 6 of the instructions)

21	Listed property. Enter amount from line 28.	**21**	
22	**Total.** Add amounts from line 12, lines 14 through 17, lines 19 and 20 in column (g), and line 21. Enter here and on the appropriate lines of your return. Partnerships and S corporations—see instr.	**22**	4,535
23	For assets shown above and placed in service during the current year, enter the portion of the basis attributable to section 263A costs **23**		

For Paperwork Reduction Act Notice, see separate instructions.   Cat. No. 12906N   Form **4562** (2002)

FIGURE 12.5

Form **8829**	**Expenses for Business Use of Your Home**	OMB No. 1545-1266
	File only with Schedule C (Form 1040). Use a separate Form 8829 for each home you used for business during the year.	**2002**
Department of the Treasury Internal Revenue Service (99)	See separate instructions.	Attachment Sequence No. **66**

Name(s) of proprietor(s) Judy Jackson	Your social security number 999 ¦ 11 ¦2222

Part I Part of Your Home Used for Business

1	Area used regularly and exclusively for business, regularly for day care, or for storage of inventory or product samples (see instructions)	1	150
2	Total area of home	2	2,000
3	Divide line 1 by line 2. Enter the result as a percentage	3	7.5 %

For day-care facilities not used exclusively for business, also complete lines 4–6.
All others, skip lines 4–6 and enter the amount from line 3 on line 7.

4	Multiply days used for day care during year by hours used per day .	4	hr.
5	Total hours available for use during the year (365 days 24 hours) (see instructions)	5	8,760 hr.
6	Divide line 4 by line 5. Enter the result as a decimal amount . .	6	
7	Business percentage. For day-care facilities not used exclusively for business, multiply line 6 by line 3 (enter the result as a percentage). All others, enter the amount from line 3 . . . ▶	7	7.5 %

Part II Figure Your Allowable Deduction

			(a) Direct expenses	(b) Indirect expenses		
8	Enter the amount from Schedule C, line 29, **plus** any net gain or (loss) derived from the business use of your home and shown on Schedule D or Form 4797. If more than one place of business, see instructions	8				27,408
	See instructions for columns **(a)** and **(b)** before completing lines 9–20.					
9	Casualty losses (see instructions) . . .	9				
10	Deductible mortgage interest (see instructions) .	10		8,250		
11	Real estate taxes (see instructions). . .	11		2,658		
12	Add lines 9, 10, and 11.	12		10,908		
13	Multiply line 12, column (b) by line 7 . .	13		818		
14	Add line 12, column (a) and line 13. . .				14	818
15	Subtract line 14 from line 8. If zero or less, enter -0- .				15	
16	Excess mortgage interest (see instructions) . .	16				
17	Insurance	17		733		
18	Repairs and maintenance	18	50	367		
19	Utilities	19		1,421		
20	Other expenses (see instructions) . . .	20				
21	Add lines 16 through 20	21	50	2,521		
22	Multiply line 21, column (b) by line 7 . .	22		189		
23	Carryover of operating expenses from 2001 Form 8829, line 41 .	23				
24	Add line 21 in column (a), line 22, and line 23				24	239
25	Allowable operating expenses. Enter the **smaller** of line 15 or line 24				25	239
26	Limit on excess casualty losses and depreciation. Subtract line 25 from line 15				26	26,351
27	Excess casualty losses (see instructions)	27				
28	Depreciation of your home from Part III below	28		201		
29	Carryover of excess casualty losses and depreciation from 2001 Form 8829, line 42	29				
30	Add lines 27 through 29				30	201
31	Allowable excess casualty losses and depreciation. Enter the **smaller** of line 26 or line 30 .				31	201
32	Add lines 14, 25, and 31				32	1,258
33	Casualty loss portion, if any, from lines 14 and 31. Carry amount to **Form 4684,** Section B .				33	
34	Allowable expenses for business use of your home. Subtract line 33 from line 32. Enter here and on Schedule C, line 30. If your home was used for more than one business, see instructions ▶				34	1,258

Part III Depreciation of Your Home

35	Enter the **smaller** of your home's adjusted basis or its fair market value (see instructions) .	35	120,000
36	Value of land included on line 35	36	12,000
37	Basis of building. Subtract line 36 from line 35	37	108,000
38	Business basis of building. Multiply line 37 by line 7	38	8,100
39	Depreciation percentage (see instructions)	39	2.247 %
40	Depreciation allowable (see instructions). Multiply line 38 by line 39. Enter here and on line 28 above	40	201

Part IV Carryover of Unallowed Expenses to 2003

41	Operating expenses. Subtract line 24 from line 24. If less than zero, enter -0-	41	
42	Excess casualty losses and depreciation. Subtract line 31 from line 30. If less than zero, enter -0- .	42	

For Paperwork Reduction Act Notice, see page 4 of separate instructions.   Cat. No. 13232M   Form **8829** (2002)

FIGURE 12.6

Index